MOTHER
AND
FETUS

Recent Titles in
Contributions in Medical Studies

MOTHER AND FETUS

Changing Notions of Maternal Responsibility

ROBERT H. BLANK

Contributions in Medical Studies, Number 36

GP

GREENWOOD PRESS
New York • Westport, Connecticut • London

Library of Congress Cataloging-in-Publication Data

Mother and fetus : changing notions of maternal responsibility /
   Robert H. Blank.
      p.   cm.—(Contributions in medical studies, ISSN 0886-8220 ;
   no. 36)
   Includes index.
   ISBN 0-313-27639-0 (alk. paper)
   1. Prenatal care—United States—Moral and ethical aspects.
2. Unborn children (Law)—United States.   3. Pregnant women—Legal
status, laws, etc.—United States.   I. Series.
   [DNLM: 1. Fetus.   2. Maternal Welfare—trends—United States.
3. Prenatal Care—trends—United States.   4. Public Policy—United
States.   5. Women's Rights—trends—United States.   W1 CO778NHE no.
36 / WA 310 R642m]
RG960.B55   1992
618.2′4—dc20   91-38029
DNLM/DLC

British Library Cataloguing in Publication Data is available.

Library of Congress Catalog Card Number: 91-38029
ISBN: 0-313-27639-0
ISSN: 0886-8220

First published in 1992

Greenwood Press, 88 Post Road West, Westport, CT   06881
An imprint of Greenwood Publishing Group, Inc.

Printed in the United States of America

∞™

The paper used in this book complies with the
Permanent Paper Standard issued by the National
Information Standards Organization (Z39.48-1984).

10 9 8 7 6 5 4 3 2 1

Dedicated to the memory of
Thomas C. Wiegele,
a true scholar and friend

Contents

Preface

The relationship between a pregnant woman and the developing fetus is becoming an increasingly volatile and problematic social issue. The reasons for this include the diffusion of a wide array of prenatal diagnostic and therapeutic technologies, a growing understanding of the impact of maternal behavior on the health of the fetus, and an expanding variety of legal intrusions into what until recently was a private relationship. As a result, public concern for the fetus is putting social pressure on pregnant women to change behavior, accept medical intervention, and in some cases give up their preferred employment. Pregnant women increasingly have become targets of educational campaigns, discriminatory work place policies, and even criminal prosecution aimed at protecting the unborn.

This book examines the public policy dimensions of these changing notions of the relationship between mother and fetus. It describes in detail the changing legal context, both civil and criminal, as it affects the pregnant woman. It also critically analyzes current policy initiatives in the United States and attempts to provide useful suggestions for balancing the rights of the woman with the interests of the fetus. My view is that the current trends that tend to pit the mother against the fetus are counterproductive and do little to serve the interests of either the mother or the fetus. Although the challenges of maximizing fetal health without unduly constraining the rights of the pregnant woman remain daunting, hopefully this book will contribute to a rational dialogue that leads to enlightened policy.

Although many individuals have had an impact on this book, the contributions of a few warrant special acknowledgment. The manuscript was strengthened considerably by the thoughtful review of Lori Andrews of the American Bar Association. Cynthia Harris and Catherine Lyons of Greenwood Press were instrumental in turning my manuscript into the final product. Marie Chase of the Program for Biosocial Research and Karen Blaser of the Liberal Arts and Sciences manuscript services at Northern Illinois University deserve special thanks for transforming my handwritten copy into a processed manuscript. Although the book is substantially stronger because of their contributions, all remaining shortcomings are solely my responsibility. I want to thank my wife, Mallory, and my children, Jeremy, Mai-Ling, and Maigin, for their cooperation and patience.

MOTHER
AND
FETUS

1

Reproductive Rights and Responsibilities: A Framework

A superior court judge in the District of Columbia orders a thirty-year-old pregnant woman convicted of second-degree theft to 180 days in jail to protect the fetus she is carrying from her alleged drug abuse. A Florida woman is found guilty of delivering cocaine through her umbilical cord to two of her children. A woman in Illinois is charged with manslaughter of her baby based on her alleged drug abuse during pregnancy. In Wyoming a prosecutor files charges against a pregnant woman for felony child abuse after her blood alcohol level is found to be above the standard to determine drunken driving. Meanwhile, in Arizona, a judge sentences a young mother who deserted her two sons in a sweltering apartment to lifetime probation and orders her to present written proof to her probation officer for the rest of her childbearing years that she is using birth control. Also, in California and other states women have been charged with fetal neglect for refusing to follow their physicians' orders, including advice to refrain from sexual intercourse. Although these cases make news because they are dramatic instances of state involvement in procreative decision making, the scope of such intervention by the courts is accelerating and altering traditional legal notions of maternal rights and responsibilities.

These and other cases illustrate the sensitive new legal and policy issues facing us in the midst of a revolution in biomedical technology, especially in human genetics and reproduction. Rapid advances in prenatal diagnosis and therapy are joined with new reproductive-aiding technologies such as *in vitro* fertilization and more precise genetic tests. Combined with the burgeoning knowledge of fetal development and the causes of congenital illness, these technologies are altering our perception of the fetus. As a result, prevailing values are being challenged by the new biology.

1

One critical set of values undergoing re-evaluation centers on the relationship of mother and fetus. The technological removal of the fetus from the "secrecy of the womb" through ultrasound and other prenatal procedures gives the fetus social recognition as an individual separate from the mother. The emergence of *in utero* surgery gives the fetus potential patient status that at times might conflict with that of the pregnant woman who carries it. Moreover, evidence that certain maternal actions during pregnancy, such as cocaine and alcohol abuse, can have devastating effects on fetal health threatens maternal autonomy. Together, these trends represent a broadside attack on women's rights achieved only recently after decades of battle. In the words of legal scholar George J. Annas, "The bodies of pregnant women are the battleground on which the campaign to define the right of privacy is fought. The ultimate outcome will likely be shaped at least as much by new medical technologies as by politics or moral persuasion" (1989, 329). No single area of medicine, therefore, promises more acrimonious and intense debate in the coming decades than the impact on the maternal-fetal relationship.

On the one hand, proponents of fetal rights contend that the health of the unborn fetus must be protected even at the expense of maternal rights. They argue that the state interest in protecting fetal health must take precedence over the maternal right to privacy. In contrast, proponents of maternal autonomy argue that no one but the pregnant woman can make such intimate choices. Any attempt at state or third-party intervention, therefore, represents unjustifiable constraints on women and is a return to the days when enslavement of women was justified as biological destiny.

This book examines the legal and political framework of this debate in the 1990s. It reviews scientific evidence, but focuses attention on trends in case law and social values relating to procreative rights and responsibilities. The conflict between the maternal right to privacy and the state's interest in protecting the fetus is bound to intensify and be fought out in the political arena. Although on the surface this issue mirrors the abortion debate, this book attempts to demonstrate that it is even more complex and, thus, more problematic.

A NOTE ON TERMINOLOGY

I have consciously chosen to use the term "mother" in this book despite the understandable objection by some observers that a pregnant woman is not a mother. Ethicist Frederik Kaufman, for instance, argues that a "logically necessary condition for being a mother is having a child" (1990, 3). By using the term "mother" in conjunction with a fetus, therefore, presupposes that the fetus is a child and thus gives the unborn a unjustified moral status. Mary B. Mahowald, too, rejects the use of the term "mother" in this context and argues that the term can be used appropriately only "after the fetus has been taken or expelled from the uterus, when the fetus is no longer a fetus but an abortus or a newborn" (1990, 43). Similarly, she states that the man responsible for the pregnancy is not the father.

Although there may be a danger that the use of "mother" and "father" in relation to a fetus might raise the moral status of the fetus at least for persons who already feel it should have such status, I disagree that this is a misuse of the terms within our social and legal tradition. Substantial emphasis in law and custom is focused on the contribution of the genetic mother who provides the ovum and the genetic father who provides the sperm. Moreover, the term "biological" or "gestational mother" is often attached to the woman who carries the fetus to term. Furthermore, women concerned that surrogate mothers be able to retain custody of the baby they contracted to a couple might be advised that to discount a maternal role during pregnancy undercuts her claim to the child. Therefore, although some will argue that a more accurate title for the book is "Pregnant Woman and Fetus" or "Gestational Mother and Fetus," the title used here purposefully demonstrates that a pregnant woman has both the rights and responsibilities of the mother of a potential child should she decide to carry it to term.

FRAMEWORK FOR REPRODUCTIVE RIGHTS

Few areas of human intervention are as sensitive or engender as much intense debate as those relating to human reproduction. This is not surprising because the whole existence of the living is organized for reproduction. The basic instinct of reproduction supplies societies with the members who maintain and perpetuate the social order. Reproduction also satisfies an individual's natural drive for sex and provides continuity with past and future generations. "It fulfills cultural norms and individual goals about a good or fulfilled life, and many consider it the most important thing a person does with his or her life" (Robertson 1983a, 408). Although some limits are placed on procreative choice in all societies, in most Western societies procreation is viewed as a fundamental right inherent in the very survival of the individual. The United Nation's Universal Declaration of Human Rights (1948) emphasizes the right to marry and found a family free from constraint, and affords special care and assistance to motherhood. According to Article 16, the family is the natural and fundamental unit of society and is entitled to protection by the state. Moreover, the United Nation's Declaration of the Rights of the Child, adopted in 1959, states: "The child shall enjoy the benefits of social security. He shall be entitled to grow and develop in health; to this end special care and protection shall be provided both to him and to his mother, including adequate prenatal and postnatal care. The child shall have the right to adequate nutrition, housing, recreation and medical services" (p. 1).

Similarly, in the United States procreative rights are viewed as fundamental human rights. Justice William D. Douglas applied the concept of "fundamental interests" to procreation when he placed compulsory sterilization within the confines of the equal protection clause of the Fourteenth Amendment: "We are here dealing with legislation which involves one of the basic civil rights of man. Marriage and procreation are fundamental to very existence and survival of the race" (*Skinner* v. *Oklahoma* 1942). Since *Skinner,* the constitutional status of reproductive choice has been expanded. Justice Arthur Goldberg, in a concurring opinion in *Griswold* v. *Connecticut* (1965), viewed the marital relationship as a fundamental area of privacy protected by the Ninth Amendment. The state can interfere with marriage and procreation only upon proof of a "compelling state interest." This philosophy was reiterated by the Supreme Court in *Roe* v. *Wade* (1973), where it ruled that the right of privacy protects a woman's right to decide whether to terminate a pregnancy, and in *Eisenstadt* v. *Baird* (1972), where the Court recognized "the right of the individual, married or single, to be free of unwarranted government intrusion into matters so fundamentally affecting a person as the decision whether to bear or beget a child." The Court restated this theme in 1986 (*Thornburgh* v. *American College of Obstetricians and Gynecologists*) holding that the right of privacy is a "central part" of liberty (p. 772).

According to Bernard M. Dickens, "the power of the individual to resist intrusions of the state into major decisions in the individual's life is perhaps more celebrated among the population of the United States than among people elsewhere" (1983, 269). Ethicist Paul Ramsey contends that "parenthood is certainly one of those 'courses of action' natural to man, which cannot without violation be disassembled and put together again" (1975, 238). Some observers argue that society has no right to intervene in childbearing decisions, except in very rare exceptions. Despite acknowledging statistics on social costs, ethicist Marc Lappé states: "I know of no such decision . . . where the decision to procreate or bear children should be the choice of other than the parents" (1972, 425). Daniel Callahan, director of the Hastings Center, agrees that an affluent society should be able to absorb the social costs that might accrue (1973). He contends that it is difficult enough to resolve conflicts among individual rights, much less between individual rights and some nebulous greater social good. On the other hand, parents should not be forced to bear defective children. Geneticist Aubrey Milunsky contends that a child has a right to begin life with a sound mind and body, but admits that ultimately the parents should have the right to make the final decision (1977, 185). There must be a "presumption in favor of the parents to reproduce."

In discussing reproductive rights, there is a danger of vastly oversimplifying what procreation itself entails and a tendency to focus on particular aspects of it at the exclusion of others. Contemporary debate, for instance, has focused on the right of a woman to control her body and terminate an un-wanted pregnancy through abortion or, conversely, on the protection of in-dividuals from being sterilized against their will. Often overlooked is that procreation is a complex process that develops over time and involves a se-ries of disparate though interrelated decisions. Its importance eminates from the genetic and biological as well as social experiences that comprise it.

Claims of procreative freedom logically extend to four components of reproduction: conception, gestation, labor, and child rearing. Although these aspects "combine to create a powerful experience," each of them has independent personal value and meaning (Robertson 1983a, 408). Only recently has attention focused on the biological experience of bearing and giving birth as aspects of procreative freedom. Child rearing is a fulfilling experience deserving respect, whether or not the person who raises the child also provided genes or bore it. There is a tendency today to deal al-most exclusively with reproductive choices about who may conceive, bear, and rear a child, again with a clear emphasis on the woman's rights to avoid or terminate a pregnancy. These choices, however, are distinct from choices about the conduct that occurs in the process of conceiving, bear-ing, and rearing. Legal scholar John Robertson distinguishes between the "freedom to procreate" and "freedom in procreation":

Freedom to control every activity related to procreation—to determine how con-ception will occur, to manage the pregnancy, decide how, when, where, and with whom parturition occurs, or how the neonatal period will be managed—may be of great significance to individuals and may also deserve protection. Although these activities may be lumped under the broad rubric of procreative freedom, analyti-cally they involve choices distinct from the decision to procreate, which is the deci-sion to conceive, gestate, or rear another person (1983a, 410).

Considerable effort is needed to clarify this critical expansion of the no-tion of procreative rights, especially in light of recent advances in genetics and medicine. No longer is the genetic linkage unambiguous. Virtually any kind of combination of germ material is now possible. Artificial insem-ination, *in vitro* fertilization, and various embryo transfer techniques also are displacing the traditional premise that the woman who conceives the child also bears it and raises it. In other words, the process of procreation itself is undergoing continuous change. It is dangerous, therefore, to focus too closely on one predominant procreative right at the exclusion of oth-ers. For instance, by stressing the right of one woman to terminate preg-nancy through abortion, we could be voiding what might be viewed by some people as the right of an infertile woman to adopt that potential child and fulfill her desire to rear a child she biologically cannot conceive or bear. Although not yet an option, fetal transfer technologies might be de-veloped in the future.

CONSTRAINTS ON STATE INTERVENTION IN DEFINING RESPONSIBLE PARENTHOOD

The preceding discussion demonstrates that the procreative freedom of parents is valued highly in our society, but is not absolute. The state does have an interest at times in intervening and limiting those freedoms. Most often, this occurs when the parents inadequately care for their children, either through ignorance or deliberation. The critical issue here is whether or not, and under what circumstances, the state is justified in intervening directly in prenatal care by imposing restrictions or requirements on expectant mothers. What limits are there, constitutional and other, that constrain the actions of the state in controlling maternal behavior to protect the life or health of the developing fetus, and how might such constraints be circumscribed?

Three constitutional rights limit the power of the states to intervene in the health care decisions of a pregnant woman: the right to bodily integrity, the right to make intimate family decisions, and the right of parents to make decisions about how to raise their child. Although each of these rights could be used to limit state intervention, they must be balanced with the right of the child to be born with sound mind and body.

The Right to Bodily Integrity

The Supreme Court in *Union Pacific Railway* v. *Botsford* (1891) held that "no right is held more sacred or is more carefully guarded . . . than the right of every individual to the possession and control of his own person, free from a restraint or interference of others, unless by clear and unquestionable authority of law" (p. 251). The origins of the right to bodily integrity lie in the Fourth Amendment "right of the people to be secure in their persons, houses, papers and effects against unreasonable searches and seizures," and in the due process clause of the Fourteenth Amendment. This right to self-determination and bodily integrity has long been applied to decisions involving medical treatment: a doctor who does not obtain consent before treating the patient can be charged with battery (*Schloendorff* v. *Society of New York Hospital* 1914). Since that time consent has come to be interpreted as informed, thus allowing the individual to weigh the risks and benefits of a proposed treatment (*Canterbury* v. *Spence* 1972). Implicit in the concept of informed consent is the right to refuse treatment, even if it might lead to the patient's death (*Bouvia* v. *Superior Court* 1986; *In re Farrell* 1972).

Although the right to bodily integrity is basic, it is a qualified right. The courts have not prohibited all state action that interferes with the right, but have applied a balancing test that weighs the invasion of bodily integrity against the legitimate state interest in taking that action. In fact, much of modern constitutional jurisprudence has engaged in balancing private rights and the public good. Although some rights are more fundamental than others, not even those highest in the hierarchy are absolute. If the right is fundamental, the interest of the state in countering it must be necessary and compelling. If, however, the right is not fundamental, or the encroachment on the liberty is insignificant, then the state must only show some legitimate state purpose and a rational relationship to the achievement of that purpose. When less intrusive means do not accomplish the state's goal, the courts have upheld intrusions. One example is compulsory vaccination (*Jacobson* v. *Massachusetts* 1905). When state action would invade an individual's bodily autonomy, however, the courts have required certain procedural safeguards.

The Constitution, then, allows states to intrude into an individual's bodily integrity only if the intrusion is essential to achieve a legitimate state goal more important than the individual's bodily privacy. For instance, in some cases the courts have held that the state's compelling interest in protecting the life and health of dependents outweighs the mother's right to bodily integrity (see *In re President and Directors of Georgetown College, Inc.* 1964, where the court ordered a blood transfusion for a woman against her will when it found that her death would jeopardize the welfare of her minor children). The state's interest in taking the intrusive action, however, must outweigh the individual's privacy interest. Furthermore, the state must not be able to achieve its goal through any less intrusive means. Additionally, the state must grant the individual adequate procedural rights if his or her rights are adjudicated.

Janet Gallagher and others, however, dispute the use of *Georgetown* and similar rulings as precedents for state interests in overriding the woman's right to bodily integrity to protect the fetus (1987, 35). Although *Georgetown* is often cited as authority for the proposition that judges may order medical treatment in the interest of dependent minor children, it turns instead on the religious character of the patient's refusal and competence to make that decision. Furthermore, the 1964 case is dated and does not "reflect the current emphasis on respect for individual self-determination and bodily integrity" in contemporary medical decision making. Finally, these blood transfusion cases, according to Gallagher, provide little insight in the context of more intrusive, risky, and painful procedures of coerced Cesarian sections and other pregnancy-related procedures (1987, 36).

The Right to Make Intimate Family Decisions

The Supreme Court in *Griswold* v. *Connecticut* (1965) enunciated a right to marital privacy that protects couples from governmental efforts to prevent their use of contraceptives. In *Griswold,* the Court struck down a Connecticut statute proscribing all individuals and couples from using birth control. The Court held that the Bill of Rights implicitly protects a "zone of privacy." While there is no explicit mention of the term "privacy," the Court forged this right in the "penumbra" of rights emanating from the First Amendment right of association, the Third Amendment prohibition against quartering soldiers in peacetime, the Fourth Amendment prohibition against unreasonable searches and seizures, the Fifth Amendment protection against self-incrimination, and the Ninth Amendment vesting in the people those rights not enumerated in the Constitution (p. 484).

In *Eisenstadt* v. *Baird* (1972), the Court extended the right to use contraceptives to nonmarried couples by applying the equal protection clause of the Fourteenth Amendment. The right to autonomy in intimate decision making rests on two principles: a person should be free from governmental intrusion into his or her home or family, and a person has a right to autonomy in making certain personal decisions. The second principle led to the *Roe* v. *Wade* (1973) decision invalidating the Texas statute prohibiting abortion. The *Roe* Court elaborated on the principle of autonomy, holding that it prevents a state from interfering in fundamental intimate decisions in the absence of a compelling state interest. The right to terminate pregnancy involves rights "implicit in the concept of ordered liberty" (p. 152) and falls within the zone of privacy protected by the Constitution. To deny a woman the right to make this decision would cause distress and the risk of harm inherent in imposing an unwanted child on the woman. Only after viability of the fetus could the state demonstrate a compelling interest to intervene.

According to a *Virginia Law Review* note, *Roe* is interesting in its acceptance of state authority to regulate abortion procedures after the first trimester ("Constitutional Limitations" 1981). The disparity in the Court's treatment of state prohibition of abortion and state regulation of abortion procedures implies that the Court is willing to apply a less demanding scrutiny to state actions short of denying the woman the right to decide.

It appears, therefore, that a less demanding form of scrutiny, such as a "balancing test," is appropriate when a state action restricts or burdens a protected individual decision but does not completely remove individual autonomy. The slighter the impact of a state action, the less compelling the state interest necessary to justify it; thus, state actions carefully tailored to serve their purposes would seem likely to survive the Court's scrutiny ("Constitutional Limitations" 1981, 1059).

In *Harris* v. *McRae* (1980), for example, the Court held that the denial of Medicaid funding even for medically necessary abortions does not interfere unduly with the freedom of choice protected in *Roe,* even though it makes "childbirth a more attractive alternative, thereby influencing the woman's decision" (p. 2687). Freedom of choice does not impose an obligation on the state to subsidize all alternatives equally for the *Harris* Court. Although the Court is adamant in prohibiting any absolute denial of the constitutional right to make autonomous procreative decisions, for lesser intrusions it is willing to apply a balancing analysis varying in intensity according to the means employed and the extent of intrusion on privacy rights. It requires considerable care on the part of the state in framing any regulations that affect childbearing decisions, but upon a compelling state interest the Court is willing to permit lesser forms of interference with procreative rights (*Webster* v. *Reproductive Health Services* 1989).

The Right to Parental Autonomy in Childbearing

There is a traditional preference in our society for minimal state intervention in childbearing decisions. It is based on the assumption that parents are able and willing to pursue the course of action that is in their child's best interest. According to the Supreme Court:

The law's concept of the family rests on a presumption that parents possess what a child lacks in maturity, experience, and capacity for judgment required for making life's difficult decisions. More importantly, historically it has recognized that natural bonds of affection lead parents to act in the best interests of their children (*Parham* v. *J.R.* 1979, 602).

The parent-child relationship, then, is special and comprises deep psychological and social bonds as well as physical and material dependence. When in doubt, the courts have chosen to err on the side of nonintervention in order to preserve the stability of the parent-child relationship. "The state should usually defer to the wishes of the parents, it has a serious burden of justification before abridging parental authority by 'substituting its judgment' for that of the parents" (*In re Phillip B.* 1979, 51). In a challenge to the law that mandated aggressive treatment of ill newborns over the refusal of parents (*Bowen* v. *American Hospital Association* 1986), the Supreme Court held that the state should intervene only in "exceptional" cases. In the Court's words: "Traditional law concerning the family, buttressed by the emerging constitutional right of privacy, protects a substantial range of discretion for parents" (p. 2113). Furthermore, the courts have been hesitant to allow state intervention in childrearing decisions because it might undermine the diversity of views and life styles promoted by allowing families to raise children in a wide variety of living situations. There is an implicit grounding of this right to the autonomy of parents' decisions in the First Amendment freedom of religion, which has played prominently in many of the cases involving medical decisions (*Jehovah's Witnesses* v. *King's County Hospital* 1967).

LIMITING PARENTAL CHOICE IN PROCREATION

The prevailing value orientation in the United States continues to give pre-eminence to the right to procreate without restriction as an interest so fundamental that society should not interfere. However, technological advances, described in Chapter 2, are shifting emphasis gradually to a less rigid viewpoint. There has been a serious questioning of the heavy reliance on the parent-child relationship, especially the assumption that parents will make good faith efforts to act in the best interests of their children even if they are capable of knowing what is best. Issues in child abuse, state support of dependent children, medical decision making, and lack of fertility control by those often least able to raise their children heighten this concern. As this book demonstrates, there is increased emphasis in both case law and literature on the parental duty to provide an adequate environment so that children have a chance to succeed: a growing view is that a child has a corresponding right to as sound a body and mind as possible. Although procreative rights are still fundamental under the Constitution, there are considerable new pressures for setting limits when exercise of this right conflicts with the health and life of children, including the unborn under some circumstances.

Within the context of emerging technologies for procreative control, there exists an alternative view that society has not only the authority but also a duty to intervene in reproductive decision making. Whether out of concern for affected children, future generations, the health of the gene pool, or some other general or societal good, there appears to be a growing agreement that some constraints ought to be placed on human reproduction when persons abuse those rights. Many advocates of this approach contend that even if procreation is an inalienable right, it can be regulated by a society concerned with the existence of the child to be born and with its own survival as a society. Reproduction in these terms is a right shared with society as a whole and is but part of a larger complex of rights, responsibilities, and obligations. State intervention might be justified under certain circumstances, although each case must be addressed with caution. For example, while sociologist Amitai Etzioni expresses concern for individual rights, he sees the tendency to give the individual "unlimited priority" over society as counterproductive, because "the individual is part of society and needs it for his or her survival and well-being" (1974, 51).

Philip Reilly, a lawyer and physician, asserts that no rights are absolute, and that it is erroneous to conclude that state action to control reproduction on genetic grounds could never survive a constitutional challenge (1977, 132). He concludes on a cautious note however:

The right to marry and the right to bear children are so fundamental that a heavy burden of proof should be placed on those who claim that society should give special priority to the reduction of genetic diseases. . . . I would demand a convincing demonstration that a really impressive societal benefit could be derived from more intrusive programs (1977, 148).

Similarly, ethicist Sumner Twiss concedes that since procreation is not an absolute right, parents may have a duty to avoid bearing children with serious genetic defects, especially when it would "affect adversely the welfare of other extant children of whom the parents bear a prior responsibility" (1974, 259). Still, he concludes that considerations against recognizing a societal right to intervene in parenthood and reproductive behavior are eminently more persuasive than the utilitarian-based affirmative considerations. Society does not have an unmitigated right to preclude fundamental procreative rights.

Although many individuals would impose tightly controlled restraints on procreative rights in order to protect affected children, others take an even stronger stand for societal intervention in reproductive choice. For instance, a strict utilitarian approach such as ethicist Joseph F. Fletcher's "situational ethics" gives society wide discretion in reproductive matters when circumstances warrant intrusion to achieve the greatest good (1974). Fletcher contends that one must compute gains and losses following several courses of action or nonaction, and then select that alternative offering the most good, whatever its implication for individual rights. The common welfare must be safeguarded, by compulsory state control if necessary: "Ideally it is better to do the moral thing freely, but sometimes it is more compassionate to force it to be done than to sacrifice the well-being of many to the egocentric 'rights' of the few" (p. 180). Fletcher thus favors mandatory controls on reproduction if they are needed to promote the greatest good for the largest number.

Bentley Glass suggests that advances in human genetics in the near future will result in a reordered priority of rights. These changes in technology will demand that the right of individuals to procreate must give way to a more "paramount" right—"the right of every child to enter life with an adequate physical and mental endowment" (1975, 56–57). With primary concern for the gene pool, geneticist Hermann Muller holds that those who are "loaded with more than the average share of defects" must refrain from engaging in reproduction "to the average extent" (1959, 590). Finally, Michael Bayles explains that it is justifiable to limit the procreative liberty of some persons if it increases the quality of life for those already alive: "If it could be shown, for example that most persons with a certain genetic defect such as Tay-Sachs did not have a quality of life of level 'n', then there would be sufficient grounds for the principle to support a law to prevent their birth" (1976).

Justifying Limits on Procreative Choice:
Ethical Considerations

Although opinions vary considerably both in degree and kind as to what conditions justify state intervention in reproductive choice, all but the most committed opponents to state interference consider such action appropriate within certain boundaries. The problem is largely one of defining the boundaries of action that can be justified. According to ethicist Tom L. Beauchamp, "the acceptability of these liberty-limiting laws ultimately depends on the adequacy of the justification offered for them" (1976, 361). Although the "general welfare" or "societal good" are too abstract to be of any aid in clarifying this problem, several other principles frequently are used to justify state interference and establish conditions for it. Among the most commonly stated justifications are paternalism and the public health. Although neither is without conceptual and practical problems that accompany any attempt at state intervention in reproduction, paternalism is the more problematic.

According to Gerald Dworkin, paternalism is "the interference with a person's liberty of action justified by reasons referring exclusively to the welfare, good, happiness, needs, interests, or values of the person being coerced" (1972, 65). Under this principle, restriction of individual liberty is justified if it is for that person's "own good." State imposition of helmet safety laws, drug usage laws, and preventive medicine are often justified on paternalistic grounds. John Rawls sees paternalism as a protection against one's own irrationality: "Others are authorized and sometimes required to act on our own behalf and to do what we would do for ourselves if we were rational, this authorization coming into effect only when we can not look after our own good" (1971, 249). There are, however, obvious problems with this justification: Who determines what is best for others? How is irrationality defined?

Beauchamp (1976, 362) rejects the paternalistic principle as a valid ground for reproductive intervention, but Gerald Dworkin (1972, 84) suggests that it might be appropriate in some situations. Dworkin argues, however, that such intervention should be kept to a minimum, and that the least restrictive alternative in each case must be adopted. Moreover, in all cases of paternalistic legislation, the authorities bear a heavy burden of proof to demonstrate that the action is in fact to the benefit of those restricted.

It appears that many types of reproductive intervention would have difficulty in meeting Dworkin's criteria. Compulsory PKU (Phenylketonuria) screening of newborns, where treatment is available to avert mental retardation and even some types of carrier screening, might be justified on paternalistic grounds; it is considerably more difficult to defend procedures that result in the abortion of a defective fetus. The uncertain status of fetal rights, and the improbability of demonstrating that, for the fetus, death is preferable to a life of abnormality, makes any paternalistic argument here weak at best. Most nontherapeutic forms of reproductive research must be justified on grounds other than paternalism.

The public health argument usually justifies restrictions on the liberty of some individuals by demonstrating that such restrictions help protect the health of others in the community. Beauchamp cites the "moral" force behind this argument as generated by the "harm principle" (1976, 361). Although he agrees that the harm principle is an acceptable justifying principle, Beauchamp concludes that "those who invoke it for purposes of genetic intervention . . . have not shown that the potential of harm to others . . . is sufficient to warrant the loss of liberties which would accompany the adoption of coercive genetic laws" (1976, 362). It has not been determined that the genetic health of the population would be improved substantially through enforced intervention in the procreative process.

Despite this, reproductive legislation has often been justified by reference to the need to protect the public health. Philip Reilly, for instance, notes that mass neonatal screening is "rapidly becoming established as a valid public health enterprise" (1978, 31). There are oft-cited precedents for state intervention into the reproductive activities of its citizens, for instance, compulsory rubella vaccination and premarital tests for syphilis. Compulsory immunization for highly contagious diseases has been accepted on public health grounds, but mandated genetic screening and compulsory sterilization are less immediate and viable concerns, because the disorder to be averted is not contagious and there is no danger that it will become epidemic. Also, the lack of treatment for most genetic diseases suggests a qualitative difference between reproductive intervention and communicable diseases. Although the long-term impact of nonaction might be a threat to the health of people in the remote future, obligations to those generations are seldom given much weight and play little role in current perceptions of public health. For those reasons, Lappé minimizes the public health aspects of genetic disease (1973, 154). Any considerations of the harm principle must balance the risks to individual rights with the health benefits gained.

Most policy decisions in the United States are at their base rooted in consequentialist criteria. Paternalistic and public health principles are often cited as the prime rationale for particular programs, but pragmatic political reasons are often at the core. Justification often rests on cost-benefit criteria; for example, what alternative action will maximize benefits and minimize costs to those interests able to influence the decision? Normally, the policy will be adopted that decreases the costs to society. If at the same time it serves humanitarian or other goals, so much the better, but the pragmatic considerations still predominate. Although the costs and benefits considered are often primarily monetary, they need not be. For instance, one political cost to be weighed heavily is the cost involved in abrogating fundamental individual rights. In a society where such rights are jealously guarded, they become an integral element in the decision-making context and must be reflected in resulting policy decisions. Within such a framework, however, procreative rights might be constrained when they interfere with broader social concerns.

Parental Obligations to Children

The importance of children as a link to the future and the survival of one's own identity has led to "an extraordinary heightening of emotional expectations of children" (Fletcher 1983, 297). Parents' longing for their own emotional fulfillment are projected to their children; in many ways, they live through their children. It seems reasonable that, as the number of children preferred by parents has declined, the expectations for each new birth have risen accordingly. Parents who have only one or two children, particularly in a society that puts so much emphasis on competition, want those children to be as "perfect" as possible, within the meaning of their own value system. The state, too, has a profound interest in the aggregate quality of progeny, especially when social preference is for one or several children per family. One clear predisposition in Western society is against those persons who are different—the mentally and, to a lesser extent, the physically retarded. The amount of prejudice now expressed toward disabled persons is already more than that expressed toward other minority groups. The availability of technologies to treat or eliminate those with "defects," along with the trend toward fewer children per family, is bound to accentuate the emphasis on quality of progeny.

Pressures on the mother to use available fetal therapies will increase as the techniques are transformed from experimental status to routine therapeutic procedures. Although fetal surgery and therapy are now at a primitive stage, and immediate concern focuses on possible harm to the fetus and the mother, rapid advances in instrumentation, technique, and skills will soon lower the risk to fetus and mother and expand substantially the options available for intervening *in utero* to surgically correct fetal defects. Once this occurs, women as a whole are likely to accept or demand therapy for their unborn child. Major dilemmas will arise, however, when a pregnant woman, for whatever reason, refuses to consent, and third parties apply pressure on her to comply to their demands for intervention.

The failure of a woman to consent to fetal therapy might lead to state intervention, primarily through court action. According to ethicist John Fletcher, as long as the experimental stage of fetal therapy persists, the obligation of parents to participate is not compelling. However, if the therapy becomes standard practice, the obligation to accept it for the fetus becomes much stronger. Law professor John Robertson comes to a similar, but even stronger, conclusion regarding maternal duty:

When prenatal surgical techniques are still experimental the mother and physician have no duty to use them. When the procedures are medically established, the question of whether they may choose to use them vanishes. It becomes good medicine and proper parental behavior to employ them. In such cases the benefit to the fetus from the intervention clearly outweighs the risks of the intervention (1982, 351).

One problem with this argument is the danger in our medicalized society that new technologies might be offered to, or even forced upon, pregnant women without adequate proof of benefit. Our dependence on technological fixes, reinforced by a medical community trained in the technological imperative, often gives us a false degree of security as to what medicine can accomplish (Blank 1988, 35). Many therapies come into widespread use without adequate assessment as to their risks and benefits (Blank 1991b). Increasingly, as demand for medical fixes escalates, the line between experimentation and therapy is a tenuous one. Arguments that a pregnant women has a legal duty to use "established" medical procedures, therefore, must be approached critically. We cannot assume that because a procedure is accepted as routine, that the benefit to the fetus warrants state intervention under force of law.

Parents in our society are legally, as well as morally, obligated to optimize the well-being of their children and protect them from imminent dangers to the maximum extent. Some of the most consequential dangers to developing humans take place during the fetal stage. With expanding knowledge of fetal development and new techniques to ameliorate or reduce these dangers, the moral status of the treatable fetus is enhanced. This trend is reinforced by the advancing social recognition of the fetus as a human being, because new technologies allow us to view, study, and eventually help the fetus prenatally. The bonding process between parents and fetus occurs far before birth, when the parents are able to see the fetus move, discover the sex of the fetus, or realize the fetus has a correctable problem. "The more living persons actually see the fetus by ultrasound or any future method to be developed, the more human and valuable the fetus will become" (Fletcher 1983, 307). Individual parents, as well as society in general, are likely to elevate the moral status of the fetus. In turn, the courts will continue their movement toward aggrandizing the legal status of the fetus at earlier and earlier stages of development.

It is clear that the well-being of the fetus is inextricably bound to the actions of the mother. Although the courts largely are cognizant of traditional maternal rights and have been hesitant to constrain those rights, recently they have shown a willingness to overrule maternal autonomy where the woman's actions harm or represent probable danger to the life or health of the developing fetus. As scientific evidence corroborates the deleterious effects of maternal behavior, the trend of the courts toward finding a cause of action against a pregnant woman for conduct injurious to her unborn child is bound to heighten.

In the last decade there has been a clear intensification of policy issues involved in attempts to define maternal responsibility. Unfortunately, the current policy context and the government response to date have been, thus far, inconsistent, haphazard, and often contradictory. Considerable activity has focused on the development of case law and the activity of the courts in redefining responsible maternal behavior and the standard of care owed the unborn. It is clear that the courts already are involved heavily in revising conventional views of maternal autonomy and discretion in procreative matters. Trends in both tort and criminal law appear to be on a collision course with the traditional predominance of maternal autonomy.

An alternative to emphasizing maternal responsibility is the social responsibility to provide all pregnant women with access to nutrition counseling, mental health and substance abuse services, and adequate general health care. Although there is a growing tendency for the public and the courts to emphasize maternal responsibility and castigate mothers of the unborn who fail to act "responsibly," less emphasis has been directed toward encouraging healthful behavior through public health education. We have a health care system that emphasizes efforts to treat the medical problems at the expense of efforts to prevent them (Blank 1988). The most pressing health problems of children continue to be related to deficiencies in access to essential basic health services. Programs to provide adequate prenatal care to pregnant women usually return many dollars in benefits for each dollar spent, not to mention the reduction of less tangible social costs. The costs of providing adequate maternal-child health care programs to educate pregnant women is meager compared to the neonatal intensive care costs of treating premature or defective infants in fully preventable instances. Therefore, before society takes action to coerce responsible maternal behavior, substantial effort must be made to provide proper education, counseling, and health care to pregnant women, particularly those in high-risk groups, such as teenagers.

Even the most comprehensive and effective prenatal health program, however, will not resolve the problems of some pregnant women unable or unwilling to change behavior harmful to the unborn. Chronic alcoholics, drug addicts, and others whose actions are undisputably harmful to the developing fetus and who are unresponsive to preventive efforts might be precluded from enjoying the rights of parenthood or legally required to pay the consequences for their behavior. Guidelines are needed that encourage proper maternal behavior, but that also protect against unwarranted state intrusion into the procreative choice of individuals. This is a very difficult, though critical, balance to achieve. The central question for policy makers is whether society has a duty to intervene in reproductive decisions in order to protect the health or life of the unborn. If so, what are the boundaries of governmental intrusion? It will be clear from the review of court action in this book that the first question has been answered in the affirmative, and that the major debate now centers on the parameters of government involvement.

THE ROLE OF GOVERNMENT IN REDEFINING PROCREATIVE RIGHTS

The progression of Supreme Court decisions on procreative privacy culminating in *Roe* v. *Wade* (1973) and reiterated in *City of Akron* v. *Akron Center for Reproductive Health, Inc.* (1983) and its companion cases clearly enunciates the right of a woman *not to have* a child if she so desires. Contraception and abortion, in theory at least, are guaranteed for all women, whatever their age and marital status. Although abortion continues to be a volatile issue, the complementary question of whether all women, whatever their age, marital status, or other characteristics, have a corresponding right *to have* children is even more problematic. If there is a right to have children, can any limits be imposed on the number or quality of progeny? Just as the right to abortion is not absolute—limits can be set after first trimester—it might be that the general right to have children ought to be circumvented under some circumstances. If so, who sets the limits and on what basis?

Furthermore, if a right to have children is granted, do infertile couples or singles have a legitimate claim to new reproduction-aiding technologies such as *in vitro* fertilization and embryo lavage? Should Medicaid or some similar public program fund these procedures for those who cannot afford the high costs? Or does this right, if recognized, apply only to those who can pay for it? If a couple requires the services of a surrogate mother in order to have children, who pays? A public furor arose recently in response to a well-publicized case in which a woman on welfare had a child via artificial insemination by donor (*Hastings Center Report* 1983). Although this case may be uncommon, it is a cogent illustration of the dilemmas that arise in interpreting reproduction as a positive entitlement.

Another policy issue regarding the right to have children relates to persons who carry genetic diseases, particularly dominant traits such as Huntington's disease. As noted throughout this book, social and legal pressures are likely to increase that will label parents as irresponsible who knowingly reproduce children with genetic disorders. More directly, do chronic alcoholics, drug abusers, or women with other high-risk conditions have an absolute right to procreate without concern for the burden placed on their progeny and society? The burdens to the child range from slight competitive disadvantages in society to severe physical, mental, and emotional problems. The burdens to society, in addition to seeing children suffer, are largely economic because frequently these children become wards of the state. Furthermore, the long-term costs of raising these children is often heightened by the need for special medical, educational, and social services. In the case of young teenagers who are emotionally and physically immature, is it fair to their potential children, others in society, or themselves to guarantee them an unfettered right to reproduce?

If one answers affirmatively that all women have a positive right to reproduce when they desire, then the social policy goals are reasonably straightforward: eliminate to the maximum extent possible any institutional and political infringements on individual reproductive choice. The legal trends described here that place emphasis on maternal responsibility for the health of the fetus represent a threat to this notion of absolute procreative freedom, because they make women who choose to have children legally accountable for the consequences of their decision. Overall, in a democratic society, the policy issues in assuming complete reproductive freedom are less troublesome than those surrounding efforts to limit this freedom because of difficulties of setting the boundaries of legitimate government involvement.

The government's potential role in constraining reproductive rights can take many routes, depending to a large extent on how these rights are defined in the prevailing value system. Because of the tradition that strongly supports the right of married couples to have children, there is a near consensus that few, if any, restraints ought to be placed on them. The use of new reproduction-aiding technologies by infertile couples appears to enjoy widespread popular support if it enhances their chances of reproducing. Although there is less support for the right of single, unmarried persons to procreate, this hesitancy has eroded in the past several decades in part because of the growing proportion of "nontraditional" families.

In those cases where state intervention seems warranted, social policies that focus on educating high-risk parents to refrain from reproduction or that provide other options for having children are likely to enjoy considerably greater support than coercive policies. Voluntary, not mandatory, genetic screening and prenatal diagnostic programs are most compatible with prevailing values concerning procreation in the United States. Although other inducements such as tax incentives, the provision of free services, or monetary rewards might offer the means to supplement education efforts, they result in inequities based on wealth. Conversely, the elimination or reduction of public support for the indigent, combined with the provision of a full range of family planning services, might encourage some people not to have children, but again the impact on various groups is not equitable.

Historically, more explicit policies to limit procreative choice have centered on involuntary sterilization programs. These misguided programs failed to reach even their most modest objectives and continue to personify state intrusion at its extreme for many people. Although new technologies in reversible sterilization and long-term subdermal implant contraceptives promise to ease rationalization of such policies (Blank 1991a), they will continue to be most controversial in the United States, because of the high value we place on reproductive choice.

Certainly, the licensing of parents is abhorrent to supporters of prevailing values in U.S. political culture. Even if it could be demonstrated that requiring parents to undergo a series of genetic, medical, social, and personality exams would assure that children born have an adequate chance to compete in this complex world, any policy of this type understandably would be widely attacked. Also, from a practical standpoint, it would be unenforceable within the U.S. pluralistic framework. It is doubtful that any public officeholder in command of his or her senses would propose a policy that would delimit who can and who cannot have children. Despite these caveats, the trends toward legal acknowledgment of fetal rights, torts for wrongful life, torts for prenatal damage, and criminal liability of parents for abuse of their unborn children demonstrate a growing acceptance by the courts and by the public to place limits on the reproductive choice of individuals. Also, the growing knowledge of fetal development in combination with the emergence of intervention technologies further shifts attention from the idea of reproduction as an unmitigated right to a responsibility to produce healthy children. Those persons who knowingly beget unhealthy children are increasingly likely to be viewed as acting irresponsibly. They will have to endure mounting social pressure to conform to standards of "responsible" procreative action.

REGULATING MATERNAL BEHAVIOR: THE NEED FOR A BALANCED APPROACH

The critical questions raised in following chapters center on the proper role of the government with regard to defining the parameters of maternal responsibility, specifically:

1. When, if ever, ought society to intervene in order to ensure as safe as possible a fetal environment for its unborn members?

2. What degree of intrusion into a pregnant woman's privacy and autonomy is justified—from education and counseling to forced *in utero* surgery?

3. If society has a responsibility to intervene in maternal life style, what means are appropriate for maximizing maternal compliance, and what means are inappropriate?

4. If society intervenes for its own benefit (i.e., to save money) or severely limits a woman's behavior to protect its interest in the potential child, what recompense, if any, is owed the woman?

5. In particular situations of conflict between the mother and the fetus, whose
   rights takes precedence?

Underlying all of these questions is the basic problem of who decides. Who
or, more accurately, which public agents establish priorities, standards of
duty, and mechanisms for mediating conflicts? In a pluralist society with a
tradition of individual choice, considerable emphasis is directed toward resolving as many of these dilemmas as possible in the private sphere. Issues
become public only when they can no longer be handled at the private
level.

Until recently, decisions concerning the behavior of the pregnant
woman were largely left to the woman and her personal physician under
the assumption that both parties had the best interest of the fetus in mind,
and that the decision was a shared one. The advent of the new era in knowledge of and technology for the fetus, along with the new medical field of
neonatology, however, has vastly increased the complexity of the decisions
to be made, thus bringing other parties into the deliberations and increasing the probability of conflict. Ethicist John C. Fletcher credits the development of the neonatal intensive care units as leading to an ethos of "a fair
trial of available therapy" and a heightened concern for the interest of the
premature newborn (1983, 308). Reinforced by the fear of liability, hospitals and physicians increasingly are turning to the courts for decisions that
they, themselves, made in the recent past. This trend is illustrated by one
case of a woman who refused to have a Cesarian section, which had been
recommended by the medical staff because of fetal distress. When the
woman refused, the hospital's attorney petitioned the juvenile court for an
order to precede with a Cesarian against the patient's wishes. Within two
hours the judge and attorneys representing the mother and the fetus met in
the patient's hospital room and a hearing was conducted. The court ruled
that necessary medical treatment including coerced surgery could be administered against the will of the mother. Although the courts might not
always be willing or able to intervene because of the time constraints, there
is a need for hospital staffs to "discuss and plan for the eventuality of situations of disputed fetal versus maternal rights" (Bowes and Selgestad 1981,
214). For reasons discussed throughout this book, such situations are certain to multiply in the near future.

Most pregnant women are deeply concerned about the health of their
unborn children; in fact, their commitment is likely to be more intense
than anyone else's. Once educated as to their responsibility to the developing fetus, they desire to reduce the risk of damage to the fetus throughout
pregnancy. As discussed later in the book, access to good prenatal and even
preconception medical services is highly correlated with healthy pregnancies. Similarly, the availability of alcohol and drug treatment programs for
all women on a voluntary basis is preferable and more likely to succeed

than coerced treatment of a pregnant woman. Amelioration of the cycle of poverty, illiteracy, unemployment and other core problems of U.S. society would do more to ensure healthy women and babies than many of the legal efforts discussed throughout this book, but such major changes are unlikely in the political and economic context of the 1990s.

Experience demonstrates, however, that a significant minority of women continue to dismiss or ignore education efforts and refuse to change life styles that are harmful to the fetus. Increasingly, public policies that include both implicit pressures to act responsibly and explicit measures, such as coerced surgery and criminal sanctions for behavior injurious to the unborn child, will be directed toward these women. Although persuasive strategies, if they work, are always preferable to coercion, in some rare cases coercion may be necessary. The discussion of court action here indicates that trends in that direction are already apparent and likely to gain considerable strength in this decade. Although there is reluctance on the part of many persons to face these difficult policy questions and a tendency to ignore or minimize the dilemmas, these problems will not dissipate. Work place hazards, teenage pregnancies, and fetal injuries caused by maternal behavior raise questions of public policy and beg immediate attention and cautious, yet rigorous, action.

Certainly, these are not politically attractive issues in a society with a tradition of individual autonomy and privacy in parenting. It is difficult at best to revise notions of parenting such that responsibility to progeny takes precedence over the right to have progeny. Unless a balanced and reasoned public dialogue begins soon over the question of maternal responsibility for fetal development, pressures will continue to build to explosive proportions in the not-so-remote future. Although the most comfortable response is to rationalize traditional values of parental autonomy, a more prudent response is to address these challenges head on and to re-evaluate our notions of parenthood within the new technological, social, and legal context.

CONCLUSION

Within a strong tradition of affording unlimited reproductive choice in U.S. culture, it is not surprising that challenges to this central value are met with intense opposition. Despite this, forces of change, often subtle, are at work to place procreative rights in a less secure framework. This book proceeds under the assumption that all rights, including reproduction, are relative to other rights, not absolute. Although society cannot indiscriminately violate the rights of parents and their reproductive autonomy, it is reasonable that society also has a responsibility to protect the rights of other individuals, including progeny and future generations. It is unfair to concentrate on the rights of today's parents without accounting for the corresponding rights of those potentially or actually afflicted, or for some broader societal needs. Certainly the fundamental right to bear children, although at the core of any genuine democratic society, has limits. Whether or not the imposition of any specific reproductive intervention is justifiable within a broader social context depends on the characteristics of each particular program.

In order not to exaggerate the conflict presented here, it is critical to note that the rights of the parents, affected offspring, and society at large will be congruent in most cases: all parties benefit in the birth of healthy children and work toward that goal. Despite this fact, it is imperative to examine the emergence of new medical knowledge and technologies in terms of the intense debate certain to surround questions concerning fetal rights. These technologies, in use now or available in the near future, promise to sharpen disagreement as to whether state intervention in reproductive decisions is ever justifiable and, if it is, under what conditions.

2

The Fetus in the Womb

A recent and rapid expansion in knowledge regarding the environment of the fetus has been accompanied by a re-emergence of concern for the rights of the fetus to have as safe as possible a sanctuary in the womb. This, in turn, has led to questions by some observers regarding the mother's obligations to provide such an environment for the fetus. The assertion of maternal control over her body is being challenged by mounting evidence that particular behavior of the mother during pregnancy might endanger the life or health of the fetus. For Patricia A. King this "increasing awareness that a mother's activities during pregnancy may affect the health of the offspring creates pressing policy issues that raise possible conflicts among fetuses, mothers and researchers" (1980, 81). Although the scientific data are new, the idea that a pregnant mother intuitively takes on an obligation to provide a healthy setting for the developing fetus is certainly not of recent origin. Aristotle in the *Politics* for instance, exhorts pregnant mothers to "pay attention to their bodies . . . take regular exercise, and follow a nourishing diet" (VII, xvi, 14).

To what extent should society take an active role to ensure a healthy fetal environment? Aristotle proposed strict state control over breeding and the conditions of pregnancy to back up his concern for the new generation of citizens. Given the traditional emphasis on parental privacy in reproductive matters, the legislatures and courts have avoided this dilemma to date by refusing generally to intervene. *Roe,* therefore, offered no guidance whatsoever for resolving conflicts of interests where a mother's treatment of her own body might cause harm to the unborn child.

STAGES OF FETAL DEVELOPMENT

During the 280 or so days between fertilization and term birth, the human zygote increases in weight by a factor of several billion and grows from a single cell to a complex organism. Contrary to the beliefs of many individuals and groups, there is no single point at which a fully defined human life begins. Instead, the gestation process represents a continuing, dynamic developmental continuum. Although conception is the point at which the newly fertilized egg contains all the genetic material of a unique individual, many concepti never implant, thus naturally precluding their continued development. Quickening and, more recently, viability have been used as critical stages in gestation, but again, they are subjective lines on the continuum. The selection of any point along this developmental progression, although often intuitively attractive, is arbitrary and varies as to the criteria of humanhood used.

On anatomical grounds, however, it is useful to classify stages of development in order to distinguish among the attributes of the organism at each stage. It should be noted that every categorization necessarily oversimplifies the complex process taking place and obscures significant variation from one individual to the next. Table 2.1 shows just how complex embryonic and fetal development is and lists some of the major stages.

The pre-embryo period covers the first seven or so days after conception. Following fertilization, the egg undergoes a series of cell divisions called cleavage that produce a package of cells. With each division, the cells are of

Table 2.1
Stages of Embryonic and Fetal Development

Period	Time after Conception	Stage	Time after Conception
Embryo			
"Preembryo,"	First week	Zygote	1 to 2 days
"preimplantation		Cleavage	2 to 4 days
embryo," or		Blastocyst	4 to 6 days
"conceptus"		Implantation begins	7 days
Embryonic	2 to 3 weeks	Primitive streak	7 to 8 days
		Gastrula	7 to 8 days
		Neurula	20 days
	3 to 5 weeks	Limb buds	21 to 29 days
		Heart beat	21 to 29 days
		Tail-bud	21 to 29 days
		Complete embryo	35 to 37 days
	6 to 8 weeks	Body definition	42 to 56 days
Fetus	9 to 40 weeks	First fetal	56 to 70 days
		Second fetal	70 to 140 days
		Third fetal	140 to 280 days

Source: Office of Technology Assessment (1988) adapted from Blank (1984).

diminishing size so that there is relatively little increase in size over this period. After seven cell divisions, the blastocyst is formed with about one hundred cells. This period ends with implantation of the blastocyst on the wall of the uterus and the beginning of placenta growth.

The embryo period covers the development of the organism from the end of the first week to about fifty-six days after conception. This is a critical phase of development, since cell differentiation of the embryo occurs at an accelerated pace. Southgate and Hey state that "partitioning of the heart and its development as a functional organ is virtually complete by 31 days" (1976, 205). Furthermore, although the heart increases in size by a factor of about one hundred during the fetal period, as a proportion of the body weight it remains virtually constant after the embryo period. The same holds for the liver, kidney, and other internal organs. During this six- or seven-week period, the embryo increases in diameter from about .1 millimeter to approximately 25 millimeters. By seven weeks, the embryo manifests primitive limbs and a head with equally crude facial features. By the end of this period of eight weeks, human limbs become evident and fingers and toes are present. Facial features, although still crude, become more clearly humanlike. Also, by seven weeks the brain stem has developed, and the brain can be seen as a continuous folding tube expanding in the head region to form elementary cerebral lobes. According to Clifford Grobstein, human embryos by the seventh or eighth week respond to stimuli by slow and weak turning of the head away from the stimulus (1988, 31). For Grobstein, this indicates that by this point in development, some nerve cells are mature enough to transmit impulses and transfer them from cell to cell. The metamorphosing embryo already has emerged as a highly differentiated organism with some visibly identifiable though primitive "human" features.

The longest period, and, therefore, the least unique, is that of the fetus, which extends from about nine weeks to full term at forty weeks. Because of the duration of this period, it is usually subdivided into three stages. The first fetal stage lasts about fourteen days, during which time the eyelids form, the umbilical hernia is withdrawn into the fetus, and external genitalia are differentiated. Spontaneous movements have been observed under ultrasound by the tenth week. Weight of the fetus by the end of this period is approximately 5 to 10 grams. The second fetal period, which extends from about ten to twenty weeks after conception, culminates in a form definitely that of a tiny human infant of approximately 45 grams. During this stage the spinal column hardens into bone, the eyelids are sealed, and the hair follicles are formed. At about eighteen weeks, quickening normally occurs with spontaneous movements of the fetus now detectable by the mother. According to Benirschke, at the end of the fifth month the fetus weighs just under 500 grams and has reached one-half the size of its term length (1981, 43). From twelve to twenty-six weeks after conception, the biparietal diameter of the head increases from 23 to 75 millimeters, and the fetus grows remarkably in length as well as in weight.

The last stage of fetal development extends from twenty weeks to term. During this stage, which encompasses the entire second half of gestation, continuous maturation of function and growth occurs. Weight normally increases from about 45 grams to full birth weight, which averages 3,400 grams. Fetal growth curves indicate that weight gains are fairly consistent across this entire stage. Organs rapidly mature and ready themselves for functioning outside the maternal environment. By the seventh month, subcutaneous fat fills out the wrinkled skin. Most crucial is the lung development and the maturation of the respiratory system.

This brief review of the stages of development generally accepted by developmental biologists demonstrates again that there is no single point at which the organism becomes something substantially different than it was at the preceding stage (Biggers 1983). It must be emphasized that any particular fetus will develop more or less quickly than the norm. When examined within the context of the concept of viability, these data imply that choosing any strict cutoff point for defining humanhood is not only arbitrary, but also misleading.

DELETERIOUS IMPACTS ON FETAL DEVELOPMENT

From the moment of conception, a developing human organism is exposed to a multiplicity of factors, all of which are capable of affecting the health of the fetus. These factors include the womb conditions, that is, the temperature, pressure character, and turnover of amniotic fluid; maternal emotions as expressed in hormonal changes that reach the embryo or fetus; all drugs administered to the mother, prescription and nonprescription; nutrition; infections; and maternal-fetal incompatibilities such as Rh blood factor (see Figure 2.1). It also includes a range of extramaternal factors, such as environmental pollution, radiation, noise (Verni and Kelly 1981), abuse by men, motor vehicle accidents, and a host of other potentially dangerous actions inflicted upon a pregnant woman (see Figure 2.2). Although the focus of this book is on maternal factors, it is emphasized here that factors beyond the control of the mother often have disastrous effects on the developing fetus and must be considered in any efforts to maximize the health of children. Any one or, more likely, combination of these maternal and extramaternal factors significantly affect the developing fetus and can cause congenital deformities, high-risk pregnancies, and numerous other problems.

Recent innovations and refinements in biomedical research and data collection have produced growing evidence of the deleterious effects of the uterine environment on the fetus's development. The behavioral patterns

Figure 2.1
Fetal Development and Maternal Behavior

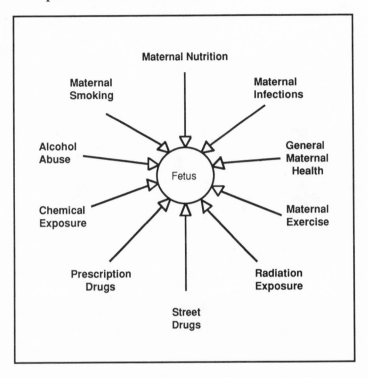

of the mother during gestation and, in some instances, prior to conception have been linked to a variety of congenital disorders ranging from reduced IQ and impaired motor coordination to mental retardation, high-risk premature births, and, in some cases, physical deformation or perinatal death (Harrigan 1980, 292). Although the exact causal nature of these factors often remains inconclusive and appears to be interrelated with the mother's physiological constituency, the evidence of fetal damage resulting from the behavior of the mother is mounting.

It is not known precisely to what extent congenital malformations (teratogenesis) are due to genetic damage, tissue injury in the developing embryo, a combination of these two factors, or environmental interaction manifested only in genetically susceptible persons. However, the evidence of the teratogenic effects of a variety of substances is growing. Although thalidomide is the most conclusive example, other drugs, including the widely prescribed Valium, are suspected teratogens. Nonmedical drugs such as caffeine, nicotine, and marijuana are also suspected, although causal evidence is limited. For other factors such as alcohol consumption

Figure 2.2
Extramaternal Impacts on Fetal Development

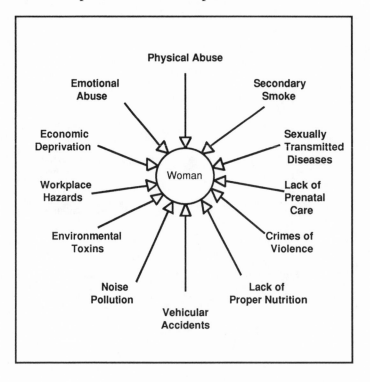

and cocaine use, however, the data are more conclusive. Also, studies indicate that many of the hundreds of thousands of chemicals that now exist in our environment, as well as direct radiation from X rays and other sources, cause chromosomal damage (Berg 1979). Exposure to LSD, cylcamates, methyl mercury, benzene, and vinyl chloride, among others, have been linked to human chromosomal aberrations.

In order to direct attention to those factors largely controllable by the mother, this discussion focuses on maternal behavioral habits that have been linked to fetal maldevelopment. Most conclusive are the data on poor nutrition, alcohol consumption, drug abuse, and smoking. Furthermore, these factors are cumulative in that multiple risk factors increase the possibility of a poor pregnancy outcome. For instance, it is not uncommon that an alcohol abuser will suffer from malnutrition and be a smoker as well. Also, these behavioral habits are often connected with medical problems such as hypertension, anemia, and certain infectious diseases, as well as such social patterns as teenage pregnancy, lack of adequate prenatal care, and minimal compliance with health care instructions.

Maternal Nutrition

All fetal nutrition comes from the mother's blood through the semi-permeable membrane of the placenta and the umbilical cord. The fetus is, therefore, totally dependent on the mother for all nutrients necessary to proper development and growth. When the fetus is deprived of an adequate and balanced supply of critical vitamins, minerals, and other nutrients, a wide range of developmental problems is possible. It is hardly surprising, therefore, that malnutrition of the mother during pregnancy can have adverse affects on fetal growth and infant vitality.

What is surprising is that, until the last several decades, the adverse effects of maternal malnutrition on the fetus were not commonly recognized. As stated by Winick: "During intrauterine life all organs of the fetus are in the hyperplastic (rapidly multiplying) phase of growth. At no other time should the organism be more susceptible to nutritional stresses, and yet only recently has any information about fetal malnutrition been forthcoming" (1976, 103). This ignorance was partially due to the difficulty in obtaining experimental data on the human fetus. Also, there was no apparent demand for such research because it was assumed that the fetus was a "perfect parasite," and that somehow the fetus would get the nutrients it needed regardless of what the mother ingested. Another myth widely accepted until recently was that if a woman was able to become pregnant, she was nourished enough to carry the fetus to term. As a result of these misconceptions, little attention was paid to maternal diet. Often physicians even recommended strict weight control during pregnancy.

It was not until the 1940s that substantial evidence became available that linked malnutrition to reduced birth weight and a range of other deleterious effects on the fetus. Massive statistical studies of the Dutch famine (Smith 1947) and the Leningrad siege of World War II (Antonov 1947) distinctly demonstrated that severe problems are associated with malnutrition during pregnancy and provided the impetus for nutrition research using animal models and human population statistics. More recently, results of the Leeds Pregnancy Nutrition study in England suggest that poor nutrition may be a causal factor for neural tube defects (NTD) (Smithells et al. 1983). The highest correlation with NTD was a vitamin C deficiency. Ongoing studies have established this finding more conclusively, and researchers are now trying to determine the extent to which preconceptual vitamin supplementation of mothers who have previously had a NTD infant will reduce its recurrence (Lipsett and Fletcher 1983). Although crucial questions remain unanswered and many findings are as yet inconclusive, "many authorities in the field of prenatal development feel that inadequate nutrition still constitutes the greatest potential threat to optimum development of the unborn child" (Annis 1978, 63).

Most attention has focused on the retardation of fetal growth resulting in low birth weight. According to Winick, twenty thousand extra calories are required during pregnancy to provide the requisites for a proper fetal birth weight (1976, 29). This means that approximately two thousand calories, carefully selected to provide protein and other essential components, are needed each day for the mother and fetus. According to Annis, the need for protein and riboflavin increases by about 45 percent during pregnancy, while the need for calcium increases by about 100 percent (1978, 64).

Importantly, research shows that nutritional reserves cannot be suddenly accumulated during pregnancy to compensate for earlier deficiencies. Instead, it appears that fetal growth is responsive to the overall nutritional status of the mother upon entering pregnancy, as well as adequate nutritional maintenance during the gestation period. Although the mechanisms are far from clearly understood, somehow the fetus is able to draw upon reserves stored up by the mother throughout her life. This evidence is critical for women who are underweight or malnourished going into pregnancy (Naeye 1980, 206) and for adolescent mothers. Over 200,000 babies are born each year in the United States to young women, many under fifteen years of age, who have not completed even their own physical growth. Annis points out that the situation is further aggravated by the total lack of concern for nutrition among some of these young mothers and by the poor prenatal care that many receive (1978, 73).

Insufficient levels of nutrition during fetal development increase substantially the risk of "small-for-date" or "small-for-gestational-age" births. Unlike true premature babies who are the right size for their fetal age but who are born too soon, these infants are born on time (thirty-eight to forty-two weeks), but because they have not developed properly, they are small upon delivery. Although there are many possible causes of small-for-date babies, including genetic disorders, one major cause is malnutrition. Winick terms growth failure mediated by abnormalities in the fetal environment as "extrinsic" (1976, 26). Extrinsic growth failure, in turn, could be the result of reduced blood supply to the fetus caused by maternal vascular problems or by maternal malnutrition.

Although adequate nutrition is important throughout pregnancy, the "most unequivocal" effects of the Dutch famine on infant mortality were found among those birth cohorts exposed to the height of the famine in the third trimester (Susser and Stein 1980, 184). Moreover, exposure to malnutrition during the third trimester was most clearly related to a low birth weight syndrome due to retarded fetal growth. Despite the prominence of the deleterious effects of malnutrition in late term, there is considerable evidence that inadequate maternal nutrition in the first trimester as well is related to shortened gestation periods, a heightened risk of central nervous system disorders, a sharp increase in perinatal and newborn death, and a retardation of fetal lung development (Naeye 1980, 201). Furthermore, nutrition throughout pregnancy has a direct effect on brain growth because without sufficient nourishment, the rate of brain cell division is slowed. Chase and associates, for example, found a significant decrease in the brain weights of six small-for-date infants and a corresponding 31 percent reduction in cerebellar DNA (1972).

The cumulative costs of treating very low birth weight (VLBW) babies (variously defined in the literature, but usually less than 1,500 grams) is staggering. By 1985, over $2 billion a year was spent on neonatal intensive care (NICU) for some 200,000 infants (Gustaitis and Young 1986, 213). With the costs of NICU reaching $2,400 per day, it does not take long to run up large bills, many of which fall on public agencies to pay. Moreover, 30 to 40 percent of low birth weight babies require rehospitalization (Shankaran et al. 1988, 372). The economic costs of care for the survivors of NICU, however, mask the full costs because, despite the remarkable strides in saving VLBW infants over the last decades, these babies account for 50 percent of all neonatal deaths even though they represent only 1.15 percent of all live births in the United States (Lantos et al. 1989, 91). As compared to normal birth weight babies, infants with very low weight at birth have a relative risk of neonatal death almost two hundred times greater.

In addition to evidence linking the overall nutritional status of the mother with growth retardation of the fetus, considerable research has been conducted on the effects of specific nutrient deficiencies on fetal development. Several human cases have linked severe vitamin A deficiency with malformed infants, while vitamin B12 deficiencies have been linked to neural tube defects (Briggs, Freeman, and Yaffe 1986, 473, 477). Similarly, vitamin C and D deficiencies in fetuses result in increased risk of physical, especially skeletal, deformities. Iodine deficiency is related statistically to malfunction of the thyroid gland and might result in stunted and malformed bodies and slowed mental development (Briggs, Freeman, and Yaffe, 1986, 364). Finally, zinc, manganese, and magnesium deficiencies may have adverse effects on fetal development. It should be noted, however, that nutritional supplements and megavitamins must be used with extreme caution during pregnancy, since excessive quantities could be harmful to the fetus. Winick, for instance, notes that excess levels of certain heavy metals might lead to impaired brain cell growth, again demonstrating the extreme sensitivity of the developing brain to environmental stimuli (1976, 112).

In spite of the extensive evidence of the risks to the fetus of malnutrition during pregnancy, most undernourished mothers have babies of adequate size and vitality (Dodge et al. 1975, 223). Again, this illustrates the complexity of fetal development and the difficulty in isolating the effect of prenatal nutrition from the multitude of relevant internal and environmental factors. As noted earlier, the factors contributing to the fetal environment are cumulative in nature and often exacerbated by successive generations of dysfunctional behavioral patterns and nutritional deficiencies.

Irrespective of these caveats, however, prenatal malnutrition is clearly associated with a broad assortment of serious and sometimes severe fetal developmental defects. Furthermore, it is an area in which prevention could in theory be fully effective if proper nutritional levels were maintained. In practice, therefore, the results of malnutrition are especially distressing because in most cases they could have been averted. In light of the relatively recent, though yet rudimentary, understanding of the importance of adequate maternal nutrition, it is vital that prospective mothers be fully educated as to their role in providing a safe environment for the rapidly developing fetus they plan to carry (Public Health Service 1989). Unfortunately, proposing such a program is easier than effectuating it. Therefore, while two decades ago the Committee on Maternal Nutrition reiterated the need for close monitoring of maternal weight and diet during pregnancy and made substantive recommendations for reducing the scope of malnutrition among pregnant women (National Academy of Sciences 1970), many infants still suffer, if they survive, because they are denied adequate nutrients during their critical formation period prior to birth.

Maternal Alcohol Consumption

There is a risk that any drug ingested by a pregnant woman will cross the placenta and enter the bloodstream of the vulnerable embryo or fetus. Even if the mother has built up immunities to particular drugs, the fetus does not have similar protection. The fetus appears especially susceptible to danger early in gestation when it is a rapidly proliferating and highly differentiating organism, "constantly changing in size, cell type, percentage of cells in mitosis, length of cell cycle, dependence on the maternal organism, and ability to replace dead cells" (Brent 1980, 147).

Although concern over the adverse effects of maternal alcohol consumption on the developing fetus can be traced back at least to the early Greeks (Warner and Rosett 1975), it was not until the 1970s that researchers were able to delineate a recognizable pattern of fetal abnormalities associated with chronic maternal alcoholism. Fetal alcohol syndrome (FAS) has since received considerable attention, and effort now is being directed at better understanding the sources of variability in the effect of alcohol consumption and timing on the fetus. Chernoff notes that findings about FAS are especially significant because of the magnitude of alcohol abuse in the Western world (1980, 321). Furthermore, there was a significant increase in the reported frequency of alcohol abuse during pregnancy over the last decade (Little, Snell, Gilstrap, Gant, and Rosenfeld 1989). According to Abel, the public health implications of drinking during pregnancy are enormous (1982, 60–61). He estimates the minimal number of pregnancies at risk based on "the most conservative published values."

1. About 3,350,000 women in the United States carried a child past the twentieth week of gestation in 1980.
2. The lowest level of drinking at which fetal risk is well documented is two or more drinks daily. Between 2 percent and 6 percent of pregnant women, depending on the section of the country, are drinking at this level.
3. Taking the average of these percentages, an estimated 134,000 pregnancies in 1980 were marked by alcohol use at levels that pose a hazard to the fetus.
4. If the risk level is expanded to include binges (five or more drinks on occasion), an estimated 8 percent or 268,000 pregnancies are involved.

Brandt estimates that there are between 1,800 and 2,400 cases of FAS annually in the United States, all of which are preventable (1982). Maternal consumption of alcohol during pregnancy is now the leading somatic cause of mental retardation in the United States, surpassing Down syndrome (Public Health Service 1989, 82).

According to Clarren and Smith, malformation patterns of FAS can be placed in four major groups: distinctive facial features, central nervous system dysfunction, growth retardation, and associated physical abnormalities (1978). It has been estimated that 30 to 50 percent of infants born to women who consume eight or more drinks a day have FAS (Little, Snell, Gilstrap, Gant, and Rosenfeld 1989, 547). Table 2.2 illustrates the frequency of the most common symptoms of FAS (see Abel 1982 for more details). Chernoff notes that FAS is the third most commonly recognized cause of mental retardation, exceeded only by Down syndrome and neural tube defects (1980, 324). In addition to the striking facial appearance of FAS children, growth deficiency, both gestationally and postnatally, is common, resulting in a "failure to thrive." Growth in head circumference is below normal, and mental retardation, ranging from minor deficiencies to severe retardation, is heightened. Poor coordination, hyperactive behavior, and tremors are also commonly reported in FAS babies. It should be noted, however, that not all of the offspring even of chronic alcoholics display these problems. Also, there are numerous instances of children born with only partial manifestations of FAS, especially to mothers who drink at lesser levels (Hanson 1981, 47).

Although initial concern was expressed that the cause of the fetal abnormalities could be some other factor associated with maternal drinking, such as malnutrition, considerable mammal research as well as human statistical studies demonstrate that the effects of alcohol consumption are independent of maternal malnutrition or a specific nutritional deficiency. "Although not conclusive, these studies would suggest that maternal nu-

Table 2.2
Symptoms of Alcohol Embryopathy

Symptom	Frequency
Intrauterine Growth Retardation	89%
Microcephaly	84
Mental Retardation	89
Hyperactivity	68
Congenital Heart Defects	29
Genital Anomalies	46
Muscular Hypotonia	58
Epicanthic Folds	66
Drooping Eyelids	38
Short Upturned Nose	49
Nasolabrial Furrows	71
Small Lips	61
High Arched Palate	39
Defective Development of Jawbone	74
Anomalous Creases on the Palm	69
Abnormal Depression of the Sternum	28

(Source: Abel, 1982:67)

tritional status is not responsible for the abnormalities seen in children with the fetal alcohol syndrome" (Hanson 1981, 46). Also, recent findings indicate that the frequency and severity of defects are more closely associated with maternal blood alcohol level than actual alcohol intake alone. This implies that women unable to effectively metabolize ethanol are at greater risk of producing an FAS child. Obviously, maternal blood alcohol level is a function of the amount of alcohol consumed, as well as the maternal genetic ability to metabolize it.

Although progeny of chronic alcoholics are at highest risk to manifest extreme FAS characteristics, considerably less maternal alcoholic intake is also linked to a variety of fetal problems. As noted earlier, a major study found that 43 percent of the offspring of chronic alcoholic women have features of FAS. However, consumption of as little as one ounce of absolute alcohol per day results in 11 percent of the offspring exhibiting FAS features. At consumption levels above two ounces, this increased to 19 percent. Because these latter two categories represent a substantially larger proportion of the population than the chronic alcoholics, prevention of FAS requires considerably more understanding of the effect of these lower consumption levels on the fetus.

In response to these data, the Food and Drug Administration in 1977 announced that while six drinks per day is sufficient cause to establish a major risk to the fetus, as little as two drinks per day could increase the risk of abnormal fetal growth and performance (Food and Drug Administration 1977). In a study of over thirty thousand pregnancies, consumption of at least one to two drinks daily was associated with a substantially increased risk of producing a growth retarded infant, while less than one drink daily had a minimal effect on intrauterine growth and birth weight (Mills et al. 1984). According to Hanson, no safe level of maternal alcohol intake during pregnancy has been established (1981, 49). Until it is, a growing number of experts are recommending that women abstain from alcohol during pregnancy. In 1987 Congress finally recognized this risk and required a warning label on all new alcoholic beverage containers that reads: "Government warning: According to the Surgeon General, women should not drink alcoholic beverages during pregnancy because of the risk of birth defects." Although this political compromise measure does not convey all the information it should, and is neither clear nor prominent on all containers because manufacturers were given free license on how and where to label, it does represent a weak attempt at health promotion.

There is a complicating factor, however, concerning maternal alcohol consumption. Crucial but as yet preliminary evidence relates to the timing of exposure to alcohol. In their study of the effect of moderate levels of alcohol consumption, Hanson and associates found that the consumption level in the first month of pregnancy was a better predictor of fetal outcome than amounts consumed later in the pregnancy (1978). "This result is not unexpected as a knowledge of embryology would predict that in order to produce major abnormalities of morphogenesis, prenatal insults to development must occur relatively early" (Hanson 1981, 49). Despite this evidence, it should not be assumed that alcohol consumption during the later stages of pregnancy is risk free. Rosett and associates (1983, 539), for instance, found that while sustained heavy drinking represents a major risk, reduced consumption in midpregnancy can benefit the newborn. Brain growth as well as the development of other organ systems proceeds throughout pregnancy and might be affected by maternal alcohol consumption late into the pregnancy.

The data that point to the critical early stages as the danger period for major central nervous system malformations caused by maternal alcohol abuse, however, are devastating for efforts at preventing FAS, since they imply that FAS is far along before most women are even aware of their pregnancy. By the time the woman knows she is pregnant, damage may have already taken place, and it is, thus, too late to avert the most severe malformations. This means that "even with full knowledge of the syndrome, some women not contemplating pregnancy will conceive and expose their developing embryo to high blood alcohol levels during critical stages of development" (Chernoff 1980, 327).

Therefore, what is required for the prevention of FAS is to "have all women of childbearing age who are not practicing contraception modify their drinking habits to be compatible with normal prenatal development" (Chernoff 1980, 326). This is an unlikely possibility in Western society, even if considerably more funds are spent on public education efforts

(Council on Scientific Affairs 1983). Given the aggregation of evidence demonstrating the deleterious effect of alcohol consumption on fetal development, though, it is certain that significantly greater attention will be directed toward the responsibility of the mother to provide an alcohol-free environment for her developing fetus.

Maternal Smoking

The increased incidence of smoking by women of childbearing age in recent decades has stimulated considerable research on the effects of cigarette smoking on the development of the fetus. According to the 1980 National Neonatal Survey, 31 percent of all married mothers and 47 percent of all teenage married mothers were cigarette smokers prior to becoming pregnant (Prager et al. 1983, 20). The comparable rates among unmarried mothers is, undoubtedly, higher. Although data remain inconclusive concerning the full impact of maternal smoking, several decades of major research studies and substantial statistical findings confirm a variety of deleterious effects of tobacco on fetal development and pregnancy outcome. Among these effects, maternal smoking during pregnancy is associated to varying degrees with retarded fetal growth resulting in low birth weight, premature birth, complications in pregnancy, heightened rates of spontaneous abortion, stillborn birth, and newborn mortality (U.S. Surgeon General 1979). In response to these data, the Surgeon General's warning is printed on cigarette packages and states: "Smoking by pregnant women may result in fetal injury, premature birth, and low birth weight." To date there has been no study to determine whether this warning has had any impact on cigarette smoking by pregnant women.

The most clearly corroborated finding to date is that mothers who smoke are at higher risk than nonsmoking mothers of giving birth to low birth weight babies (Longo 1982). Basing its conclusions on over forty-five separate studies, the U.S. Surgeon General's report *Smoking and Health* confirmed that maternal smoking reduces birth weight, even when statistically controlled for a broad range of demographic and situational factors (1979). The average weight of a smoker's baby is 200 grams less than a nonsmoker's across all categories. One study found that women smokers over thirty-five years of age had babies weighing on average 301 grams less than nonsmokers of that age (Wen et al. 1990). Reinforcing this, a significantly greater proportion of smokers' infants weigh less than 2,500 grams at birth, putting them at higher risk for a range of potential complications. One observer reports that 25 percent or more of infants born to women who smoke ten or more cigarettes per day are born with moderate to severe intrauterine growth retardation (Risemberg 1989, 150). Research also shows that the greater the number of cigarettes a woman smokes during pregnancy, the greater the chances of bearing a low birth weight baby. Moreover, actual birth weight declines steadily as the number of cigarettes smoked increases, implying a cumulative effect of smoking on the fetus.

Although birth weight is determined by a complex of "genetic, environmental, and pregnancy-related factors" (Heinonen et al. 1977), maternal smoking reduces birth weight regardless of the other factors at work. Meyer and associates concluded that of all relevant factors studied, the largest decline in birth weight was attributable to maternal smoking (1976). However, Rush notes that the effect of smoking is mediated by the nutrition of the mother, and that depressed birth weights associated with smoking can be "normalized" through nutritional supplements (1980, 211). Rush surmises that the relationship between heavy smoking and poor nutrition accounts for the markedly worse effect of smoking on the poor, possibly because "more affluent smokers are protecting themselves by sustaining their weight gain, presumably by maintaining dietary intake, in spite of their smoking, while poorer smokers are not" (1980: 211). Although these findings are inconclusive, they further demonstrate the complexity of isolating causal relationships in fetal growth and development.

Although many hypotheses have been advanced to explain why smoking causes reduced birth weight, the preponderance of evidence points to carbon monoxide and nicotine (Eriksen et al. 1983). Because fetuses are especially vulnerable to oxygen deprivation, the increased levels of carbon monoxide in the fetal bloodstream resulting from maternal smoking appear capable of retarding proper fetal growth. According to Meyer and Tonascia, the small size of the infant might be a result of fetal adaptation to reduced oxygen supply during gestation (1977). Similarly, nicotine, with its vascular constricting action, is likely to reduce placental blood flow, thereby augmenting the deleterious effects of the carbon monoxide.

In addition to retarding fetal development as measured by lowered birth weight, maternal smoking has also been linked to shortened gestation periods (Meyer et al. 1976), increased incidences of spontaneous abortion and complications in pregnancy, and a higher risk of late-term and newborn deaths. Kline and associates, for instance, found that the risk of spontaneous abortion among mothers who smoked during pregnancy to be 80 percent higher than among mothers who did not smoke (1977). Coleman and associates present a summary of fifteen studies in which late-term or newborn deaths were found to be associated with maternal smoking (1979, L16–L17). According to Meade, "Smoking in pregnancy is probably responsible for an excess of nearly 30 percent in the perinatal death rate of babies whose mothers smoke while pregnant" (1976, 75). Significantly, Meyer and associates found that the risk of perinatal death increased as the number of cigarettes smoked increased (1976). For those smoking at least one pack a day, the risk was 35 percent higher than for nonsmokers. At least a portion of the increased mortality of smokers' babies is attributable to complications arising in pregnancy, including premature rupture of membranes, bleeding during pregnancy, and premature detachment of the placenta (Coleman et al. 1979, L14).

Given evidence of the effects of maternal smoking on fetal development, it is not surprising that children of smokers run a higher risk of being slightly disadvantaged physically and intellectually, although in many studies the differences are not statistically significant. Meade, however, recommends that despite the limited evidence of long-term effects of maternal smoking, "pregnant women should be discouraged from smoking on this score" (1976, 75).

One consolation that emerges from research on the teratogenic effects of maternal smoking is that smoking habits prior to pregnancy appear to have no appreciable effect on birth weight. Furthermore, unlike alcohol, the effects of tobacco are not concentrated in the early pregnancy period. Therefore, a woman who quits smoking or even reduces the amount consumed during pregnancy can reduce the risk of fetal developmental retardation and increase the birth weight and length of the infant (Sexton and Hebel 1984). Contrarily, however, the proportion of female teenagers who smoke has increased significantly over the last decade. Given the trend toward elevated rates of normally high-risk pregnancies among teenage women, this trend is not encouraging.

OTHER TERATOGENS AND ENVIRONMENTAL HAZARDS

Primary attention here has been directed toward the effects of maternal malnutrition, alcohol consumption, and smoking on the developing fetus. This seems reasonable since a large proportion of American women of reproductive age exhibit one or several of these conditions. However, there are a wide variety of other exposures, over which the mother has some degree of personal control, with potential teratogenic effects. These include prescription, over-the-counter (OTC), and street drugs; maternal infections and chronic disorders; and high-energy radiation such as X rays. Although most of these possible teratogens affect only a small proportion of pregnant women, Montagu contends that the proportion is "significantly large enough to cause us to take every practical prophylactic step to ensure optimum health in the mother and in this way ensure the optimum conditions of development for the fetus" (1962, 321).

Pharmaceuticals

There is no question that we live in a drug-oriented society. In addition to the large amounts of nicotine, alcohol, caffeine, and food additives ingested, as a society we are heavily dependent on a variety of pharmaceutical products. Over 1.2 billion drug prescriptions are written each year in the United States, some of which are written without clear evidence of their benefits and risks. Furthermore, because pregnancy is a symptom-producing situation, it has the potential of causing women to increase their intake of drugs and chemicals, with the potential that the "fetus will be nurtured in a sea of drugs" (Yaffe 1986, xiv). The drug industry is a multibillion dollar business with large outlays for advertising its products, many of which are available for unlimited self-administration on an OTC basis. According to the director of the Center for Research for Mothers and Children of the National Institutes of Health (NIH), Sumner Yaffe, "Exposure to drugs, both prescribed and over the counter, among mothers to be continues unabated throughout pregnancy. It is possible that this exposure to drugs and chemicals may be responsible for the large numbers of birth defects which are seen in the newborn infant and in later development" (1986, xv). Roe reports that there are about 500,000 OTC drugs on the market, and that approximately 65 percent of pregnant women take at least one of these. The major classes of OTC drugs include: antacids, antidiarrheal agents, cold remedies, cough mixtures, laxatives, nonnarcotic analgesics, nutrient supplements, sedatives, stimulants, tonics, and weight-reducing agents (1982, 191).

Given the availability of drugs and the cultural proclivity to use them, spawned by the "magic bullet approach" to which many in the medical profession adhere, it is no surprise that pregnant women in the United States are heavy users both of prescription and nonprescription drugs. The Collaborative Perinatal Project (CPP), a major government-sponsored epidemiological study of over fifty thousand mother-child pairs from 1958 through 1965, found relatively high proportions of their subjects exposed to a wide range of drugs. Table 2.3 shows the percentage of women in the CPP study who reported taking specific categories of drugs during pregnancy. The most common were analgesics (mostly aspirin), which over two-thirds of the women reported taking.

In addition to the scope of drug exposure presented in Table 2.3, the cumulative use of these drugs by the respondents is consequential. Only 5.8 percent reported taking no medication during pregnancy, and another 14.9 percent reported using only one drug. The vast majority of women used multiple preparations during pregnancy. Overall, 48.7 percent took two to four drugs, 27.1 percent took five to ten drugs, and 3.4 percent took more than ten. More distressing is that, despite attempts to minimize drug usage during pregnancy by expanded education efforts, usage increased considerably during the period of study. In 1958 the mean preparations per mother was 2.6, and by 1965 it was up to 4.5. Moreover, the proportion taking over five preparations increased from 14 percent in 1958 to 40.1 percent in 1965. Although Heinonen and associates conclude that the vast publicity directed toward avoiding unnecessary use of

Table 2.3
Reported Drug Usage of Pregnant Women, CPP Study

Drug Category	Mother-Child First 4 months	Pairs Exposed Anytime Prior to Labor
Analgesic and antipyretic drugs	31.6	67.3
Immunizing agents	18.3	45.2
Antinauseants and antihistamines	10.4	25.2
Antibiotics	8.8	19.0
Sulfonamides	2.9	11.3
Barbiturates	4.8	25.1
Tranquilizers	1.9	6.4
Anesthetics, anticonvulants, stimulants	5.3	13.9
Caffeine and other xanthine derivatives	11.5	26.9
Diuretics	0.6	31.2
Drugs affecting autonomic nervous system	9.2	24.9
Cough medicines	1.9	15.8
Hormones, hormone antagonists and contraceptives	4.6	7.0
Inorganic compounds and vitamins	5.1	20.1

drugs, generated in part by the thalidomide disaster in 1962, was a failure, we really do not have data on the extent to which it prevented women from trying new, unproven drugs (1977, 265). The evidence we have, however, points overwhelmingly to a secular increase in drug use by pregnant women, again reinforcing the reality of dependence on drugs, despite the potential risks of taking any drug. "Recognition of the fact that drugs administered during pregnancy can affect the fetus should lead to decreased drug consumption. Nonetheless, studies conducted in the past few years indicate drug consumption during pregnancy is increasing" (Yaffe 1986, xv). Such orientations must be accounted for in any attempt to alter behavioral patterns of pregnant women and of the physicians that prescribe the drugs.

The deleterious effects of most drugs on the fetus are not clear, but as Hook and Porter state, "it appears plausible that any agent, operative procedure, or infection which directly affects the structure of the female reproductive system may also influence indirectly the rate of embryonic and fetal deaths" (1980, 16). No drug is without risk to the fetus, the level of risk depending on dosage, timing, and so forth, because most chemicals will cross the placenta in some form or amount. Even a drug of low risk to the mother might pose a serious risk for the fetus. Because the fetus lacks a fully developed liver and kidneys, the placenta takes on the detoxification and excretion functions of the organs that act to protect the adult from the toxic effects of a chemical. If the placenta is unable to accomplish these functions, the fetus will suffer. Even if the placenta is able to detoxify a chemical, what might be a reasonable dose for an adult woman might be an overdose for the developing embryo or fetus.

Female sex hormones, both estrogens and progesterones, should not be used during pregnancy, especially in early pregnancy where their use may seriously damage the developing fetus. Several reports suggest an association between intrauterine exposure to female sex hormones and congenital anomalies, including congenital heart defects and limb reduction defects. One study estimated a fivefold increased risk of limb reduction defects in infants exposed *in utero* to sex hormones, including oral contraceptives and hormone withdrawal tests for pregnancy, even though some of these exposures were very short, involving only several days of treatment (Janerik et al. 1974; see discussion of DES case in Chapter 3).

Shepard lists over one thousand agents in his *Catalog of Teratogenic Agents* (1989). Only a handful of these are unquestionably associated with human congenital malformations. Care must be taken not to exaggerate available hard data, which is sparse and open to controversy. The complexity of isolating the effect of any chemical is described by Heinonen and associates (1977, 1-29). One set of problems arises because some teratogens might be nonspecific, producing malformations in general; some might produce recognizable patterns of deformity; and others might be highly specific. Although drugs such as thalidomide that are both potent and striking in their effects are identified relatively easily (still, ten thousand babies were born with phocomelia before thalidomide was isolated as the common factor), others that are less potent and cause less obvious or severe teratogenic deformations are extremely difficult to detect. Heinonen and associates suggest that any yet-undetected teratogenic drugs currently in use are probably of this latter type (1977, 7). Another problem in demonstrating causality is that human experimental research is precluded (see Lipsett and Fletcher 1983); thus, evidence must come from two types of data, both with inherent constraints. Much data come from controlled experiments on animals, usually entailing replications with several species. Although animal data are suggestive for humans, they are not readily generalizable. A clear case is thalidomide, which gave no evidence of teratogenic effects in certain animal studies but had devastating effects on humans when released in Europe for clinical use. Although extrapolation from animal models to humans is always difficult, they still remain a basic source of knowledge of potential teratogens.

The second primary source of data on the effects of drugs are retroactive epidemiological studies of specific populations. These studies examine a large number of relevant factors, controlling where possible to isolate factors common to particular malformations or to specific patterns of drug use. The results in most every case are a set of statistical associations indicating increased risk related to drug usage. In addition to the normal problems of inferring causality from aggregate measures of association, epidemiological studies on teratogens have special problems because the effect of any drug depends on many mediating factors, such as dosage, timing of exposure in the developmental process, and constitutional differences among individuals. A growing body of evidence suggests that the genotype of the fetus can influence the likelihood of the teratogenic effects of a drug (Phelan et al. 1982). As a result, Spielberg cautions against the use of epidemiological risk data in specific cases: "The existence of human genetic polymorphisms in susceptibility to teratogens, however, suggests that we may be dealing with a large population at no risk and a few selected patients with a very high risk" (1982, 116). This means that a relative risk factor for a drug derived from epidemiological data could be misleading in that some exposed fetuses would be at high risk and others would be at low risk, despite similar timing of exposure, dosage, and so forth.

As noted earlier, the most definitive epidemiological study to date is the CPP. Although many of the drugs examined, including aspirin, were associated with a variety of fetal malformations, Heinonen and associates conclude: "No commonly used drugs were identified whose potency as teratogens could be regarded as even remotely comparable to thalidomide" (1977, 420). They caution, however, that less easily identifiable drug teratogens might have escaped detection. Furthermore, they contend that we should not have a false sense of security, even though the most commonly used agents were found to be relatively safe. They find it reassuring that the marked secular increase in drug use during the study period was not accompanied by a similar increase in the malformation rate. Conversely, they find it distressing that had a powerful teratogen been made available to the public for some common indications, it most likely would have been used widely. The CPP urged more focused follow-up studies and continued surveillance of all drug exposure, especially during the first forty-five days of gestation.

One drug labelled as a dangerous cause of birth defects is Accutane, a very effective treatment for patients with severe cystic acne. At least sixty-two deformed babies have been born to women undergoing Accutane therapy since the drug went on the market in 1982 (Sun 1988, 714). Fetuses exposed to this drug develop major malformations at about 25 times the normal rate.

The defects are catastrophic. Most commonly affected are the head and face, with small or absent ears, small jaw, and abnormal shape of the skull. Hydrocephalus and abnormalities in brain formation, as well as life-threatening deformations of the heart and large blood vessels are also prevalent. The thymus gland, needed for normal immunity, is often underdeveloped ("Accutane Alert" 1986, 1).

A fetus exposed to Accutane for even a brief period is at very high risk. If the woman discontinues taking this drug at least a month before conception, there appears to be no hazard. Unfortunately, because of Accutane's therapeutic use on acne patients, many young women who are unaware of their pregnancy might be exposed to this potent teratogen.

Although epidemiological studies and animal research have failed to reveal large numbers of drugs that, like Accutane, have clear teratogenic effects, certain associations have been confirmed. For instance, the drug Danazol, which is the treatment choice for endometriosis, like all androgens crosses the placenta and causes pseudohermaphroditism when taken in the first trimester of pregnancy. At least twenty-nine cases of Danazol use in pregnancy have been documented (Wentz 1982). Of these seven were aborted, five spontaneously and two for medical reasons. Although ten of the sixteen female babies were normal, six had abnormalities of the genital organs. Niebyl (1982) reviews in detail the evidence of teratogenic effects of many prescription drugs, Briggs and associates (1986) establish a risk factor for over five hundred of the most commonly used drugs in pregnancy and lactation, and Wilson (1977) cites reports on drugs that have been directly associated with human fetal death. Anticonvulsants, for instance, commonly used to control epilepsy, are associated with fetal growth retardation, head and face abnormalities, and mental retardation (Annegers et al. 1974). High doses of aspirin may be related to increased perinatal death, intrauterine growth retardation, and teratogenic defects (Briggs et al. 1986, 28).

Despite the lack of hard data indicating severe teratogenic effects from commonly used drugs, most observers urge caution in the use of any drugs during pregnancy. Spielberg recommends maximum use of epidemiological studies and the choice of a drug with the "widest human exposure and with data suggesting no increase in risk for birth defects" in situations where a drug is necessary (1982, 116). In contrast, Friedman and associates argue that while prescription drugs are a recognized cause of less than 1 percent of congenital anomalies, many patients fear fetal damage from any medication taken during pregnancy (1990, 594). This fear, they contend, may complicate necessary treatment of pregnant women and cause undue anxiety. Davis, however, advises caution: "It is argued that until more is known about fetal pharmacology the administration of untried drugs to pregnant women should be carefully monitored as a public health exercise and that the onus of proof should be on those who assume that a drug is harmless rather than vice versa" (1976, 57). The *American Journal of Nursing* recommends that whenever a drug is prescribed for a pregnant woman by someone who does not specialize in expectant mothers—for example, a dentist or psychiatrist—the prescription should be checked by her obstetrician before it is filled ("Nurses' Alert" 1982, 981). If the drug prescribed is not the safest that can be used, the obstetrician should write a new prescription for a safer drug with comparable therapeutic action. The

Journal also states that no diuretic should be used during pregnancy unless it is absolutely necessary, because the risk to the fetus may outweigh the benefit to the mother.

Street Drugs

As difficult as it is to isolate the effects of legal drugs and to monitor their consequences, illegal drugs present an even greater problem. However, with the use of these drugs becoming more common among many groups in U.S. society, it is imperative that attention be directed toward their effect on the developing fetus. It is estimated that as many as 11 percent of all newborns in the United States have been exposed to illegal drugs in utero (Pinkney 1990, 8). This translates to about 375,000 infants annually. Moreover, the high rate of pregnant women abusing drugs is not confined to urban areas and is not limited to hospitals serving a high proportion of low-income or public-aid patients. Although the drug of choice might differ, abuse of illegal drugs by pregnant women crosses all socioeconomic lines.

In the late 1980s, considerable attention was directed to the teratogenic effects of cocaine use by pregnant women (National Library of Medicine 1990 lists 468 journal citations on this subject between January 1988 and March 1990). In part, this reflected the dramatic increase in the incidence of cocaine and crack abuse by women of childbearing age (Neerhof et al. 1989) and from a pattern of highly publicized court cases in which women who used cocaine during pregnancy and gave birth to an affected infant were prosecuted for crimes, including delivery of a controlled substance to a minor and child (or fetus) abuse. It also resulted from growing medical evidence concerning the magnitude and scope of harm to the developing fetus caused by cocaine abuse of the pregnant women and to the heightened social burden and expense of caring for these very ill newborns. During a one week period at one hospital, 20 percent of black infants and 10 percent of white infants were born on cocaine. A commonly cited figure from urban hospitals is a prevalence of cocaine abuse of about 10 percent of all NICU cases (Neerhof et al. 1989, 637, and conversations with neonatal staffs). Because of the economic status of many of these women, "Taxpayers usually end up paying the health-care bill—a bill that can exceed $100,000 per infant" (Office of Technology Assessment 1990, 10).

A number of clinical studies have concluded, similarly, that cocaine abuse during pregnancy is associated with a wide range of neonatal morbidity and mortality. Infants born to cocaine abusers have significantly lower average birth weights, increased frequency of congenital anomalies, and heightened rates of preterm birth, neurologic deficits, and intrauterine growth retardation (Little, Snell, Klein, and Gilstrap 1989; Neerhof et al. 1989; Keith et al. 1989; Hoyme et al. 1990). According to Mercado and associates, many of the adverse perinatal affects associated with cocaine use might be explained by the fact that cocaine is a potent vasoconstrictor, thus producing a "significant increase in uterine artery resistance and resultant decreases in uterine blood flow and fetal oxygenation" (1989,467). Other research found eye and skeletal defects associated with fetal exposure to cocaine (Isenberg, Spierer, and Inkelis 1987).

Although the biochemical and neurobehavioral effects are more difficult to document, they are just as real (Office of Technology Assessment 1990, 10). Clearly, newborns who have been exposed to cocaine exhibit a high degree of irritability and other signs of withdrawal as their source of cocaine is removed.

Many of the abnormal characteristics seen in the cocaine-exposed newborn persist through at least 4 months of age. When comparing motor development of cocaine-exposed infants to non-drug-exposed infants, some striking differences can be noted in muscle tone, primitive reflexes, and volitional movement patterns. . . . Tremors are common, especially in their arms and hands, when they reach for objects (Chasnoff 1988, 1407).

Also troubling is the possibility of an increased incidence of sudden unexplained infant death in the offspring of cocaine-abusing women (Hume et al. 1989, 685). According to MacGregor and associates (1989, 882), comprehensive prenatal care may improve the outcome of cocaine-affected pregnancies, but morbidity associated with cocaine abuse cannot be eliminated solely by improved prenatal care.

A complicating factor in isolating the effects of cocaine on the fetus is that women abusing cocaine are likely to have abused multiple substances during their pregnancies. Table 2.4 shows the extent of multiple substance use found in one study (Little, Snell, Klein, and Gilstrap, 1989). Furthermore, cocaine and multiple-substance abusers tend to have poor nutritional habits and often adverse socioeconomic situations that lead to very limited prenatal care. Moreover, the pregnant cocaine users themselves are at heightened risk to develop hypertension, seizures, respiratory arrest, and cardiac failure, all of which could be harmful to the fetus as well. Finally, because of the recency of research on cocaine abuse, data on the long-term costs of dealing with the problems of children born under cocaine is now sketchy. Many of these children end up wards of the state, suffer learning problems, or are at risk for continual abuse.

Conclusive evidence associates maternal heroin addiction to growth retardation and fetal addiction while in the uterus. Fortunately, the numbers of heroin addicts who carry the fetus to term is small. Although there have been sporadic reports of birth defects associated with the use of marijuana by pregnant mothers, the findings have been inconsistent. Actually, there is surprisingly little hard data in this area. While there is no evidence of

Table 2.4
Multiple Substance Abuse During Pregnancy

Substance	Cocaine-exposed Infants (N=53)	Unexposed Infants (N=100)
Tobacco	29	14
Marijuana	10	1
Alcohol	12	0
Methamphetamines	8	2
Ts and Blues	4	0
Heroin	2	1
Valium	2	0
Touluene	1	0
Opium	1	0

Source: Little et al. (1989:158).

human teratogenicity, likewise, there is no assurance that marijuana exposure is safe for the fetus (Anderson and Globus 1989, 125). It seems logical that, at the least, heavy marijuana smoking might reduce the oxygen available to the fetus and increase the absorption of carbon monoxide into the bloodstream.

Despite the publicity about the deleterious effects of LSD and PCP, evidence is sparse and reports conflicting. Lubs and Ruddle (1970), for instance, concluded that LSD usage is at most a trivial factor in birth abnormalities, while Berlin and Jacobson (1970) found the rate of central nervous system defects in children born to LSD users was about sixteen times that of the general population. Similarly, Strauss and associates found symptoms of drug withdrawal present in the infants of two mothers who used PCP during pregnancy (see Freeman and Pescar 1982, 62). As with cocaine use, one of the problems in ascertaining the teratogenic effect of these drugs is that many of the users have compounding behavioral patterns. Berlin and Jacobson found that 81 percent of their LSD users also smoked, 25 percent used narcotics, and 36 percent had undergone extensive X rays (1970). Malnutrition, infections, and alcohol usage are also common among many of these women, thereby complicating attempts to single out the effects of each drug.

Maternal Infections

Rubella (German measles) is the most striking reminder of the potential effect of maternal disease on the fetus. During the last major epidemic in the United States (1963–65) approximately fifty thousand fetuses were affected. About 60 percent of these died before birth, and the remainder were born with serious birth defects including microcephaly, heart malformations, deafness, and cataracts. As with many maternal situations, the most deleterious effects of rubella occur upon exposure during the first trimester, especially the first four weeks of pregnancy.

Happily, widespread use of effective vaccines have reduced the occurrence of congenital rubella dramatically in the United States, although it remains a major threat in many countries. Because the vaccine contains live viruses, it should not be given to pregnant women nor to a woman within sixty days prior to conception. Otherwise, the effect will be the same as if the woman had rubella. As a result, immunization programs are targeted at young children on the assumption that exposure to women of childbearing age will thus be diminished.

Congenital toxoplasmosis is thought to occur only after primary maternal infection. Most affected infants do not exhibit symptoms of the disease at birth, but regardless of the initial presentation of the infection, prognosis is very poor. Of those infected 10 to 15 percent die, 85 percent of the survivors display severe psychomotor retardation by age two to four, and 50 percent develop visual problems detectable by age one. Although the progression of the disease can be controlled medically, neurological damage cannot be reversed (Devore, Jackson, and Piening 1983).

Another infection that can be transmitted from mother to child is viral hepatitis, particularly hepatitis B virus. Most frequently, the infant becomes infected during delivery or soon after birth. The transfer rate is highest when the mother contracts the virus in the third trimester. When viral hepatitis is transmitted to the fetus, the risk of prematurity, stillbirth and perinatal mortality heighten. Although infants who develop hepatitis B virus often become chronic antigen carriers, very few infants develop acute hepatitis or chronic liver disease. For the few who do, however, the effect is calamitous.

An infection with devastating effects on the fetus is syphilis. Although the incidence of congenital syphilis declined in the 1950s after the introduction of penicillin therapy and prenatal serologic testing, a steady increase has occurred in the past decade. In 1986, more cases of congenital syphilis were reported to the Centers for Disease Control (CDC) than in any of the preceding fifteen years (Ricci, Fojaco, and O'Sullivan 1989, 687). Approximately 250 to 400 infants are born annually in the United States with congenital syphilis. According to a CDC study, 80 percent of women with primary and secondary syphilis are in their reproductive years ("Maternal Age" 1984). Transmittal of the disease to the fetus is associated conclusively with brain damage, cardiovascular system abnormalities, blindness, and increased rates of spontaneous abortion and perinatal deaths. Evidence indicates that the fetus is at high risk for damage throughout the gestation period, and that nearly every organ in the body can be affected. Prevention of fetal damage depends on early diagnosis of syphilis and treatment with high doses of penicillin for mother and child. Mascola and associates argue that congenital syphilis can be reduced primarily through improving prenatal care for high-risk populations (1984).

Exposure of a baby to gonorrhea as it passes through the cervix upon delivery can result in serious eye infection and blindness. However, this condition is prevented effectively with the application of silver nitrate in the newborn's eyes upon birth. Because gonorrhea often is present without symptoms of infection in a woman, as a public health measure most states require silver nitrate treatment for all newborns. Another danger of gonorrhea to women is a heightened risk of pelvic inflammatory disease (PID), which might result in sterility.

The most common sexually transmitted disease is chlamydia trachomatis, which has been cultured from 10 percent of U.S. women during pregnancy. Although there are mixed research findings concerning the impact of chlamydia on pregnancy and newborn health, there is some evidence of an association with premature labor, preterm premature rupture of the membranes, and up to ten times the relative risk of neonatal mortality compared with noninfected women (Thorp et al. 1989).

The frequency of genital herpes infections has increased markedly in the last decade, leading some observers to term it an epidemic. There is now evidence suggesting that infection in the first trimester may lead to increased risk of spontaneous abortion, although more research is necessary for confirmation. In one study of 184 cases of herpes simplex infection of newborns, 41 percent were of low birth weight. By one week after birth, 59 percent of infected babies had experienced seizures or had developed a fever, conjunctivitis, or lesions of the skin (Stone et al. 1989). Herpes infections at term are also clearly associated with heightened risk of microcephaly, retinal dysplasia, mental retardation, and perinatal death. "Neonatal herpes is a relatively devastating disease with a fairly high morbidity and mortality. The major risk is the acquisition of the disease from exposure to infection in the birth canal in a woman who develops herpes for the first time during pregnancy" (Corey 1982).

Whether or not the mother has visible lesions, 30 to 50 percent of newborns delivered through the birth canal contaminated with herpes virus are infected, and of these half will die or be severely damaged. Approximately 70 percent of all neonatal herpes infections are disseminated, affecting the internal organs, especially the liver, adrenals, and central nervous system. Of those infants who contact the disseminated form, 60 to 90 percent die (Devore, Jackson, and Piening 1983, 1661).

Although disseminated herpes simplex virus (HSV) infection during pregnancy is uncommon, at present it is accompanied by high maternal and fetal mortality and morbidity (Peacock and Sarubbi 1983). Jacob and associates in a study of 215 middle-income, white, suburban women, revealed that 4.6 percent had positive herpes cultures near term, though none bore a child with neonatal herpes (1984). However, Sever contends that herpes infections will require "considerable" emphasis in the 1980s because of the explosive increase in the rate of infection among women of reproductive age, the recurrences of infections after dormant periods, and the current lack of satisfactory treatment (1980, 174). Corey recommends virologic surveillance in pregnant women (1982). He advocates that women with a history of genital herpes, or whose current or past sexual partners have had herpes, be monitored to identify those with clinical or asymptomatic viral shedding at or very near term. Those who test positive are candidates for a Cesarian section, although Lagrew and associates argue that treatment with the antiviral agent for HSV, acyclovis, presents less risk than an emergency Cesarian section and has produced encouraging results (1984).

One of the most troubling trends in the incidence of AIDS is the vertical transmission of the virus from mother to fetus, reported to range from 20 to 60 percent (Hoff et al. 1989). Approximately one-third of the infants born to women testing positive for the human immunodeficiency virus (HIV) antibody will die or show evidence of infection within one year of birth (Witwer 1989, 282). Many of these infants will be become "boarder babies" who spend their entire short life in a hospital. Although the prevalence of babies infected with the AIDS virus varies depending on the specific population and geographical location, average figures for the United States are two per one thousand pregnant women, or approximately two thousand infants per year. In New York City and other urban areas the prevalence is considerably higher—as high as 20 percent in some hospitals. Rates of HIV are significantly higher among black and Hispanic infants than among white infants.

Furthermore, infants born to mothers with AIDS-related conditions are at high risk for other infections, including hepatitis B and congenital toxoplasmosis (Scott et al. 1985). Although Scott and associates conclude that their observations do not clarify the source of infection in the mother (twelve of the sixteen mothers were Haitian, three reported using intravenous drugs, and one was an acknowledged prostitute), they support the argument that infant cases likely result from transmittal from the mother rather than from other household members (1985, 363). Also, because the infants developed symptoms of AIDS at a mean age of four months, the data suggest that transmission occurs either *in utero* or during the perinatal period.

Radiation

It is a fact that radiation damages cells, especially cells that are dividing rapidly. Mammal studies clearly demonstrate that high-energy radiation leads to congenital malformations, growth retardation, and embryonic death. Although the effects on human fetuses are less clear, "there is reasonable corroboration of the teratogenic and growth-retarding effects of x-ray in the human" (Brent 1980, 177). High-energy radiation is associ-ated with microcephaly and mental retardation in humans, especially with exposure in the first three weeks of pregnancy. "It has been estimated that low doses of approximately 0.2 rads can increase the chance of a child developing cancer by fifty percent. Nurses, physicians, and technicians involved in radium treatments and nuclear medicine have been found to be exposed to double or triple this dose" (Hunt 1978).

There is clear evidence that radiation exhibits a cumulative dosage effect, and that fetal tissue may be as much as twenty-five times more sensitive to radiation than adult tissue. Furthermore, unlike adult irradiation, fetal irradiation is essentially a whole body exposure, thereby exposing all organs, including the gonads. Finally, there is a small but increased risk of childhood leukemia and other malignancies in children who have been exposed to X rays early in pregnancy (Rubin 1980, 149). Despite these potentially deleterious effects, Brent concludes that while it is advisable to limit diagnostic X-ray procedures on women of reproductive age, it is also crucial that "the exaggeration of low dose diagnostic radiation risks do not interfere with appropriate medical care or create unnecessary anxiety in exposed women of reproductive age" (1980, 180).

THE FETUS IN THE WOMB:
A SUMMARY OF EVIDENCE

A wide range of behavioral patterns and maternal characteristics have been found to be associated with deleterious effects on the fetus. In most cases, it appears that the critical period of development occurs between the third and twelfth weeks of human gestation (Nishimura and Tanimura 1976). However, each organ has its own critical period, and for some, such as the brain, where cell proliferation does not cease until at least six to eight months after birth, sensitivity to environmental teratogenic agents extends throughout the pregnancy. Although the exposure to potential teratogens later in gestation might not result in gross organ system abnormalities, it might still be associated with other serious dysfunctions.

Furthermore, research on teratogens indicates that most teratogenesis probably is caused by the combined effects of a number of more subtle teratogens acting in consort, rather than a "single-hit massive teratogenic action." According to Melnick, a "simple one-to-one correspondence does not exist for birth defects" (1980, 453). The problem is vastly more complex, and the solution depends on unraveling the unique contribution of each of a multitude of intimately related factors.

Despite the complex nature of fetal development and the variation of effects any single stimulus might have on a specific fetus, the evidence demonstrates that there are many ways in which maternal behavioral patterns and health status can impair the proper maturation of the fetus and cause irreparable harm in some cases. Although the data remain inconclusive, there is growing evidence of the importance of providing as risk-free a setting for fetal growth as possible. Maternal smoking, drinking, eating, and general life style can and do have an effect on the fetus. As more is known about the specific deleterious effects of certain maternal behaviors, increased attention likely will be directed toward the responsibility of the mother to assure the fetus as normal an environment as possible throughout the gestation period. Unlike most other prenatal disorders, many of these threats to the fetus and newborn are completely avoidable. Hanson, for instance, exclaims that fetal alcohol syndrome is a "national tragedy made particularly poignant" because it can be prevented if the commitment is made to do so (1980, 221).

Within the context of the growing knowledge of these hazards, the question re-emerges as to what right a child has to a safe uterine environment and as normal a start in life as possible? In turn, this demonstrates the potential conflict of rights between the developing fetus and the mother. It is certainly a tragedy that in an affluent country such as the United States, children continue to be born with birth defects caused primarily by a lack of proper nutrition or the behavior of the mother during pregnancy. Despite clear evidence that extramaternal factors can be a significant danger to the mother and the fetus, in a democratic society the woman, at times perhaps unfairly, bears responsibility for her actions. She alone is the direct link to the fetus and she alone makes the ultimate decision as to whether or not to smoke, use alcohol or other drugs, maintain proper nutrition, and so forth.

Although emphasis here on the responsibility placed on the woman could be interpreted as sexist, the actions of the mother, not the father, do in fact more directly affect the fetus. Emerging evidence of perinatal mortality associated with coitus near delivery clearly demonstrates the shared responsibility of the father and mother in providing a risk-free fetal environment (Naeye 1981). The effects of secondary smoke and other paternally initiated behavior are yet to be seriously evaluated. In recognizing the rights of women, not men, to reproductive choice in matters of abortion (*Roe* v. *Wade* 1973), however, the Court has not so tacitly ruled that the pregnant woman has the prime responsibility to the fetus. Although this does not excuse a father and other parties from playing a positive role in guaranteeing a risk-free environment for the fetus, the final choice should be that of the woman.

3

Prenatal Injury: Emerging Legal
Causes for Action

In the past several decades, major changes have occurred in the body of case law surrounding the processes of birth and pregnancy. Preconception, conception, and prenatal legal actions are commonplace in part due to alterations in social values regarding birth and pregnancy. Major causes of the growing legal attention to these subjects include the recent advances in medical science, discussed earlier, that have brought about significant change to the physiological aspects of the birth process and altered perceptions of it. "In short, the advances in medical science have reshaped the way American society thinks about birth" (Winborne 1983, 4).

Along with altered values and advances in medical science, many legal controversies have arisen regarding prenatal and even preconception injuries, as well as the birth process. The growing number of these birth and pregnancy cases are forcing judicial considerations of many new and novel causes of action. This cluster of topics surrounding prenatal injury "presents a series of anguished questions, inevitably enmeshing the torts watcher in which Darwin called 'the web of life'" (Lambert 1983, 65). Terms like "wrongful pregnancy," "wrongful life," and "wrongful birth" are quickly emerging, resulting in substantial questioning of previous legal and policy assumptions. It is not surprising that there is wide divergence in the reaction of the courts to these novel cases, both in recognizing a cause of action and determining the appropriate amount of damages, if any, to be awarded. According to Winborne, the law in this area is far from being settled; it is just beginning to develop (1983, 5). This chapter attempts to review systematically court action in the area of prenatal injury. Although much of this discussion is not concerned directly with the maternal-fetal relationship, these trends in case law have a significant, cumulative impact on it. The following chapter focuses on the issues raised by an emerging trend in case law to accept a cause of action against the parents for prenatal injury.

FRAMING A CAUSE OF ACTION
FOR PRENATAL INJURY

The child's right to recover from a third party for prenatal injuries, though largely unquestioned today, is a very recent judicial development. Prior to 1946, the courts largely accepted the precedence of *Dietrich* v. *Inhabitants of Northampton* (1884), where the Massachusetts Supreme Court disallowed recovery for negligently inflicted prenatal injuries in a wrongful death action of a child that did not survive its premature birth. In that case a woman four to five months pregnant slipped and fell, because of a defect in the highway, and subsequently had a miscarriage. The plaintiff was alive when delivered, but too premature to survive. In arriving at its decision, the *Dietrich* court relied on the lack of precedent and on the concept that the fetus was part of the mother and not a separate entity: "Taking all of the foregoing considerations into account, and further, that, as the unborn child was a part of the mother at the time of the injury, any damage to it which was not too remote to be recovered for at all was recoverable by her" (p. 17).

Similarly, in *Walker* v. *Railway Co.* (1891), after an accident on a train whereby the mother and her unborn fetus were seriously injured, so that the child was born crippled and deformed, all of the judges agreed that the suit could not be maintained because: "As a matter of fact, when the act of negligence occurred the plaintiff was not in esse, —was not a person, or a passenger, or a human being. Her age and her existence are reckoned from her birth, and no precedent has been found for this action" (p. 71). Subsequently, in *Allaire* v. *St. Lukes Hospital* (1900), the Illinois Supreme Court following *Dietrich* held that an action for injuries could not be maintained by a plaintiff who at the time of injury was a prenatal infant with no separate legal existence. In this case, the infant plaintiff's claim came from injuries sustained while in the womb, when his mother was severely injured in an elevator accident. As a result of the accident, the child's left side and limbs were "wasted, withered, and atrophied" and he was "sadly crippled for life" (p. 638). Interestingly, the court rejected the cause of action of the child against the owners of the elevator because it might set a precedent for a child to sue its mother: "If the action can be maintained, it *necessarily follows* that an infant may maintain an action against its own mother while pregnant with it. We are of the opinion that the action will not lie [italics added]" (p. 640).

The strong dissent of Judge J. Boggs in *Allaire* is also very illuminating. Just because no precedent could be found for a plaintiff awarded damages for injuries inflicted upon his or her person while in the womb does not mean that a new principle cannot be established when the facts warrant it. According to Boggs, at some point of "viability" the fetus reaches a stage where destruction of the life of the mother does not necessarily also end its life. Furthermore:

Medical science and skill and experience have demonstrated that at a period of gestation in advance of the period of parturition the foetus is capable of independent and separate life, and that, though within the body of the mother, it is not merely a part of her body, for her body may die in all of its parts and the child remain alive, and capable of maintaining life (p. 641).

Boggs asks: why should the infant that survives be denied the right to recover damages resulting from the same injury in which the mother has such a right? He, therefore, rejects the precedents of *Dietrich,* where the fetus did not survive, and *Walker,* where the issue centered on the lack of contractual obligations to the unborn child. Compensation should not be "denied on a mere theory—known to be false—that the injury was not to his person, but to the person of the mother (p. 641)."

Judge Boggs's thinking, although rejected by the majority in *Allaire,* soon began to gain momentum in many jurisdictions. As medical science learned more about prenatal development, the *Dietrich* rule was attacked for its illogical legal bases and for its inconsistency with biological knowledge. That the unborn child's property and contract rights were protected legally under common law while its personal rights were not was criticized as inconsistent. Also, it was argued that, at least after viability, when a child is capable of maintaining independent life, it is a separate entity and not simply an appendage of its mother. Another objection to this cause of action, that proof of causation is more difficult in prenatal injury cases, was weakened as medical knowledge about the causes of congenital damage expanded.

Despite the growing realization that *Dietrich* reasoning was faulty, it was relied upon as controlling until the U.S. District Court of the District of Columbia dismissed it in *Bonbrest* v. *Kotz* (1946). In the case, infant Bette Gay Bonbrest by her father attempted to recover for injuries sustained when she was removed negligently by a physician, a clear instance of injury to a viable child. In order to distinguish itself from *Dietrich,* the court emphasized that the plaintiff was viable and capable of surviving outside the womb.

As to a viable child being 'part' of its mother—this argument seems to me to be a contradiction in terms. True, it is in the womb, but it is capable now of extrauterine life—and while dependent for its continued development on sustenance derived from its peculiar relationship to its mother, it is not a "part" of the mother in the sense of a constituent element. . . . Modern medicine is replete with cases of living children being taken from dead mothers. Indeed, apart from viability, a non-viable foetus is not a part of its mother (p. 140).

The *Bonbrest* court, therefore, reasoned that once the child demonstrated it was capable of survival outside its mother's womb, the argument that the fetus had no independent existence was inexplicable. If a child after birth is denied right of action for prenatal injuries, there is a wrong inflicted for which there is no remedy. "If a right of action be denied to the child it will be compelled, without any fault on its part, to go through life carrying the seal of another's fault and bearing a very heavy burden of infirmity and inconvenience without any compensation therefor" (*Bonbrest*, 141–42).

After *Bonbrest*, the right to recover for injuries sustained *in utero* gained rapid and widespread acceptance. For instance, in *Woods* v. *Lancet* (1951) a New York appellate court concluded that "To hold, as a matter of law, that no viable fetus has any separate existence which the law will recognize is for the law to deny a simple and easily demonstrable fact. This child, when injured, was in fact, alive and capable of being delivered and of remaining alive, separate from its mother" (p. 694).

In *Williams* v. *Marion Rapid Transit, Inc.* (1949), the Ohio Supreme Court held that a viable fetus was a "person" within the mean of the Ohio Constitution, and thus after birth could maintain an action for tortious prenatal injuries. Shortly thereafter, the Minnesota Supreme Court in *Verkennes* v. *Corniea* (1949), following the reasoning of Justice Boggs in *Allaire,* held that the representative of a stillborn child could maintain an action for wrongful death because it was viable at the time of the injury. Likewise, the New Jersey Supreme Court in *Smith* v. *Brennan* (1960), a case where the infant plaintiff sustained injuries during an automobile collision while in his mother's womb, stated:

Regardless of analogies to other areas of the law, justice requires that the *principle be recognized that a child has a legal right to begin life with a sound mind and body* [italics mine]. If the wrongful conduct of another interferes with that right, and it can be established by competent proof that there is a causal connection between the wrongful interference and the harm suffered by the child when born, damages for such harm should be recoverable by the child (p. 503).

The *Smith* court concluded that the semantic argument of whether an unborn child is a "person in being" is irrelevant to recovery for prenatal injury. Furthermore, the difficulty of proving fact of prenatal injury to the infant in the mother's womb is not sufficient reason for blocking all attempts to prove it (p. 503).

According to respected legal commentator William L. Prosser, the trend toward allowing recovery after the abandonment of *Dietrich* was "the most spectacular abrupt reversal of a well settled rule in the whole history of the law of torts" (1971, 336). Today, all states recognize a cause of action for prenatal injury by a subsequently born child against a third party.

Despite the consensus of the courts to recognize a cause of action for prenatal injury, many inconsistencies remain. One of the most critical differences focuses on whether a fetus must reach a certain stage of development at the time of injury before there can be a settlement. Other crucial distinctions center on the scope of liability, the standards of causation required, and whether or not the injured child must be born alive. Before examining the various types of prenatal actions, the difficult issue of viability will be discussed (see Chapter 4 for further discussion concerning viability and personhood).

The Viability Rule for Prenatal Torts

Although there is a clear case law trend in favor of allowing a claim for prenatal injury regardless of the stage of gestation during which the injury occurred, there is far from unanimity in the courts on the question of viability. The viability rule developed originally as a means of distinguishing cases from *Dietrich,* which assumed the fetus is part of the mother. In *Bonbrest,* the court refuted *Dietrich* by concluding that a viable fetus can sustain life independent of the mother and is, therefore, a distinct legal entity. Courts relying on *Bonbrest* thus often limited the authority of their decisions to suits involving injuries incurred after viability. For instance, in *Albala* v. *City of New York* (1981), the New York Supreme Court, Appellate Division, upheld the viability requirement when it refused recovery for injuries suffered by a previable fetus (see also *Evans* v. *Olson* 1976). The court held that a cause of action did not lie in favor of the child, whose injuries allegedly resulted from the perforated uterus suffered by the child's mother during an abortion performed prior to the child's conception. A primary rationale used by many courts sustaining the viability rule is that proving causation is difficult when the injury occurs in the previable stages of fetal development.

Increasing numbers of courts, however, have either expressly renounced the viability rule or ignored it. The Georgia Supreme Court in *Hornbuckle* v. *Plantation Pipe Line Co.* (1956) held that viability was not the deciding factor in a prenatal personal injuries action, and that recovery for any injury suffered after the point of conception should be permitted.

The petition alleges that the plaintiff, who is now in life, received prenatal injuries caused by the alleged negligent operation of an automobile by the defendant, which caused it to collide with the automobile in which the plaintiff's mother was riding while pregnant, which resulted in the plaintiff being born with a deformed right foot, right ankle, and right leg. . . . If a child born after an injury sustained at any period of its prenatal life can prove the effect on it of a tort, it would have a right to recover (p. 728).

In another case arising out of an automobile collision, the New Hampshire Supreme Court in *Bennett* v. *Hymers* (1958) held that the fetus from the time of conception becomes a separate organism and remains so.

It is not our intention to engage in an abstruse and technical discussion of the exact moment when conception occurs and the life of a new being starts. However, it seems to us that if an infant is born alive and survives bearing physical or mental injuries medically provable to have been incurred by it while *en ventre sa mere* it is being oblivious to reality to say that the mother alone was injured by the tortious act and not the child (p. 109).

According to the court in *Smith* v. *Brennan* (1960), "Whether viable or not at the time of injury, the child sustains the same harm after birth, and therefore should be given the same opportunity for redress" (p. 504). In *Sylvia* v. *Gobeille* (1966) a Rhode Island appellate court stated: "We are unable logically to conclude that a claim for injury inflicted prior to viability is any less meritorious than one sustained after" (p. 226).

The trend toward abolition of the viability rule is a just one because the harm sustained by the child may be the same whether the injury occurred before or after viability. "Once the child is born alive, it is a separate human being deserving of compensation, regardless of whether it was a separate legal entity at the time the injury was originally inflicted. At birth, and throughout its life, the child exhibits the injury which was caused by the prior negligent act" (Simon 1978, 55).

In *Wilson* v. *Kaiser Foundation Hospital* (1983), the California Court of Appeal, Third District, agreed with this reasoning and concluded that birth is the condition precedent that establishes the beginning of the child's rights. A tort action may be maintained if the child is born alive—whether the injury occurred before viability or after is immaterial once birth takes place. However, if the injured child is not born alive, a cause of action for prenatal injuries does not arise on its behalf, because a stillborn fetus is not a person within the wrongful death statute of California (p. 650). In fact, as pointed out in Chapter 2, injuries inflicted in the first trimester are likely to produce the most severe congenital deformities. Thus, the viability rule precludes many of the most meritorious claims. The presumption here is that the fetus from the time of conception, becomes a separate organism and remains so throughout its existence.

Another reason for rejecting viability as a pivotal point in defining the legal rights of the fetus is its arbitrariness. As discussed later in Chapter 4, the medical parameters of viability are in a constant state of flux. As neonatal intensive care technology improves, viability, or that point at which the fetus can survive outside the mother's uterus, will be pushed back earlier in gestation. Also, there remains considerable disagreement over which of many criteria, including fetal age and weight, is most adequate in determining viability, and over the precision of any such measures. In addition, the viability rule is difficult to apply because it is an indeterminate concept that depends on the individual development of a specific fetus, the health of the mother, the quality of neonatal care available, the competency of the attending physician, and a host of other factors. As a result, there is no way of determining whether or not a particular fetus was viable at the time of injury, unless it was born immediately. Insofar as viability is usually impossible to ascertain, the theory is impractical as a measure of liability and ought to be abolished as a criterion. Lambert, too, favors discarding the "arbitrary" viability rule on these grounds (1983, 65).

In a further extension of this logic, some courts recently have recognized a cause of action for personal injuries prior to conception. In *Renslow* v. *Mennonite Hospital* (1977), a physician was held liable for injuries suffered by an infant girl as a result of a blood transfusion to the mother nine years before the child's birth. These "preconception torts" arise when a negligent act has been committed against a person not yet conceived, but whose eventual existence is foreseeable (see also *Turpin* v. *Sortini* 1982 and *Harbeson* v. *Parke-Davis* 1983).

Wrongful Death of the Unborn

Under common law, the death of a person may not be compensated by civil court. In order to alleviate the harsh common law rule of no liability for the death of a person, wrongful death statutes in all jurisdictions are designed to fill the void and provide compensation to survivors. There are, however, many problems in bringing wrongful death actions for the death of an unborn child. First, the provisions of the statutes themselves vary considerably across the fifty states. Moreover, variation in judicial construction and interpretation of the statutes is even greater. Therefore, it is not surprising that the courts remain divided as to whether a fetus may be the subject of a wrongful death action and, if so, under what conditions. Despite these inconsistencies, however, there are clear patterns that indicate a growing acceptance of a cause of action for wrongful death of a fetus.

In addition to the difficulties raised by variations in the statutes and their interpretation, requirements for the existence of a right of action in wrongful death also make application to the unborn problematic. Typical requirements of the statutes include: the existence of a "person" who has died; the death of the person from injuries resulting from a wrongful act, neglect, or default that would have conferred a cause of action upon the person who has died, had that person survived; and the act, neglect, or default that caused the fatal injury must have been performed by another. Although the third requisite is generally amenable to proof, especially in light of advances in medicine, the first two are not. Critical remaining issues are whether a child which is never born alive is a person within the meaning of the statute, and whether the plaintiff can prove that the injury caused the unborn child's death.

Causation

In considering actions for wrongful death of a fetus, early courts concluded that the action should be dismissed because of the difficulty of demonstrating causation of prenatal injury and the possibility of fictitious claims. These objections have been undercut to a great degree by advances in medical science. The Alabama Supreme Court ruled that proof of the cause of an unborn child's death can be made by expert testimony, as in other wrongful death torts: "The problems of proof of causation do not impose a bar to bringing an action for the wrongful death of a stillborn fetus as any difficulty in proof of causation would inure to the benefit of the defendant" (*Eich* v. *Town of Gulf Shores* 1974, 355). As noted in Chapter 2, a variety of prenatal diagnostic techniques such as ultrasound can be used to establish trauma or injury to the fetus immediately after an accident. Furthermore, advances in pathology provide more objective data for evaluating causation of an unborn's death.

In addition to the availability of more precise medical evidence of causation, courts increasingly have rejected the arguments of denying causes of action on the basis of the difficulty of proving causation or of the possibility of fictitious claims. The court in *Woods* v. *Lancet* (1951), for instance, concluded that difficulty in proving legal and factual causation should not affect substantive rights. The *Smith* v. *Brennan* (1960) court stated that proof is no more problematic in a prenatal injury case than in any other personal injury case. In *Presley* v. *Newport Hospital* (1976), the Rhode Island Supreme Court reiterated that the "legal right of a child to begin life with sound mind and body should not be abridged by difficulties in proof of causation" (p. 748). Finally, it is argued that the rules of evidence are adequate to prevent fictitious claims, and that a cause for action should not be denied on those grounds (*Eich* v. *Town of Gulf Shores* 1974, 354).

Is the Unborn a Person?

The major remaining basis of the inconsistency of establishing the rights of the unborn to a cause of action for wrongful death is the question of whether or not a fetus is a person under the appropriate statutes and, if so, at what point in gestation? (A related question is whether or not the fetus must be live born before action is allowed.) This issue is crucial, because if the fetus is defined as a person, the action will be recognized; if not, the action will be dismissed. Ordinarily, the courts focus on three elements to determine if a fetus is a person: First, they examine the legislative intent in the enacting statute. If a fetus is not specifically included in the statute, the court can either extend by implication a cause of action for the fetus (*Group Health Association* v. *Blumenthal* 1983) or defer to the legislature to make explicit their intention to include the unborn as a person (*Justus* v. *Atchison* 1977; *Egbert* v. *Wenzl* 1977).

In situations where the statutes are not explicit, the courts will be attentive to the legal status of unborns traditionally enjoyed in the state for other types of action. Finally, they will consider community knowledge and attitudes about the unborn (Kader 1980, 653). Here again the role of medicine is critical in shifting the balance toward recognizing a cause of action for the unborn. It will be demonstrated in Chapter 4 that social recognition of the fetus as a person has been heightened by a variety of techniques that allow visualization of the fetus early in gestation, as well as the increase in fetal surgery and therapy. According to Scofield, "parental concern with the unborn has increased with advances in medical science, and this reality supports inclusion of the unborn within the meaning of death statutes" (1982, 803).

As a result of amended wrongful death statutes that facilitate inclusion of the unborn and the other social and legal forces above, a majority of jurisdictions now allow a cause of action for the death of an unborn. However, as stated earlier, there is a significant variation in the criteria used to qualify a fetus for legal status, primarily focusing on viability and whether the fetus was live born, if even for a few minutes. Concerning viability, in some cases it has been held that a fetus, regardless of viability at the time of injury, is a person for purposes of the wrongful death statute. In *Presley* v. *Newport Hospital* (1976), for instance, the Rhode Island Supreme Court held that the fetus, whether viable or previable, was a person within the meaning of the Rhode Island statute.

Of all the arguments in the plaintiff's favor, the most simple and perhaps the one that underlies all others is that it is simply illogical and therefore arbitrary to cut off the right of action at birth. The myth perpetuated by Mr. Justice Holmes in 1884, [in *Dietrich*] that the unborn fetus is but a part of its mother's body, has long since been laid to rest in both the law and medicine (p. 753).

Similarly, in *Danos* v. *St. Pierre* (1981), the Louisiana Supreme Court affirmed an award under the wrongful death statute for the death in a car crash of a fetus in the sixth month. A concurring opinion stated that the word "person" should include an unborn child from the moment of fertilization and implantation (see also *O'Grady* v. *Brown* 1983). In a case involving maternal exposure to hepatitis in the work place when she was three months pregnant (*Jarvis* v. *Providence Hospital* 1989), the Michigan Court of Appeals ruled that wrongful death action could be maintained on behalf of a fetus that was nonviable at the time of the negligent conduct, but viable at the time of injury resulting from the negligence. In another case involving an automobile accident, the same court (*Fryover* v. *Forbes* 1989) held that a nonviable fetus not born alive is a person within the meaning of the Michigan Wrongful Death Act.

In contrast, other courts have held that a fetus is a person under a wrongful death statute only if viable at the time of injury. In *Shirley* v. *Bacon* (1980), the Georgia Supreme Court ruled that wrongful death action was contingent on the fetus being "quick" at the time of its death. The California Supreme Court (*People* v. *Hamilton* 1989) ruled that murder of a viable fetus comes under the homicide statute. Likewise, the Massachusetts Supreme Court in *Commonwealth* v. *Lawrence* (1989) held that a viable fetus is considered a human being for purposes of common-law murder. In *Williams* v. *State* (1988) the Maryland Court of Appeals held that "criminal infliction upon a pregnant woman of prenatal injuries resulting in the death of her child after live birth" (p. 216) could constitute manslaughter. In two cases involving vehicular homicide, the Wisconsin Court of Appeals in *State* v. *Cornelius* (1989) and the Georgia Court of Appeals in *State* v. *Hammett* (1989) agreed that an infant who is born alive, but who subsequently dies of injuries inflicted *in utero,* falls under the homicide statutes. In an interesting case (*Matter of Klein* 1989), a New York appellate court held that a nonviable fetus was not a person for whom guardianship could be appointed. It thus rejected attempts of strangers to obtain guardianship of the fetus of a comatose pregnant woman.

In *Green* v. *Smith* (1978), the court drew a clear distinction between the common-law cause of action on behalf of an infant for injuries suffered prior to viability and a statutory cause of action for destruction of a fetus not yet viable. The loss incurred by a live-born child burdened with defects resulting from a prenatal injury is the same whether the injury is suffered prior to or after viability. However, the wrongful death statute provides for the recovery of the death of a "person," and the court found no basis on which to hold that one can cause the death of a fetus not yet viable. Similar decisions were rendered in *Salazar* v. *St. Vincent Hospital* (1980) and *Wallace* v. *Wallace* (1980).

In *United States* v. *Spencer* (1988) the U.S. Court of Appeals, Ninth Circuit, ruled that fetal infanticide was within the federal statutory definition of murder under 18 U.S. Code §1111. In this case Spencer assaulted a pregnant woman, kicking and stabbing her in the abdomen. The child was born alive after an emergency Cesarian section, but died ten minutes later as a result of the injuries. Similarly, the U.S. Court of Appeals, Eleventh Circuit (*Smith* v. *Newsome* 1987) declared that the Georgia feticide statute, which prohibits the willful killing of an unborn child so far developed to be ordinarily called "quick," was not unconstitutionally vague within the meaning of the Fourteenth Amendment.

Finally, to cover all possible combinations, some courts have concluded that a fetus, whether viable or previable, is not a person under the wrongful death statute and, therefore, its beneficiaries have no cause of action to seek recovery for the loss. In *Scott* v. *Kopp* (1981), the Pennsylvania Supreme Court denied recovery under the wrongful death statute for death resulting from an automobile accident injury to a fetus in the eighth month of pregnancy. The court held that plaintiffs had no right of recovery since there was "no independent life in being, surviving birth, which could have brought the action prior to death" (p. 959). Moreover, "we believe . . . that drawing the line at conception or viability or at any point other than birth will not remove the element of arbitrariness, but will merely relocate the difficulty while increasing the problems of causation and damages" (p. 961–62). Similar findings that a wrongful death action cannot be maintained for the death of a viable fetus have been forthcoming in Pennsylvania (*Hudak* v. *Georgy* 1989), California (*Wilson* v. *Kaiser Foundation Hospital* 1983), Iowa (*Dunn* v. *Rose Way* 1983), Florida (*Abdelaziz* v. *A.M.I.S.U.B. of Florida, Inc.* 1987), Texas (*Wheeler* v. *Yettie Kersting Memorial Hospital* 1988), and Michigan (*Carr* v. *Wittingen* 1990). In *Justus* v. *Atchison* (1977), a California appellate court stated that if the legislature meant the fetus to be a person under the wrongful death statute, it would determine "to confer legal personality on unborn fetuses." Likewise, in *Hamby* v. *McDaniel* (1977) the Tennessee Supreme Court concluded that it was not appropriate or necessary to judicially determine when life begins, because the creation of a wrongful death action is properly the business of the legislative branch of government: "The Tennessee Legislature's failure to change the Wrongful Death Statute to provide a right of action for a viable fetus, stillborn, implies approval of the definition given by this Court . . . and gives the judicial construction of the statute the effect of legislation" (p. 776–77). Expansion of benefits to include viable fetus, fetus, or embryo is within the legislature's exclusive province.

Of those jurisdictions that recognize any cause of action for a fetus under wrongful death, virtually all have abandoned the live-birth requirement. Most courts will allow an action when a fetus is prenatally injured and subsequently stillborn, and its representative attempts to recover for wrongful death. In *Vaillancourt* v. *Medical Center Hospital of Vermont* (1980), the Vermont Supreme Court held that a viable fetus, subsequently stillborn, is a person under Vermont's wrongful death statute. In agreement, the Missouri Supreme Court in *O'Grady* v. *Brown* (1983) held that parents may maintain a wrongful death claim for their stillborn fetus. The court agreed with the plaintiffs that there is "no substantial reason why a tortfeasor who causes prenatal death should be treated more favorably than one who causes prenatal injury" (p. 905). Similarly, the *Danos* court stated that it was illogical for the cause of action to depend on whether the child was stillborn or lived outside the womb for a few minutes. Rejecting a cause of action for the fetus's wrongful death would simply serve to benefit the person causing the injury.

In *Eich* v. *Town of Gulf Shores* (1974), the court stated that logic, fairness, and justice compel recognition of an action for prenatal injuries causing death before birth (see also *Volk* v. *Baldazo* 1982). These courts agree that the live-birth requisite is logically indefensible, in that one who injures a fetus later born alive only long enough to cause damages must pay for his or her actions, while one who injures a fetus severely enough to kill it outright does not. This would serve only to reward the tortfeasor for the severity of the injury. According to Winborne, "it would be bizarre to hold that the greater the harm inflicted the better the opportunity for exoneration of the defendant" (1983, 357).

Despite these criticisms of the live-birth requirement and the trend toward its rejection in wrongful death actions, a few courts remain adamant in its use. Some courts have argued that lines must be drawn, and that requiring a live birth has an advantage of establishing to a legal certainty that there was a living person (*Scott* v. *Kopp* 1981). From the moment of conception onward there must be some cutoff point, and to place this at the moment of live birth provides some degree of certainty to an otherwise speculative situation. Whatever the persuasiveness of these arguments, the *Justus* court held that a rejection of a wrongful death action for the death of a stillborn fetus is not illogical, nor is nonrecovery contrary to public policy, because it provides an incentive for tortfeasors to refrain from saving their victims' lives. In *Lacesse* v. *McDonough* (1972), a Massachusetts court stated that "if the fetus is not born alive, it is not such a person and will not suffer injury (p. 340)." Therefore, no recovery is allowed for a stillborn.

Damages

Another area of incongruous judicial decision making in prenatal wrongful death actions centers on recovery of damages. Although many courts are willing to recognize a cause of action, the extent of damages is difficult to prove. Damages in a wrongful death settlement are intended to benefit survivors and compensate them for their loss. In addition to determining what constitutes a fair award, the courts have to deal with how to distinguish between the lost fetuses at different stages in gestation. Is the emotional distress resulting from the death of a live born greater than that from the death of a stillborn? Of an embryo?

In *Prado* v. *Catholic Medical Center* (1988), for instance, the New York Supreme Court, Appellate Division, held that a mother could not recover for pain or emotional distress resulting from stillbirth. The claim that the plaintiff in this malpractice suit suffered prolonged pain "cannot be actionable since it was not permanent and since it could be considered as pain naturally associated with the childbirth process itself" (p. 475). Similarly, the Pennsylvania Superior Court in *Schroeder* v. *Ear, Nose and Throat Associates* of Lehigh Valley (1989) ruled that parents could not recover for loss of the society and companionship of an unborn child. Finally, a U.S. District Court in *Denham* v. *Burlington Northern Railroad Co.* (1988) ruled that parents could not recover damages for loss of the society of a fetus killed in a collision of a train and a car with a pregnant motorist.

Although the Supreme Court of Oklahoma in *Evans* v. *Olson* (1976) held that there is no more speculation as to the probability of pecuniary loss with a stillborn than with a child, and that a cause of action existed for wrongful death of a viable unborn child, other courts have held that damages associated with the loss of services and support is not recoverable because there is no competent evidence of the child's capability and potential (*Miller* v. *Highlands Insurance Co.* 1976). For the unborn none of the usual criteria, such as mental capacity, personality traits, and training, are present. (The *Miller* court did, however, hold recoverable medical and funeral expenses.) In *Jones* v. *Karraker* (1983), an Illinois appellate court affirmed a jury verdict of $125,000 in a wrongful death action involving an unborn child. Although the court admitted the difficulty of providing adequate evidence for determining pecuniary loss, it noted that the Illinois wrongful death statute provides for pecuniary compensation to the next of kin. While the appeals court said it would have awarded a substantially reduced sum, it found the question properly one for the jury to decide and let it stand.

Although the North Carolina Supreme Court ruled in a malpractice suit that the wrongful death act allows recovery of a viable but unborn child (*DiDonato* v. *Wortman* 1987), damages awarded in any such action are limited to those that are not purely speculative. Damages must be proved to a reasonable level of certainty and may not be based on pure conjuncture (p. 493). The court argued that when a child is stillborn, we can know nothing about its intelligence, abilities, interests, and other factors relevant to the monetary contribution it someday might have made to the beneficiaries in a wrongful death action (p. 494). Therefore:

Damages from lost income, loss of services, companionship, advice and the like, which are normally available in wrongful death action, cannot be recovered in action for wrongful death of stillborn child, in that such damages would be too speculative; damages for pain and suffering of decedent's parents are recoverable if they can be reasonably established, while medical and funeral expenses, as well as punitive and nominal damages, which are susceptible of proof are allowable (p. 489).

In *Danos* v. *St. Pierre* (1981) the Louisiana Supreme Court posited that in awarding damages in prenatal wrongful death cases, the trial judge may look at a number of factors for determining the extent of damages suffered by the parents. These factors include: the stage of pregnancy at which death occurs, the number of children the couple has, the probability of the pregnancy going to full term, whether the mother used artificial means to induce pregnancy, prenatal care of the unborn child, and prenatal preparation for the forthcoming child, such as house additions and baby furniture. Inherent in this approach is a recognition of the emotional ties between a mother and her unborn child. As noted earlier, new techniques, such as ultrasound and fetoscopy, that allow viewing of the fetus early in pregnancy, along with amniocentesis, which identifies fetal sex, are strengthening the emotional bonds between parent and child as well as the social recognition of the fetus as a person. Women who have undergone prenatal diagnosis often refer to the fetus as a baby and name it after learning its sex.

A California appeals court in *Johnson* v. *Superior Court* (1981) concluded that the mother forms a sufficiently close relationship with her fetus during pregnancy so that its death will cause her severe emotional distress.

In this cause of action petitioner alleges that she was a maternity patient . . . that she was negligently and carelessly permitted to remain in labor for over 24 hours "with ruptured membranes" and without definitive treatment, that she "felt and perceived her then unborn viable fetus die within her body" and as a result of sensory perception of the death of the fetus, petitioner suffered profound shock and emotional trauma (p. 63-64).

When the death results from medical malpractice or other negligence rather than natural and unavoidable causes, the loss is all the more poignant and should be legally redressable. Trends in prenatal diagnosis and monitoring are certain to enhance the measure of damages for emotional distress.

Prenatal Injury Actions

An unborn child can be injured, although not killed, through the tortious act of another person during the child's gestation. For instance, a Florida appellate court in *Singleton* v. *Ranz* (1988) held that a mother has legal cause of action for negligent or intentional tortious injury to the fetus as a living tissue of her body. Although inconsistencies exist in case law as to viability, proof of causation, and so forth, a consensus now exists in all fifty states that a child has a right to bring common-law action for injuries suffered before birth. This unanimity has been achieved in a short span in part because new medical knowledge of the deleterious effects of particular actions on the unborn permitted causation susceptible to legal proof.

As in all tort actions, the plaintiff must prove the existence of a legal duty on the part of the defendant to conform to a specific standard of conduct for the protection of the plaintiff against unreasonable risk of injury, as well as a breach of that duty by the defendant. For the breach to occur, there must be actual misfeasance: the defendant must be found to have been affirmatively negligent. Moreover, it must be proven that damage was suffered by the plaintiff, and that the proximate cause of the damage was the negligence of the defendant. Legal causation may be established even though the biological processes that bring the injury about are not understood precisely. Legal cause does not need be the sole or even predominant cause of the injury. It is only required that the defendant's conduct must be a substantial or material factor in bringing about the injury—but for the defendant's negligent conduct, the injury would not have occurred.

Tort actions predicated on prenatal injury have arisen from various factual settings, including automobile accidents and medical malpractice. To date, most prenatal injury suits have been brought against third parties, particularly physicians and other health providers, who allegedly failed to exercise the proper standard of care and caused damage through their negligence. Once the fetus was recognized as a legal entity separate from the mother, torts for prenatal injury became identical in principle to other malpractice suits. Given the growing state of medical knowledge about fetal development and the expanding array of diagnostic techniques, torts for prenatal injury have become a common medical malpractice suit.

One case that demonstrates the unique nature of many emerging causes of action in this area, *Payton* v. *Abbott Labs* (1981), was a class action suit brought by approximately four thousand women exposed to the drug diethylstilbestrol (DES). These women sued because their mothers ingested DES while pregnant and transmitted the drug to them *in utero*. As a result, they are at increased risk for a rare type of genital cancer as well as abnormalities of the reproductive organs. The defendants were pharmaceutical companies, including Abbott, Eli Lilly, Merck, Rexall, Squibb and Sons, and Upjohn, all of which manufactured and marketed DES as a miscarriage preventative between 1945 and 1976. The plaintiffs contended that the defendants were negligent in marketing DES, and that they should be compensated for the higher risk of cancer and other abnormalities they incurred. To confuse the situation even more, most of the plaintiffs were unable to identify the specific manufacturer of the DES ingested by their mothers.

Based on precedents treating *in utero* injury resulting from ingestion of a drug by the mother, the court held that the plaintiffs could maintain a cause of action. The *Payton* court rejected the defendants' argument that recovery should be denied because of the difficulty of proving causation and because of the risk of fictitious claims. The difficulties of proof or the possibility of false claims could not bar action by plaintiffs with medically demonstratable injuries. Of course, they would have to satisfy the normal requirements of any tort action.

Although *Payton* was rendered in response to a certified question by the federal court as to whether there is a cause of action in Massachusetts for those injured by a drug prior to birth, the precedental force is expected to be substantial. According to Seksay, the prenatal injury holding in *Payton* results in a potential increase in liability for anyone who negligently supplies a pregnant woman with drugs or medication (1983, 266). Under *Payton,* Massachusetts courts, in accord with the courts and legislatures of other jurisdictions, are gradually extending legal rights to the unborn.

CRIMINAL LAW AND THE UNBORN

Another area of law that demonstrates an inconsistent and at times incoherent view of the status of the unborn is criminal law, particularly homicide and child abuse. For purposes of criminal law, the fetus generally has not been recognized as a person or human being. Under common law, the unborn fetus was not considered a person to whom the law of homicide applied. In some jurisdictions no penalties were imposed for homicide unless the victim had been born. For instance, in *Giardina* v. *Bennett* (1988), the New Jersey Supreme Court held that causing the death of a fetus is not murder unless the fetus is born alive and subsequently dies of the injuries inflicted. Similarly, in *Coveleski* v. *Bubnis* (1990), the Pennsylvania Superior Court ruled that action may not be brought under wrongful death and survival statues on behalf of a fetus not yet viable at the time of the accident. The Vermont Supreme Court in *State* v. *Oliver* (1989), the Kansas Supreme Court in *State* v. *Trudell* (1988), an Oklahoma appellate court in *State* v. *Harbert* (1988), and the Maine Supreme Court in *Milton* v. *Cary Medical Center* (1988) all held that an unborn viable fetus is not a person under state wrongful death statutes. Similarly, a Michigan appellate court in *People v. Guthrie* (1980) dismissed a charge of negligent homicide where the victim was a fetus "ready for birth."

In a vehicular homicide case, the Tennessee Court of Criminal Appeals in *State* v. *Evans* (1987) agreed that a viable fetus is not a person or human life within the meaning of the vehicular homicide statute. The court argued that criminalization of the death of a fetus was a matter for the legislature, not the courts. Likewise, in *Hudak* v. *Georgy* (1989) the Pennsylvania Superior Court ruled that a cause of action for wrongful death and survival on behalf of a nonviable fetus did not exist, and creation of such a cause of action was a legislative, not a judicial, function. Finally, the Kansas Supreme Court in a first degree murder case (*State* v. *Green* 1989) concluded that imposing criminal liability for killing a fetus was a legislative function.

Therefore, the court was prohibited from construing "viable fetus" to be included in the term "human being" in first-degree murder statute.

One response to the failure of common law to provide redress for the killing of a fetus is for state legislatures to define it explicitly in the penal codes. The Iowa code (707.7, West 1979), for instance, defines feticide as the intentional termination of a human pregnancy after the second trimester, while the New York penal law (125.00) defines homicide as including the death of an unborn child of more than twenty-four weeks. The California penal code (187, West Suppl. 1982) was amended in 1976 to define murder as "the unlawful killing of a human being, or a fetus, with malice aforethought." The California legislature amended the code in response to a ruling by the California Supreme Court in *Keeler* v. *Superior Court* (1970) that a viable fetus, stillborn as the direct result of an assault, had not become a person at the time of viability for purposes of the state's murder statute, which referred only to the killing of a "human being." As the California Supreme Court noted in a later case (*Justus* v. *Atchison* 1977), the legislature included the fetus by creating a new category of murder, rather than by redefining the term "human life" to include the fetus. In *People* v. *Apodoca* (1978), a California appeals court affirmed a conviction for second-degree murder of a twenty-two- to twenty-four-week-old fetus in a case where the defendant repeatedly struck a pregnant woman with the intent to kill the unborn fetus.

The Minnesota Supreme Court in *State* v. *Merrill* (1990) upheld the unborn child homicide statute, arguing that it provides adequate notice to potential violators, even though the violator may not know the assaulted woman is pregnant, and even though the woman may not have been aware of her pregnancy at the time of the assault. Furthermore, "state's interest in protecting the potentiality of human life includes protection of the unborn child, whether an embryo or a nonviable or viable fetus, and protects the woman's interest in her unborn child and her right to decide whether it shall be carried in utero" (p. 319). Likewise, in *Willis* v. *State* (1988), the Mississippi Supreme Court upheld the conviction of the defendant for manslaughter in the death of a seven-month fetus, and in *People* v. *Bunyard* (1988), the California Supreme Court ruled that the multiple-murder special circumstance was applicable to the killing, by a single act, of a pregnant woman and her fetus.

Despite the increased tendency of courts and legislatures to provide some criminal protection for the unborn, the courts continue to define such protections narrowly. According to Parness, one reason for this hesitancy may lie in their misunderstanding of *Roe* v. *Wade* (1983, 444). In *People* v. *Smith* (1976), a California appellate court affirmed the dismissal of a homicide charge against a man who allegedly murdered a previable human fetus, even though the criminal statute had been amended to include a fetus. The court based its decision on the *Roe* Court's handling of viability:

The underlying rationale of *Wade,* therefore, is that until viability is reached, human life in the legal sense has not come into existence. Implicit in *Wade* is the conclusion that as a matter of constitutional law the destruction of a non-viable fetus is not the taking of human life. It follows that such destruction cannot constitute murder or other form of homicide, whether committed by a mother, father (as here), or a third person (p. 757).

The California court clearly misread *Roe* (Parness 1983, 445). In *Roe,* the Supreme Court held only that a previable fetus was not a person enjoying Fourteenth Amendment protection and specifically refused to resolve the difficult question of when life begins. Actually, the Court noted that while fetuses are treated differently from living persons under the law, the unborn have been accorded certain legal rights.

Other state supreme courts have shown a similar reluctance to extend legal protection to the unborn, despite clear statutory intent. For example, in *State* v. *Brown* (1979), the Louisiana Supreme Court sustained a motion to void an indictment of the defendant for the murder of a fertilized, implanted fetus, in spite of the criminal homicide statute specifying that the term "person" included a human being from the moment of fertilization and implantation (La. Rev. Stat. Ann §412[7]). Despite legislative action to reverse the common-law definition of homicide in Louisiana, therefore, the court precluded the unborn from full legal protection. At most, the perpetrators of such action are subject to prosecution under lesser offenses, such as assault and battery of the pregnant woman. According to Parness and Pritchard, "Notwithstanding the Supreme Court's recognition that legal protection of children may sometimes cover the unborn, relatively few states have enacted criminal laws protecting the unborn" (1982, 270). Although a viable fetus likely may be a victim of homicide in many states, it is unlikely that previable fetuses will be considered such.

Another set of criminal codes relevant to the unborn are the child abuse laws. Here the guidelines are even less developed and more fragmented. In *Reyes* v. *Superior Court* (1977), a California appeals court found that the felony child-endangering statute was not violated by the continued use of heroin by the mother during the last two months of pregnancy, despite warnings from a public health nurse, which led to the heroin addiction of twin boys. Conversely, in *In re Baby X* (1980), a Michigan appellate court upheld the conviction for child abuse of a woman who gave birth to a child addicted to heroin. This area of law will be discussed in substantial detail later.

TORTS FOR WRONGFUL LIFE

A related but more recent variety of prenatal torts, "by far the most unusual and troublesome set of liability issues emerging from the intersection of law and human genetics, is the tort for wrongful life" (Capron 1979, 681). A tort for wrongful life is a suit brought on behalf of an affected infant, most commonly against a physician or other health professional who, it is alleged, negligently failed to inform the parents of the possibility of their producing a severely ill child, thereby preventing a parental choice in avoiding conception or birth of the child. The unique aspect of such suits is the assumption that a life has evolved that should not have. If not for the negligence of the defendant, the child plaintiff would never have been born. Although the term "wrongful life" has been applied to a variety of situations, including those where parents are suing for damages to the child, it is more precise to limit wrongful life action to that brought solely by the affected child. Most recent suits for wrongful life have been brought on behalf of children with severe mental or physical defects and ask for monetary damages to be awarded on the basis of the children's very existence, as compared to their nonexistence. Wrongful life suits differ from traditional negligence actions in that the harm here is in being born, even though compensation ultimately is asked in the form of monetary damages: "What the infant plaintiff alleges is that the breach of duty led proximately to his birth—the maturing of the harm—and, thus, he is forced to endure life with defects which he would not be forced to do but for the defendant's breach of duty" ("A Cause" 1970, 67).

Legal questions surrounding wrongful life action, therefore, center on whether the defendant has a legally cognizable duty to the infant plaintiff, even though the plaintiff was not born or in some cases even conceived at the time of the defendant's allegedly negligent act. There is considerable disagreement, however, over whether the plaintiff is harmed by the defendant's negligence, and, if so, how such damages can be measured. A question that the courts traditionally have been unwilling to face is whether or not the infant plaintiff is damaged by being born with defects when the only alternative is nonexistence. The plaintiff here must successfully argue that he or she would have been better off never born. On public policy grounds, which have been interpreted by many legal observers as always favoring life over nonexistence, most courts have asserted that the plaintiff cannot be harmed by his or her birth.

Despite continued debate over the concepts of duty, harm, and proximate cause, recent court decisions indicate that many courts are now willing to accept such causes of action. Additionally, many legal observers have come out in support of such action. Rogers argues that recognition of wrongful life claims would promote societal interest in genetic counseling and prenatal testing, deter medical malpractice, and at least partially redress a clear and undeniable wrong (1982, 757). In agreeing with an earlier article that concludes that "the awarding of monetary damages is an appropriate remedy for the wrongful life plaintiff," Kashi argues that while the child's life is not "wrongful," neither is it as it should be (1977, 1432). He states that the rejection of causes of action for wrongful life represent "a clear case of meritorious cause of action being denied because of its ill-chosen label" (p. 1432).

Although Capron appears cautious in his view of torts for wrongful life, he supports an intermediate position—permitting recovery of some damages in severe cases but rejecting compensation of a defective child for the full amount by which his or her life differs from "normal life" (1979). Conversely, Trotzig rejects the notion of damages in such cases and states it is absurd that "anyone, no matter how deformed, should be compensated for having to be alive" (1980, 32). Tedeschi, too, doubts whether logically or legally there can be such a thing as a "damage of being born," since the plaintiff would not exist if the claimed negligent act had not occurred (1966). He argues that claims for wrongful life are "doomed to failure," since the element of damage is missing if no difference can be drawn between the results of the act and its absence: "By his cause of action, the plaintiff cuts from under him the ground upon which he needs to rely in order to prove his damage" (p. 555).

Legal Precedents and Trends

Prior to the late 1970s, the courts unanimously refused to recognize the possibility of a cause of action for wrongful life. In *Gleitman* v. *Cosgrove* (1967), the New Jersey Supreme Court declared that the preciousness of human life, no matter how burdened, outweighs the need for recovery by the infant. *Gleitman* set the precedent until well after *Roe* v. *Wade* (1973) altered public policy toward abortion. To award damages to the affected child would be counter to public policy, which views the right to life as inalienable in our society. In 1975 the Wisconsin Supreme Court in *Dumer* v. *St. Michael's Hospital* dismissed a suit filed for wrongful life but found that the parents had a cause, thus producing a clear legal distinction between torts for wrongful life and torts for wrongful birth, giving legal cognizance to the latter.

During the late 1970s the courts, while continuing to reject a wrongful life cause of action, began to make subtle distinctions that shifted toward recognition of legally cognizable harm to the child. Moreover, a number of trial courts ruled in favor of the plaintiffs, and increasingly strong dissents on the higher courts acknowledged causes of action for wrongful life. According to Cohen, *Park* v. *Chessin* (1977) "marked the first step toward judicial acceptance of the theory of 'wrongful life'" (1978, 217). The suit was brought on the child's behalf for the conscious pain and suffering resulting from the specialist's advice to the parents to have another child, although they already had one child die from polycystic kidney disease, "a fatal hereditary disease of such nature that there exists a substantial probability that any future baby of the same parents will be born with it" (Perkoff

1970, 443). Although later overruled, an intermediate appellate court held that both the parents and the child had a cause of action and declared that "decisional law must keep pace with expanding technological, economic and social change" (p. 112). For the first time, a cause of action was stated for the child, because "once having been born alive . . . said child comes within the 'orbit of the danger' for which the defendants could be liable" (p. 112).

This recognition of a legally cognizable action for wrongful life, however, was short-lived, or at least sidetracked. The *Park* decision was reviewed by the New York Court of Appeals as a companion case in *Becker* v. *Schwartz* (1978) and overruled. Although the parents in both cases were allowed to recover their pecuniary loss, the court refused to permit recovery for emotional or psychiatric damages, arguing that this would "inevitably lead to drawing of artificial and arbitrary boundaries" as well as offend public policy. The infant plaintiffs in both *Park* and *Becker* were barred from recovery of any damages because of the inability of the law to make a comparison between life with handicaps and no life at all. The court specifically refused to accept the idea that a child may legally expect a life free from deformity, and direct reference to the lower court decision stated "there is no precedent for recognition . . . of 'the fundamental right of a child to be born as a whole, functional human being'" (p. 807).

Although it is yet too early to predict whether future wrongful life decisions will recognize a cause of action for an affected child, a distinct trend continues in that direction. *Curlender* v. *Bio-Science Laboratories* (1980), in which a California appeals court agreed that a Tay-Sachs infant was entitled to seek recovery for alleged wrongful life, represents a step toward that end. The court concluded that the breach of duty of the laboratory was the proximate cause of an injury cognizable by law—the birth of the plaintiff with such defects. The court dismissed without discussion the central rationale for barring recovery in previous wrongful life cases since *Gleitman*—the value of nonexistence versus life with handicap—and focused attention instead on the resulting condition of the child.

The reality of the "wrongful-life" concept is that such plaintiff both exists and suffers, due to the negligence of others. It is neither necessary nor just to retreat into meditation on the mysteries of life. We need not be concerned with the fact that had defendants not been negligent, the plaintiff might not have come into existence at all. The certainty of genetic impairment is no longer a mystery. In addition a reverent appreciation of life compels recognition that plaintiff, however impaired she may be, has come into existence as a living person with certain rights (p. 488).

In *Curlender,* the court argued that perceptive analysis of the wrongful life concept requires recognition of the great distinctions in the conditions of the particular plaintiffs as well as in the changing policy context. The court noted the "progression in our law" toward allowing recovery in such cases, as well as the "gradual retreat" from the "impossibility of measuring damages" (p. 488) as the sole ground for barring recovery by infants. The dramatic increase in the genetic knowledge and skills needed to avoid genetic disease is also introduced as a mitigating factor. Finally, the court cited the persistence of wrongful life litigation, despite the "cool reception" from the courts as evidence of the "serious nature of the wrong" and an understanding that the law reflects, perhaps later than sooner, basic changes in the way society views such matters (p. 489). In reversing the superior court's dismissal of this tort, the appeals court stated: "We see no reason in public policy or legal analysis for exempting from liability for punitive damages a defendant who is sued for committing a 'wrongful life' tort" (p. 490).

In *Schroeder* v. *Perkel* (1981), the New Jersey Supreme Court agreed with *Curlender* and allowed an infant plaintiff born with cystic fibrosis to collect for his "wrongful," "diminished" life. In *Procanik* v. *Cillo* (1984), the New Jersey Supreme Court ruled that a congenitally defective child may maintain an action to recover at least the extraordinary medical expenses he or she will incur over a lifetime, although it refused to allow recovery of general damages for emotional distress or "diminished childhood." Moreover, in January 1983, a unanimous decision of the Washington Supreme Court in *Harbeson* v. *Parke-Davis* strongly approved the principle of wrongful life as well as wrongful birth. The court found that the parents have a right to prevent the birth of a defective child, and that health care providers have a duty to impart to the parents material information about the likelihood of birth defects in their future children. The child born with such defects has a right to bring a wrongful life action against the health provider. According to the court, it would be illogical to permit only parents, not the child, to recover for the cost of the child's own medical care. The child's need for medical care and other special costs related to his or her defect will not disappear when the child attains majority. The burden of these costs should fall not on the parents or the state, but on the party whose negligence was the proximate cause of the child's need for extraordinary care. The child should be able to collect a lifetime's worth of medical, educational, or any other costs of the deformity, according to the court. However, following the reasoning of the California Supreme Court in *Turpin* v. *Sortini* (1982), the Washington court denied the child recovery for general damages such as pain and suffering.

Other recent decisions recognizing a cause of action for wrongful life against third parties are *Call* v. *Kezirian* (1982) and *Graham* v. *Pima City* (1983). In *Call,* a California appeals court ruled that damages are recoverable for extraordinary expenses for the specialized teaching, training, and equipment needed by an unhealthy infant because of defects. In *Graham,* the Pima City Superior Court approved a settlement of $380,000 for a wrongful life action. Also see *Eisbrenner* v. *Stanley* (1981), where a physician's failure to diagnose rubella in a pregnant woman who subsequently gave birth to a deformed baby was upheld as a wrongful life claim.

Although these cases might demonstrate a trend in tort law, many courts continue to refuse to recognize wrongful life actions. In *Siemieniec* v. *Lutheran General Hospital* (1987), the Illinois Supreme Court held that a child has no cause of action on his or her behalf for extraordinary medical expenses expected to incur during his or her majority. It ruled that a child born with hemophilia could not maintain a wrongful life action against physicians allegedly negligent in failing to advise, counsel, or test his or her parents during the mother's pregnancy concerning the risk that fetus would have hemophilia. According to the court, recognition of a legal right not to be born, rather than to live with hemophilia, was contradictory to public policy.

Similarly, in *Ellis* v. *Sherman* (1986), the Pennsylvania Superior Court affirmed a lower court's refusal to recognize an infant's cause of action for wrongful life. This case involved the failure of an obstetrician to diagnose the manifestations of neurofibromatosis, a hereditary disorder that the father exhibited. Likewise, in *Alquijay* v. *St. Luke's-Roosevelt Hospital Center* (1984), the New York County Supreme Court, Appellate Division, held that there is no cause of action on behalf of an infant enabling the child to recover extraordinary expenses that would result of the disease after he or she reached majority. In this case, an infant girl afflicted with Down syndrome sued the hospitals whose personnel conducted amniocentesis that erroneously indicated the mother would give birth to a normal male child. The court reiterated its opposition on public policy grounds and concluded that recognition of such a cause of action would require legislation. Moreover, in *DiNatale* v. *Lieberman* (1982), the Michigan Appellate Court denied a cause of action for wrongful life because of the difficulty in assessing damages for being born, while in *Dorlin* v. *Providence Hospital* (1982) and *Nelson* v. *Krusen* (1982), the child's claim for wrongful life was rejected because the assessment of damages would be too speculative. The judicial landscape, then, continues to be eccentric and confusing.

Legislative Action on Wrongful Life

In response to court actions for wrongful life, at least six states (Idaho, Montana, Minnesota, Missouri, South Dakota, and Utah) have enacted measures limiting or prohibiting actions brought by, or on behalf of, infant plaintiffs for wrongful life. The 1982 Minnesota statute, for example, proscribes such tort actions, stating that: "No person shall maintain a cause of action or receive an award of damages on behalf of himself based on the claim that but for the negligent conduct of another, he would have been aborted." At least four states, including Idaho, Minnesota, Missouri, and Utah, have gone a step further and prohibited wrongful birth suits as well as wrongful life suits. Idaho law, however, specifically exempts actions against physicians for negligence in not advising prenatal testing that could have cured, prevented, or ameliorated defects. This means that parents are unable to claim damages for the birth of an unhealthy child, even if a physician fails to inform them of available prenatal tests that could have diagnosed the problem and given the parents the option of obtaining an abortion. California law prohibits children from bringing wrongful life actions against parents, but it does imply that such actions against third parties should be recognized.

Although the motivation for such legislative action undoubtedly is complex, in several instances it has been overtly a product of anti-abortion sentiment. Right-to-life groups have argued successfully that the acceptance of wrongful life torts encourages abortion not only of those fetuses identified as defective, but also of those fetuses that are marginal. Moreover, opponents of this cause of action assert that a legal atmosphere where wrongful life claims are recognized will encourage health care providers to order diagnostic tests conducted only for "search-and-destroy" purposes to avoid liability. Advocacy groups for handicapped persons have also been critical of the use of technologies directed solely toward ending selective abortion, instead of treating the handicap. Whatever the motivation behind current statutory prohibition of wrongful life and wrongful birth suits, the legislation to date has failed to appreciate the complexity of the issue and balance the many competing interests involved. By protecting health professionals from liability for not apprising the parents of their availability, the practical effect of these statutes is to discourage prenatal diagnosis and genetic screening. Because such procedures can provide valuable information and in the long run promote healthy children, these statutes fail to address the many legitimate but conflicting interests (Hackett 1987, 266).

Consequences of Wrongful Life

The literature is replete with references to the dangerous consequences of recognizing a cause of action for wrongful life. Oft-quoted is the statement in *Zepeda v. Zepeda* (1963) that the "legal implications of such a tort are vast, the social impact could be staggering." Some observers predict a "flood of litigation" and multimillion dollar settlements imposing an "intolerable burden" on the medical community, escalating maternity costs and reducing services in some cases (Trotzig 1980, 15). Chapman notes a fear that "Down's Syndrome children from all over could come into court and sue with such an action recognized" (1979, 34). Others dispute these claims and argue that relatively few children would be able to assert reasonably that they would have been better off not being born. Those in favor of awarding damages usually emphasize traditional tort functions of justice to the harmed, deterrence, and punishment.

If responses to other malpractice actions can be taken as examples, it appears reasonable to assume that many physicians and health professionals will react to torts for wrongful life by practicing defensively. Although this is a desired goal of torts when it results in better care, wrongful life situations do present a unique dilemma because the response is reflected in heightened use of prenatal diagnosis and abortion of affected fetuses. At least, successful wrongful life actions will require physicians to inform the parents of the availability of genetic diagnosis. In some cases this might result in a decision by the pregnant woman to abort a fetus that is less than perfect. In the extreme, physicians might be less prone to use heroic neonatal intensive care to save severely premature infants, for fear of later being sued for keeping them alive with defects.

Although a more realistic defense against negligence would appear to be full disclosure to the parents by the physician and referral to specialists more knowledgeable in genetics, an atmosphere likely will develop that assumes that the most effective protection from wrongful life torts is ensuring such infants are not born. Trotzig might be correct in anticipating this response from some physicians, but it seems improbable that wrongful life torts will become so pervasive as to dominate medical decision making. Such torts still require proof of duty, damage, negligence, and proximate cause, traditionally required by malpractice cases.

More crucial, however, is the potential impact of acceptance of the concept of wrongful life on perceptions by the public of those persons born with genetic or other congenital defects. The amount of prejudice now directed toward mentally and physically disabled persons is already generally more than that expressed toward various minority groups. If the courts recognize wrongful life, it is probable that these attitudes will be accentuated and social intolerance for the disabled will increase since, it might be presumed, they should not have been born. It might also be feasible under such conditions for society to sue parents for the costs of maintaining such children in public institutions, although this would require substantial value alterations in the United States. The danger of establishing arbitrary categories of individuals "rightfully" born and "wrongfully" born is obvious. "A cogent policy justification for the continued dismissal of wrongful life actions," according to Friedman, "is the possible societal acceptance of the belief that if the life of a genetically defective being is wrongful, then only his death can be 'rightful'" (1974, 154).

In addition, there is danger that widespread acceptance of selective abortion encouraged by wrongful life action will reduce even further tolerance for the living affected. Kass expresses concern for those abnormals viewed as having escaped the "net of detection and abortion," as attitudes toward such individuals are "progressively eroded" (1976, 317). In this atmosphere, such individuals increasingly will be viewed as unfit to be alive, as second-class humans or lower, or as unnecessary persons who would not have been born if only someone had gotten to them in time. Parents are likely to resent such a child, especially if social pressures and stigma are directed against them. The "right to be born healthy," according to Murphy and associates, is misleading because it actually means that "only healthy persons have a right to be born" (1978, 358). The choice of those affected is not between a healthy and unhealthy existence, but rather between an unhealthy existence and none at all. Ironically, what is viewed as protecting the rights of the plaintiff in a particular case might result in degrading the rights of those affected by genetic disease as a group. As noted by Botkin, "children with disabilities will not be better served by the further development of the concept of life without value" (1988, 1545).

CIVIL RIGHTS OF THE FETUS

In *Douglas* v. *Town of Hartford* (1982), a federal district court held that a five-and-a-half-month-old fetus is a person capable of maintaining an action under 42 U.S.C. 1983. Section 1983 provides a civil cause of action for violation of constitutional or federal statutory rights. According to the court, the viable fetus born with severe head injuries allegedly the result of an attack by a police officer on the mother was a person within the parameters of the Civil Rights Act of 1871, despite other federal court rulings to the contrary. Although *Douglas* conflicts with other federal court rulings (for instance, *Harman* v. *Daniels* 1981), that Section 1983 does not protect the unborn. According to Rice, this decision does reflect the trend of the courts to recognize an array of fetal rights in all areas (1983). It must be noted that Section 1983 creates no rights but only provides a remedy for violations of protected rights. This decision has little practical significance for the fetus unless fetuses are granted substantive rights. If Congress or the courts should grant constitutional or federal statutory rights, Section 1983 would provide a remedy for deprivations of those rights, according to *Douglas*.

Although the *Douglas* court's ruling is very limited, it is further evidence of the trend both in common law and statutory law to grant the fetus some protectable rights. Although *Roe* seems to deny a previable fetus entitlement to constitutional rights or protection, and human life bills seem at this time not to have sufficient support to become law, after viability even the *Roe* Court implicitly recognizes that the fetus may have some entitlements if the states recognize a compelling interest in the potentiality of life.

It seems logical that the federal government's interest in protecting life would be equal to the states', but this recognition would have to come from Congress. To date, the motivation for action in Congress has centered on undermining *Roe* v. *Wade* by declaring that human life begins at conception for purposes of the Fourteenth Amendment. Although any statutory action by Congress along this line presumably would fail on constitutional grounds as long as the *Roe* precedent persists, this does not eliminate the possibility of granting substantive federal civil rights to viable fetuses. The state law trend might encourage Congress or the federal courts to give legal protection to the unborn by expanding federal statutory rights, at least for the viable fetus. Such action might be necessary to overcome current inconsistencies among the various jurisdictions. To date, however, Congress has not passed a law specifically protecting fetal rights, and as long as the battle lines are drawn around the point of conception, little movement to this end appears forthcoming. Furthermore, although some state courts have interpreted state statutes as establishing protection for the unborn, federal courts have thus far refrained from interpreting any federal statutes that broadly.

According to Rice, the courts should define the fetus as a "person" with protectable rights, at least in those cases where the fetus's rights will not conflict with the constitutional rights of other persons (1983). In cases where the mother and fetus are both victims—for instance, if someone commits a violent act on a pregnant woman—the rational underlying abortion considerations no longer apply because the rights of the mother and the fetus are parallel, not conflicting. It is logical that in such cases fetuses should be given protectable civil rights under Section 1983. The *Douglas* decision represents a clear, although limited, break with the tradition of denying a civil cause of action and represents further evidence of a changing attitude among courts toward according legal rights to fetuses.

PARENTAL LIABILITY FOR PRENATAL INJURY

The high incidence of congenital defects caused by the fetal environment has given rise to increased concern for the rights of the fetus to be born free from avoidable prenatal injury. It is clear from the discussion of trends in tort law that, despite considerable variation among jurisdictions, the fetus is being accorded an expanding protection of civil law against injury caused by third parties. Although these trends appear to conflict with some aspects of the *Roe* decision, ironically the legalization of abortion aroused concern for the unborn child and has facilitated this pattern. As noted earlier, new technical innovations and knowledge of fetal development have helped clarify the deleterious effects of certain environmental influences and reinforced the acceptance of prenatal torts.

These general trends toward recognition of a legal status for the unborn have substantial consequences for redefining the legal context of maternal responsibility toward the fetus. Because the immediate cause of most prenatal injuries is the disruption of the intrauterine environment, and because the parents, primarily the mother, largely control that environment, it is logical that attention be placed on those factors over which they influence control. As noted in Chapter 2, many actions of the mother might cause harm to the fetus, either through ignorance or with knowledge of the potential dangers. Not surprisingly, there is a clear trend toward recognition of causes of action against parents by children injured prenatally. This trend produces a clear conflict between the child's right to be born free from parentally induced prenatal injury and the parental right of autonomy. By holding a woman liable to her infant for negligent care of her body during pregnancy, the woman's freedom to control her body is violated. However, because of the consequential role she plans in the development of the fetus and its total dependence on her, it might be argued that once she decides to bear a child, she has a duty to restrict her freedom in order to maximize the health of a child to be born.

Two basic legal developments have been especially critical in this emergence of parental responsibility: The first is simply the expanding sphere of liability for prenatal injury, which logically leads to those individuals most likely to cause injury—the parents. The second legal development is the abrogation of the intrafamily immunity doctrine, which traditionally protected parents from liability. The former trend was discussed above; the latter is briefly examined here.

Abrogation of Parent-Child Immunity Doctrine

Until recently, the parent-child (or intrafamily) immunity doctrine barred any tort action brought by a child against his or her parent. This doctrine was first enunciated in *Hewlett* v. *George* (1891), where the Mississippi Supreme Court reasoned that an action by a child against his or her parents would disrupt peace in the family and was against public policy. This precedent held even in cases of intentional and malicious injury to the child by the parents (*McKelvey* v. *McKelvey* 1903; *Roller* v. *Roller* 1905). According to Simon, the immunity rule was not predicated upon a lack of duty of reasonable care owed the child by the parent, but solely upon the child's procedural disability to sue: "The parent avoids liability on the theory that the child's right to recovery should be sacrificed for the public good" (1978, 61). Despite this, for nearly a century this doctrine, itself based on no precedential authority, prevented unemancipated minor children from taking legal action against their parents. As late as 1987, an Illinois appellate court (*Chamness* v. *Fairtrace*) held that the parental tort immunity doctrine precluded the father, as administrator of the estate of a viable fetus, from bringing wrongful death action against the fetus's mother, whose negligence resulted in an automobile collision that was the proximate cause of the death of the fetus. To do so, the mother could benefit from her own negligence, since the mother and father were husband and wife.

In recent decades, however, the immunity rule has come under heavy criticism, and its validity has been challenged by many courts. The traditional arguments in favor of denying tort action by children against parents—that it would destroy family harmony (*Dunlap* v. *Dunlap* 1930), disturb parental discipline and control (*Brennecke* v. *Kilpatrick* 1960), weaken the family unit (*Tucker* v. *Tucker* 1964), and result in fraud and collusion against insurance companies (*Hastings* v. *Hastings* 1960)—have gradually been dismissed by the courts either through the granting of a widening series of exceptions or by judicial abrogation of the doctrine entirely.

Abandonment of the parental relationship (*Dunlap* v. *Dunlap* 1930), emancipation of the child (*Logan* v. *Reeves* 1962), injury in the course of a business activity (*Trevarton* v. *Trevarton* 1963), and intentional or reckless injury of the child by the parent (*Teramano* v. *Teramano* 1966) have all been accepted by courts as exceptions to the immunity doctrine. According to Simon, the common denominator underlying these exceptions is that the rule of immunity is applied only where clear reasons for the rule are present (1978, 66). Although the parents should be immune for liability in torts committed in their parental status, courts have allowed action in those cases not arising directly out of the parent-child relationship, or where the parent has relinquished his or her status as parent.

Courts in other jurisdictions have gone beyond this reasoning and abrogated entirely the parent-child immunity doctrine. Since 1963, when the Wisconsin Supreme Court threw out the immunity rule (*Goller* v. *White* 1963), an increasing number of states have abandoned support of the rule and allowed tort actions of children against parents (*Ard* v. *Ard* 1982). In *Plumley* v. *Klein* (1972), for example, the court held that parent tort immunity should be overruled and that a child may maintain a lawsuit against his or her parent for injury suffered as a result of ordinary negligence of the parent. The court noted, however, that exceptions exist if the alleged negligent act involves the exercise of reasonable parental authority over the child. As noted earlier, public expectation of what is reasonable or responsible parental action are likely to change in light of knowledge provided by medical science and the available technologies.

At this point, over forty states have abrogated the immunity doctrine. In the remainder, exceptions to the rule are freely granted such that it seems unlikely prenatal injury torts against parents will be dismissed summarily. The courts generally agree that the child's personal rights are more worthy than property or contract rights, which are already protected (*Hebel* v. *Hebel* 1967). Also, it is argued that society's best interests dictate that those individuals who are tortiously injured be compensated for their injury so that they do not become wards of the state (*Streenz* v. *Streenz* 1970).

Finally, the courts see little family tranquility protected in denying a tort action soley on the basis of the immunity rule (*Peterson* v. *Honolulu* 1969). According to the Massachusetts Supreme Court in *Sorenson* v. *Sorenson* (1975), it is the injury itself, not the lawsuit, that disrupts harmonious family relations. The child's relationship to the tortfeasor should not result in denial of recovery for a wrong to his or her person (*Briere* v. *Briere* 1966).

Some jurisdictions continue to make distinctions between situations directly involving parental discretion over the control of the minor child and other negligent acts by a parent. In *Silesky* v. *Kelman* (1968), for example, the Minnesota Supreme Court abrogated parental immunity, except where the alleged negligent act involves the exercise of reasonable parental authority or discretion with respect for providing necessities for the child. One method viewed favorably by several courts is the use of a "reasonable parent standard" to determine when parental conduct is actionable. According to Atchison, such a standard strikes a balance between the child's right to recover for a tortiously inflicted injury and the parent's need to discipline and use authority judgment and discretion in raising the child (1983, 1003).

The clear trend of many state courts to disregard the parent-child immunity rule opens the way logically for expanding prenatal injury causes of action to include suits of children against parents for negligence in the prenatal period. Along with the rapidly advancing state of medical knowledge in fetal development and the growing medical evidence of the deleterious effects of maternal behavior on the fetus, there is a heightened recognition by the courts of parental liability for negligent injury to minor children. Based on these factors, an action by a child against its parents for negligent injury suffered prior to birth seems increasingly likely and logically consistent. Although no court has yet awarded damages for such an action, several recent court decisions demonstrate its imminence.

Tort Liability for Prenatal Injury

In *Grodin* v. *Grodin* (1980), the Michigan Court of Appeals recognized the possibility of maternal liability for prenatal conduct. The court upheld the right of a child allegedly injured prenatally to present testimony concerning his mother's negligence in failing to take a pregnancy test when her symptoms suggested pregnancy, and her failure to inform the physician who diagnosed the pregnancy that she was taking tetracycline, a drug that might be contraindicated for pregnant women. Noting that the Michigan Supreme Court had determined that a child could bring suit for prenatal injury and that the immunity doctrine had been discarded, the *Grodin* court ruled that the injured child's mother would "bear the same liability as a third person for injurious, negligent conduct that interferred with the child's 'legal right to begin life with a sound mind and body.'"

The key question in *Grodin* was whether or not parental immunity should insulate the mother (and her homeowners' policy) from liability where the alleged negligent act involved an exercise of "reasonable parental discretion" in medical decision making. According to the court, a woman's decision to continue taking drugs during pregnancy is an exercise of her parental discretion. The crucial point is whether the decision reached by the woman in a particular case is a "reasonable exercise of parental discretion." (Also see *Matter of Danielle Smith* [1985] and *Matter of Gloria C.* v. *William C.* [1984], where family courts found a cause of action for *in utero* neglect.)

Similarly, in *Payton* v. *Abbott Labs* (1981), the court's decision in favor of a cause of action for an infant injured prenatally against anyone who negligently supplies a pregnant woman with drugs leaves the door open for a child to sue family members for injuries resulting from the improper administration of a drug to its mother during gestation. The *Payton* opinion patently approves of recovery for any prenatal injury if the harm can be demonstrated by medical evidence and proven in court. In *Stallman* v. *Youngquist* (1988), however, the Illinois Supreme Court held that no cause of action exists by or on behalf of a fetus, subsequently born alive, against its mother for unintentional infliction of prenatal injuries. In this case, in which action was brought by the infant against the mother for prenatal injuries sustained in an automobile accident, the supreme court reversed the appellate court's finding for action.

Criminal Actions: Child Neglect or Abuse

The heightened frequency of crack and cocaine abuse by women of child-bearing age, combined with the legal trends toward defining a maternal responsibility for fetal health, has led to a number of actions against pregnant women for drug use (Logli 1990). One approach is to use maternal drug abuse during pregnancy as a basis for finding neglect. For instance, in *In re Troy D.* (1989), a California appellate court held that an infant diagnosed as being under the influence of illegal drugs taken by the mother during pregnancy is sufficient to establish a juvenile court's jurisdiction over petition to declare the infant a dependent child. It has been estimated that New York City alone holds about five thousand such child neglect hearings a year ("Coke Baby" 1990, 2), despite a recent family court ruling that a mother's prenatal cocaine use could not form a basis for a finding of neglect (*Matter of Fletcher* 1988).

One of the most publicized and controversial legal developments in the late 1980s was the increasing number of jurisdictions that tried to impose legal sanctions to deter illegal drug use by pregnant women. Women have been charged under statutes against child abuse and neglect, delivery of a controlled substance to a minor, and involuntary manslaughter. It has been reported that the district attorney of Butte County, California, announced his intention to prosecute all mothers of newborns with illegal drugs found in their urine; a conviction would carry a mandatory minimum sentence of ninety days in jail (Chavkin and Kandall 1990, 223). Likewise, other legal interventions such as civil detention have been sought to control the behavior of pregnant women deemed dangerous to the fetus. Although few of the attempts at criminal prosecution have resulted in convictions, they raise critical issues concerning the extent to which the state can intervene to protect potential fetal health.

In an early case, a Michigan appeals court convicted a heroin addict of child abuse after she gave birth to an addicted baby (*In re Baby X* 1980). In *Reyes* v. *Superior Court* (1977), a California appeals court reversed a conviction of an addict who gave birth to a child congenitally addicted to heroin on the ground that the California criminal code for child abuse was not intended to include the unborn. According to John A. Robertson,

This interpretation of the statue is erroneous, for it overlooks the fact that the abused child here is not the fetus, but the child who has been born and is suffering from injuries occurring before its birth. There is nothing in the history or wording of the statute that requires the abusive conduct to occur after birth, as long as the child who suffers from the prenatal injuries is born before the action is brought. Indeed, to limit the statute to postnatal actions would be inconsistent with California homicide law, which imposes liability for prenatal actions that cause death postnatally (1983a, 439).

Although the details of the court cases involving drug abuse by pregnant women vary, several well-publicized cases clearly demonstrate the complex issues facing the courts. In 1989, Jennifer Johnson gave birth to a daughter. At the time, she advised hospital personnel that she was addicted to cocaine and tests confirmed traces of cocaine in her daughter's system. She subsequently was reported to the Florida Department of Health and Rehabilitation and charged with child abuse and delivery of a controlled substance during the delivery of her daughter, as well as during the delivery of a son born in 1987. Although she was acquitted on the child abuse charge due to lack of evidence, she was found guilty on the controlled substance charge and sentenced to fifteen years probation, two hundred hours of community service, mandatory drug treatment, and participation in an intense prenatal program if she again became pregnant (*Florida* v. *Johnson* 1989). The judge reasoned that she had illegally introduced the cocaine into her own body and then passed it on to the newborn children in the moments after delivery, before the umbilical cords were cut. Children, like all persons, have the right to be born free from having cocaine introduced

into their system by others, according to the judge. Another headline case
of 1989 was that of Melanie Green, a young mother in Rockford, Illinois,
whose two-day-old daughter died after testing positive for cocaine. Green
was charged with involuntary manslaughter and delivery of a controlled
substance. Although the charges were dropped eventually when the grand
jury refused to indict, this case again brought national attention to questions of maternal responsibility and the proper state response when a baby
dies because of illegal behavior by a pregnant woman.

In 1988, Brenda Vaughn of Washington, D.C., pled guilty to forging
several checks (*United States* v. *Vaughn* 1989). Instead of imposing the
probation recommended by the prosecutor, however, the judge sentenced
Vaughn to prison because she had tested positive for cocaine, and the
judge wanted to ensure she would not use cocaine for the duration of her
pregnancy. Several weeks prior to the baby's delivery, when Vaughn was to
be released under a general early release order to alleviate prison crowding,
the sentencing judge issued a special order exempting her from early release for protection of the fetus she was carrying.

The fourth case that raised these issues through widespread media coverage was the prosecution of Pamela Rae Stewart for willfully omitting adequate medical attention for her "child" during gestation (*People* v. *Stewart*
1987). It was charged that Stewart abused the fetus by disregarding specific
physician's advice to discontinue amphetamine use during pregnancy, to
abstain from sexual intercourse because of placenta previa, and to seek immediate medical attention if she began to hemorrhage. Her son was born
with brain damage and traces of amphetamines in his blood, and died
within two months of birth. Stewart subsequently was reported to the California Department of Child Protective Services and charged with child
abuse. Although a state judge dismissed the charge, reasoning that the statute under which she was charged was not intended to penalize women for
conduct during pregnancy, again the specter of explicit state intervention
against a woman for fetal injury raised intense debate among legal scholars,
health care professionals, and the lay public.

Wrongful Life Action Against Parents

One extension of the concept of wrongful life that promises a severe impact on social values and on notions of responsibility is a damage claim
brought against parents charging their liability for their own child's birth
under handicap. For instance, what liability do parents have if, given accurate advice from the physician regarding the risk of genetic disease, they
disregard it and either fail to undergo amniocentesis or refuse to abort the
abnormal fetus, resulting in a child with a genetic disorder? If a claim for
damages against a physician can stand, can a suit against the parents also
succeed? Or does the exercise of the constitutional right to privacy of the

parents assure immunity from action? The answer would seem to depend on the extent to which the courts are willing to override the parent's right to refuse prenatal diagnosis or abortion with the right of a child to be born with a sound mind and body. Until now, in cases of genetic disease, parents could argue successfully that they should not be held accountable for circumstances beyond their control, and that the child's handicap is simply an unfortunate fate. However, there is evidence that, given the state of human genetic technology, the legal climate might be fluctuating toward sympathy for the affected child.

Despite suggestions that torts for wrongful life against parents by genetically affected children are improbable as well as undesirable, the thrust of the progression of decisions summarized here illustrates that the courts are, indeed, moving in that direction. The majority in *Curlender* argued that fears over the determination that infants have rights cognizable by law, thereby opening the way for such a plaintiff to bring suit against its own parents for allowing it to be born, are "groundless" (488). It goes on to note, however, that if the parents make a conscious choice to proceed with the pregnancy despite full knowledge that a seriously impaired infant will be born, "we see no sound public policy which should protect those parents from being answerable for the pain, suffering and misery which they have wrought upon their offspring."

At least partly in response to *Curlender,* in 1981 the California legislature passed and the governor signed a bill that provides that no cause of action arises against a parent of a child based upon the claim that the child should not have been conceived, or, if conceived, should not have been allowed to have been born alive. Other states that by extension prohibit wrongful life action against parents are Idaho, Indiana, Minnesota, Missouri, South Dakota, and Utah.

Margery Shaw (1980) agrees with the principle implied by *Curlender.* Women who are informed that their fetus is affected should incur a "conditional prospective liability" for negligent acts toward their fetus if they fail to use their constitutional right to abort. She would permit children harmed by the behavior of their mothers during pregnancy to sue their mothers:

Withholding of necessary prenatal care, improper nutrition, exposure to mutagens and teratogens, or even exposure to the mother's defective intrauterine environment caused by her genotype, as in maternal PKU, could all result in an injured infant who might claim that his right to be born physically and mentally sound had been invaded (p. 229).

In contrast, Annas argues that while this position might be a logical extension of permitting the child a cause of action on its own behalf, there are policy objections that focus on protecting the unborn child (1981, 9).

Rejecting the notion that there is a "right to be born both physically and mentally sound," he contends that such a "right" could easily turn into a "duty on the part of potential parents . . . to make sure no defective, or 'abnormal' children are born" (1981, 9). Dinsdale concludes that in cases where parents consciously choose to give birth despite risks of impairment to the child,

constitutional considerations preventing state intrusion upon parental rights of privacy, free exercise of religion, and family autonomy should prevail. In light of the inherently undefinable and, at least at the present time, only reluctantly recognized right of a child to be born unimpaired, more established parental rights necessitate that the decision to deem nonlife more valuable than life be left to the parent rather than to a jury after the fact. Even if a state were willing to assume responsibility for making this judgment in lieu of the parent, the state would find itself on an anfractuous drawing. Recognition of the child versus parent wrongful life cause of action would be only the beginning of more difficult and inappropriate incursion into the realm of childbirth and pregnancy, a realm which should best be governed by the parents (1982, 419–20).

Cohen contends that because of strong public policy considerations, the acceptance of wrongful life is not likely to lead to the "acceptance of intrafamily wrongful life actions" (1978, 231). Since liability in an intrafamily wrongful life action would turn on the moral question of whether the parents should have had the child, it should be beyond the scope of judicial review. Given the constitutional guarantee of parents' right of privacy, not only to choose to not have a child (*Roe* v. *Wade*), but also to give birth to a child (*Eisenstadt* v. *Baird*), "a child should not be able to sue his parents for making such a choice" (Cohen 1978, 231). This choice represents a moral, not legal, question on the part of the parents and should not give rise to a cause of action by a deformed child against his or her parents.

What are the implications, if litigation by an infant plaintiff (most likely initiated by counsel representing his or her rights) is successful, and he or she is awarded damages from the parents for birth with specific disabilities because the parents' "irresponsible" action had contributed to the disability? Had the parents given birth to a fetus known to be defective, even though the plaintiff would not exist if the parents made the opposite decision, part of the parents' responsibility might be perceived as compensating the resulting child. One result would be that parental responsibility might evolve into a legal duty to refrain from having children under a variety of circumstances or to abort all defective fetuses. Many observers view this possibility with repugnance, but Shaw envisions beneficial results in this redefinition of parental responsibility:

If the freedom to choose whether or not to have a child is limited by the threat of civil liability for having a child who is genetically defective, our posterity will be the beneficiaries. We will have decided that there is no "absolute right to reproduce" and that instead it is a "limited privilege" to contribute one's genetic heritage to future generations (1978, 340).

What might appear to be a just and humane means of compensating a child for damages suffered in a specific case in reality might serve to redefine parental responsibility in procreation more generally. Torts for wrongful life have strong potential to encourage or coerce parents to reevaluate value systems that primarily assume the child to have limited rights vis-à-vis the parents (Blank 1983). In addition to the individualist premise that each person has the "right" to be born free of defects to the maximum extent possible, such torts also include a eugenic dimension that emphasizes the responsibilities of parents to avoid bearing children who will be a burden to future generations. Both of these aspects might conflict directly with and limit the parents' procreative prerogatives. Although the eugenic implications of such lawsuits appear to be unplanned and simply a by-product of the set of individual suits, societal encouragement of such actions might reflect an underlying predisposition to control procreation decisions and consciously limit parental discretion for some perceived broader social benefit. The danger here is that once society is given the right to dictate that certain children not be born because they cannot contribute, it is a tenuous extension to require that certain women reproduce because they are likely to have children that will contribute greatly.

Although the courts continue to be unwilling to award damages based on "unavertable genetic disease," the context is being altered substantially by broadened availability and knowledge of evermore sophisticated prenatal diagnostic and screening techniques. If the parents consciously reject prenatal diagnosis in a clear case of risk, refuse to participate in available carrier screening programs, or fail to use genetic therapy once that is feasible, and a handicapped child results directly from their action or lack of action, the child would appear to have reasonably strong cause of action once the wrongful life concept is accepted. Although the actual cause of the disability does not result directly from parental negligence, their failure to take prudent action to avoid the situation might be persuasive evidence against the parents.

The merits of any case revolve around the certainty that the disability could have been avoided through actions of the parents. As the state of human reproductive technology and knowledge of the fetal environment advances to provide effective means of alleviating fetal disorders, the parents might be expected to bear legal as well as moral responsibility for their actions in accepting or rejecting available technologies. In the absence of more direct compulsory eugenic legislation, torts for wrongful life might serve as one means by which society will define "responsible" and "irresponsible" procreation decisions. If the courts recognize the right of progeny to sue for damages from their parents, this obviously would represent a strong, though indirect, mandate to parents predisposed against human genetic intervention technologies to use them. By allowing compensation to affected children through wrongful life torts, society, as reflected in its courts, would put its mark of disapproval on such parental actions.

CONCLUSION

The patterns in civil and criminal law reviewed in this chapter demonstrate a growing reluctance by the courts to deny a cause of action for prenatal injury or wrongful death of a fetus. Although there continues to be significant inconsistency across jurisdictions, the trend is unmistakenly in the direction of recognizing some form of protection of the health of the unborn and for compensation for damages incurred during the prenatal period. Legal distinctions between viable and nonviable fetuses are becoming less definitive as courts attempt to keep up with rapid changes in medical knowledge and technology.

Although few cases to date have dealt with civil and criminal liability of mothers for their actions during pregnancy, the abrogation of intrafamily immunity and the heightened awareness and evidence of the deleterious effects on the fetus of certain maternal behavior makes it likely that such suits will proliferate. Furthermore, the heightened acceptance of causes of action against third parties for prenatal injuries or fetal death is bound logically to extend to causes where prenatal injury resulted from parental negligence. As discussed in Chapter 4, the manifestation of these trends is likely to alter substantially notions of responsible maternal behavior and in some cases pit the rights of privacy and autonomy of the mother against the rights of a child to be born with a sound mind and body.

4

Maternal Rights and the Welfare of the Unborn

Many observers who study patterns in tort law have concluded similarly that continued expansion of tort recovery for prenatal injury is leading to the recognition of the fetus as a person (Kadar 1980, 643). Furthermore, the trend toward abrogating the parental immunity rule and efforts to surmount the practical difficulties of a parent-child suit clearly presage the day when a cause of action by a child against a mother for prenatal injury will be upheld. Although these trends seem incompatible with the woman's constitutional right to abortion and threaten in some cases to contradict her procreative autonomy and bodily integrity, they demonstrate a growing legal concern for the welfare of the unborn and the right of all children to be born with a sound mind and body. As noted earlier, new knowledge and technologies in medicine encourage this legal trend.

The practice in many jurisdictions of predicating a cause of action for prenatal injury on the viability of the fetus represents an effort to strike a compromise between the potentially competing interests of the mother and the unborn. Given trends in law and medicine, this dependence on an arbitrary and shifting boundary is bound to be only a temporary solution. Inevitably there will be a collision between these interests, and, somehow, the two sets of interests must be reconciled. In order for the most equitable balance to be struck, however, it is essential that the basis of the rights of each party be explicated.

WIDENING FISSURES IN MATERNAL PROCREATIVE AUTONOMY

Although the mother's right to autonomy and privacy in reproduction is fundamental, like all other constitutional rights it is not absolute. Therefore, at times she may be restrained legally from performing some action that under other circumstances would be considered a personal choice— for instance, smoking cigarettes or drinking alcohol. Although the U.S. Supreme Court has recognized that the parent-child relationship is special, entailing constitutional protection of parental discretion, it also has ruled that "the state has a wide range of power for limiting parental freedom and authority in things affecting the child's welfare" (*Prince* v. *Massachusetts* 1944, 168). Considerable deference is given the rights of the mother. However, the state also has an interest in protecting children who are under disability and has the power to do so under the *parens patriae* doctrine. Although our society places weight on the presumption that parents will act in the best interests of their children, the law is clear that parents have corresponding duties to act responsibly in the parenting role. Parental discretion can be limited when it violates the best interests of the children, whether born or unborn.

Full freedom in procreation for a woman includes the capacity to make all decisions in gestation and in giving birth, once she decides to have the child. What she eats, where she works, what type of recreational activity she participates in, and whether she smokes are her decisions alone. However, because a pregnant woman's choices in these disparate areas might adversely affect the fetus, conflicts will arise. Robertson makes a distinction between the woman's right to procreate and her right to bodily integrity during the course of pregnancy (1983a, 437ff.). The conflicts here arise in the management of the pregnancy only after the woman has made her decision to conceive and has exercised her constitutional choice as to whether to abort the conceptus. Only after she decides to forego her right to abortion, and the state chooses to protect the fetus, does the woman lose her liberty to act in ways that might affect the fetus adversely. Ironically, the constitutional right to abortion, then, has increased the feasibility of a maternal duty to the fetus because the choice to continue the pregnancy is hers alone. Although a woman is under no obligation to invite the fetus in or even to allow it to remain, once she has done these things she assumes obligations to the fetus that limit her freedom of autonomy. As stated by law professor Robertson:

The mother has, if she conceives and chooses not to abort, a legal and moral duty to bring the child into the world as healthy as is reasonably possible. She has a duty to avoid actions or omissions that will damage the fetus and child, just as she has a duty to protect the child's welfare once it is born until she transfers this duty to another. In terms of fetal rights, a fetus has no right to be conceived—or, once conceived, to be carried to viability. But once the mother decides not to terminate the pregnancy, the viable fetus acquires rights to have the mother conduct her life in ways that will not injure it (1983a, 438).

In contrast with Robertson's approach, Janet Gallagher argues that a pregnant woman's fundamental rights to bodily integrity, self-determination, and privacy protect her against any government intrusion into her medical decision making (1987). She contends that women have always put themselves at risk to bear children, and, if anything, pregnant women have been "altogether too compliant in their dealings with the medical profession and in their willingness to accept invasive procedures" (1987, 13). Even in those instances where the threat to the unborn child is real, the benefits of the proposed treatment indisputable, and the risks to the pregnant woman minimal, the courts must honor the woman's refusal. Furthermore, her decision not to abort the fetus does not imply abrogation of her continuing rights to bodily integrity and privacy. For Gallagher, the "individual and societal costs of placing the power of decision making anywhere but with the pregnant woman are simply too great" (1987, 14).

A Standard of Care for Pregnant Women

As discussed in Chapter 3, the basic principles of tort law require proof of the following: an existence of a duty; a failure to conform to that standard of duty; a close causal connection between the breach of duty and the complaint of injury; and actual loss or damage. Although the three latter elements are difficult to prove in prenatal injury cases, advances in medical knowledge concerning the fetal environment make them similar to other malpractice torts. Once a standard of care is established and one can judge what a reasonable person would do under similar circumstances, negligence can be determined. Proof of the causal relationship between the mother's action and injury to the fetus is more difficult; because she is in charge of so many actions and substances that affect the fetus, it is difficult to know whether a particular effect is an unexpected consequence of a legitimate action or a known consequence of an illegitimate one. Despite this complexity, the courts are likely to deal with causality much as they do in third-party cases. Finally, measurement of damage can be accomplished using the same methods applied in other prenatal injury suits. The only unique problem is the first element, defining the standard of care for pregnant women.

One of the practical problems, then, in implementing maternal responsibility for fetal development is the establishment of a reasonable standard of care for pregnant women. It is unreasonable to force a woman to refrain from all conduct that could remotely injure a fetus. In contrast, it is unreasonable to conclude she has no obligations to the unborn child. Somehow an equitable standard of care between the two extremes that balances the mother's right to control her body and her duty to the fetus must be established. Defining the legal duty owed by a pregnant woman is problematic but by no means impossible. In order to establish a standard of care, one must consider the nature of the maternal conduct in question, the foreseeable risks for the fetus arising out of the conduct, and the extent of infringement upon the mother's right of autonomy effected by the imposition of liability. The more severe the effect and the higher the risk of that effect, the greater the standard of care. In contrast, low-risk minor effects would warrant a less stringent standard of care for the mother.

Central to defining a standard of care, then, is the determination of the degree to which maternal behavior affects the fetus. As described in Chapter 2, the entire period of human fetal development is hazardous for the fetus. Susceptibility of the fetus to teratogenic agents is highest in the early development stages, but throughout gestation the fetus can be harmed by its environment. Moreover, because the fetus obtains all nourishment, liquid, and even oxygen from the mother and is exposed to chemicals ingested by the mother, it is totally dependent on the mother. The mother's life style becomes, in effect, the life style of the fetus, often exaggerated. The pregnant woman, therefore, has significant environmental influence over the health and even the life of the fetus throughout gestation. In contrast, the fetus is totally dependent on the mother and particularly vulnerable to deficiencies or disruptions in the environment of the womb.

As noted above, in establishing a standard of care, the risk that the negligent action foreseeably entails is critical. The individual is under an obligation to refrain from actions that are unreasonably dangerous to others. But what maternal actions constitute an unreasonable danger to the fetus? To what extent does an omission—for instance, the refusal of a woman to undergo prenatal diagnosis or consent to *in utero* surgery—constitute negligence? Moreover, foreseeability in tort law is not measured by probabilities, but rather by what a "reasonably prudent" person would consider in determining future courses of action. Clearly, this varies with the level of understanding about the effects of maternal action on the unborn. The question then becomes what information do we expect a reasonable person to have concerning risks to the unborn? Can we expect all women to be equally capable of understanding these risks, or at least of having some minimal standard of knowledge?

Under the reasonably prudent expecting parent standard, the parent would be held to a minimum standard of knowledge which would be based upon what was commonly known in the community. For example, if the community was unaware that a given course of conduct could adversely affect the unborn child, the parent would not be expected to know it either. However, if the parent should possess superior knowledge, the law would require the individual to act accordingly. The converse would not be true: it the parent did not have a sufficient experience to be aware of a fact of common knowledge, the community standard would still be applicable (Simon 1978, 85).

Establishing a standard of care for pregnant women also entails balancing the likelihood and nature of the apparent risk to the fetus against the benefit the mother must forego in order to eliminate the risk for the fetus. Again, the mother would be held to the community's standards of proper and reasonable behavior under similar circumstances. Actions that result in severe high-risk injuries, such as cocaine addiction or chronic alcoholism, are more likely to be viewed as negligent by the courts than light social drinking or an occasional cigarette. Defining a standard of care, then, depends not only on the state of medical knowledge, but also on how that knowledge is viewed by the community. Even if a foreseeable risk can be demonstrated, the community might conclude that the woman's right to a certain standard of physical comfort overrides a duty to the fetus, for instance, in the taking of cough medicine or antibiotics. "The reasonably prudent expecting parent standard would hold parents to the standards of the community. Only what the community considered to be unreasonable action in light of the risks to the fetus would result in liability" (Simon 1978, 86). Also, the more intrusive the action required of a mother, the more stringent the liability criteria should be.

The Limits of Maternal Liability: A Balance

A standard of care based on reasonably prudent action by the mother would be more fair to the woman than standards that might make her accountable for all decisions on managing the pregnancy. To minimize interference with the pregnant woman's right to control her body, Balisy suggests that negligent conduct of a high degree should be required before holding her liable for prenatal injury to her child (1987, 1237). He would limit liability to gross negligence, an almost conscious disregard for the welfare of the fetus, by the pregnant woman. Still, if it were proven that the mother knew or should have known that her conduct presented a high risk of seriously injuring the fetus and that her cost in curbing the conduct was minimal, she could be held liable for conscious and reckless disregard for the welfare of the fetus. One observer even concludes that legal recognition of a child-parent cause of action for preconception negligence is a "necessary and proper result of society's development" (Carroll 1986, 316).

Although there is a growing consensus that some state action is justified to protect the unborn from maternal negligence, the question of what specifically entails a proper standard of care remains controversial. Although Robertson (1983, 422) feels that there is no question that a state could prohibit actions by a pregnant woman that might reasonably be thought to kill a viable fetus or cause it to be born in a damaged state, other observers strongly disagree (see Gallagher 1987; McNulty 1988; Johnsen 1986). Gallagher, for instance, concludes that fetal rights advocates such as Robertson ignore the fact that women possess fundamental rights that preclude the kind and degree of government intervention they propose (1987, 12). For Johnsen (1986), Gallagher (1987), and McNulty (1988), the pregnant woman has a right to be free from any unique and discriminatory criminal or civil liability for her conduct during pregnancy and birth.

In contrast, Robertson contends that laws prohibiting only pregnant women from obtaining or using alcohol, tobacco, or drugs likely to damage the fetus would withstand a constitutional challenge (1983a, 422). Moreover, the states would not even be required to show a compelling interest, but only to pass the courts' "rational basis" test. Because there is no fundamental right to use psychoactive substances (*State* v. *Murphy* 1977), the state would only be required to convince the court that it was a rational public policy to prohibit such behavior to protect the fetus. The more difficult compelling interest test would not be needed under such circumstances.

Criminal laws also could be amended to include a wide range of behavior by pregnant women likely to cause harm to their unborn children. Attorney Barbara Shelley argues, in fact, that maternal fetal abuse should be criminalized because "a fetus injured by the conduct of its mother during pregnancy may not have the knowledge or means to vindicate its injury; consequently, the injury will go uncompensated and a wrong unredressed" (1988, 714). If criminal law was applied in this area, the state would take on this responsibility by defining the crime as an offense against the public at large. This would represent a major aggrandizement of criminal law if used to prosecute pregnant women. For Balisy, if a mother refuses to terminate substance abuse during pregnancy, the state is justified in imposing criminal sanctions and compelling enrollment in rehabilitation programs "for the benefit of the fetus" (1987, 1238). Under such laws, the state could prosecute women who refused to take necessary medication or knowingly exposed themselves to teratogenic substances. The result of such an approach, if applied to prescribed medicine, would be counterproductive because of the lack of conclusive evidence of the long-term risks and benefits to fetuses of specific pharmaceuticals. In recent times, if this was followed, we could have jailed women for not taking DES or thalidomide if their doctor ordered it. This strategy would also seem to conflict with the need to reduce our overreliance on drugs. This view also raises the criticism that such state action simply would encourage a woman at risk (e.g., a chronic alcoholic or drug addict) to abort the fetus.

Another position is that, although some causes of action for gross negligence ought to be recognized, there must be a balancing of interest between mother and unborn child, with considerable deference to the mother.

Certainly where infringement of individual rights is slight and governmental action is necessary to protect a fetus' health, intervention is proper. Yet where state action would intrude significantly into a woman's privacy, the importance of privacy to both the woman and her fetus strongly supports requiring the state to demonstrate that the intervention is truly necessary—that it prevents serious injury to the fetus and that no less intrusive means would afford adequate protection ("Constitutional Limitations" 1981, 1067).

Similarly, attorney Kathleen Rauscher contends that courts generally should defer to the decision of the mother; "only in exceptional cases," where risk to the mother is minimal and benefit to the fetus of a normal, healthy life is highly probable, should the courts be involved in balancing (1987, 793). Although Stearns admits a woman may have a duty to "properly manage" the gestation period and allow the fetus to reach its developmental potential, he argues that the state may not impose affirmative duties to undergo surgical procedures for the fetus (1986, 634). Under this perspective, the interest of the state in protecting the health of the fetus must be balanced with the mother's privacy interests in her home and in intimate decision making, the mother's interest in bodily integrity, and the fetus's psychological and physical interest in the autonomy and emotional stability of the mother. The fetus is not well served if the mother is coerced into conduct she resents. The dilemma is clear in that, if the mother is allowed unfettered freedom of action during gestation, the right of the unborn child to be born with a sound mind and body could be undermined. Contrarily, recognizing maternal liability for injury to her developing fetus would curtail maternal autonomy considerably and reduce her to a fetal container.

A third position argues that state intervention should never be used to override the decision of the mother during pregnancy. Law professor Martha A. Field, for instance, contends that controlling the woman to protect the fetus is both "unwise and unconstitutionally burdens the woman's right to reproduce." Moreover, such a strategy does not work to protect the health of newborns. "Pregnancy is a personal event. Pregnancy should not become a legal event as well—an occasion for governmental intrusion. There is no need for the law to regulate pregnancy and no net benefit from its doing so" (Field 1989, 124). Similarly, attorneys Manson and Marolt argue that criminal sanctions for prenatal negligence violate women's rights and fail to serve the "purported purpose of protecting the fetus" (1988, 181). Janet Gallagher, likewise, argues that we must defer to the choices of the person most directly involved—the pregnant woman—"out of recognition that licensing state intervention in such intimate areas ex-

acts unacceptable social costs" (1987, 57). Common themes of opponents
to government intervention is that it violates the rights of women, and that
it will not work in protecting the health of the fetus in any case.

Even prior to the birth of the child, parents do not have an unqualified
privilege to treat the fetus in any manner they choose. Also, while attention
here and in the literature concentrates on the responsibility of the mother
during pregnancy, the paternal duty to support one's minor children has
long been held to include the unborn as well as the born. Although a father
cannot, within the current technological context, directly provide the fetus
with necessities, one court (*People* v. *Sianes* 1933) reasoned that he has a
duty to supply them indirectly through the mother. If the mother is denied
proper medical care and adequate nutrients required by the fetus for proper
development, the health of both the mother and the fetus will be endan-
gered. Because of the extent to which the mother's health is so closely intertwined with the development of the fetus, the failure of a father to provide
his wife with basic necessities may be viewed as a failure to supply the fetus
with materials essential to its health. In light of the growing dependence
on an array of prenatal technologies, it would seem logical that fathers who
are financially able must provide for access to technologies demonstrated
to be necessary to protect the health of the unborn. (The potential development of procedures for fetal transfer to the abdominal cavity of a man
raises the interesting legal question as to whether he could be required to
carry a fetus for his unhealthy wife.)

Unanswered, however, are many questions as to whether or not a father
can be found guilty of negligence if he condones, or at least does not attempt to stop, behavior of his spouse that is hazardous to the fetus. Does a
husband have a responsibility to discourage his pregnant wife from smoking, drinking, or engaging in other potentially dangerous behavior? What
if he buys the alcohol, the drugs, or the cigarettes? What if he infects his
wife with genital herpes that is then transmitted to the fetus? Although evidence of the effects of secondary tobacco smoke on the fetus is not clear
(Hauth et al. 1984), does a husband as well as his pregnant wife have a duty
to refrain from smoking in the home? In *People* v. *Stewart* (1987), for instance, one of the charges against Pamela Rae Stewart was that she abused
her fetus because she did not abstain from having sexual intercourse with
her husband, despite her physician's advice that she do so because her placenta had detached. Why was her husband not also charged, at least with
contributing to the accused crime? What if he had demanded intercourse?
These and similar questions illustrate that, while prime attention is targeted at maternal behavior, the paternal contribution to fetal health should
not be neglected.

This conflict between paternal autonomy and fetal rights also raises serious questions concerning the role of third parties. Should physicians and
other health care providers who recognize that the fetus may be injured by

maternal action have an obligation to report the abuse? Increasingly, physicians are finding themselves in a dilemma. For instance, in 1983 a physician in Baltimore went to court in an effort to force a pregnant woman to stop using drugs that threatened the well-being of the seven-month fetus she carried. He contended that the woman already had one child born with injuries caused by her "willful use" of substantial amounts of Quaalude, Valium, cocaine, and morphine. Opponents from the Governor's Commission on Domestic Relations Laws argued that the doctor's request could pose an "unconstitutional imposition" on the mother. Similarly, a representative of the National Legal Resource Center for Child Advocacy and Protection stated, "What bothers me about this is that it could result in putting all pregnant women in a pen and force them to adhere to state standards of good prenatal care (1982, 16)."

George J. Annas agrees this pattern could lead to severe deprivations of the liberty of pregnant women during the third trimester (1982). He argues for the right of parents to make good-faith judgments and against the right of caretakers to make decisions for parents. As one commentator on the Baltimore case succinctly summarized the issues, "You've got to balance the rights of the state and the rights of the mother and the fetus. It's also a question of individual rights and privacy. It also raises questions of whether a fetus is legally a child" (Annas 1982, 17).

We have discussed the first two of these issues. Now attention is directed once again to the third question: is a fetus a child?

FETAL STATUS AS A PERSON: THE PROBLEM OF VIABILITY

Legal recognition of only the born child's dependence is arbitrary. The law should recognize the duty to provide and care for unborn, as well as born, children. Duties of parenthood should not commence upon the birth of the child; they should commence when the parents know or have reason to know of the pregnancy (Simon 1978, 81).

At the core of the debate over the legal parameters of maternal responsibility for assuring a safe fetal environment is the question of the legal status of the fetus. Part of the difficulty in defining the legal status of the fetus is that there are currently two separate and seemingly conflicting legal developments in the United States that appear to pit "disparate visions of the unborn against each other" (Kadar 1980, 640). On the one hand, the Supreme Court in Roe v. Wade (1973) and succeeding decisions has clearly stated that the fetus is not a person within the meaning of the Fourteenth Amendment. The Court, therefore, has granted immunity from liability for a death intentionally caused and maternally desired prior to the third trimester. On the other hand, case law in most jurisdictions permits the imposition of third-party liability for death or injury negligently caused at the previable stage and is moving toward acceptance of similar causes of action against the mother. This leads to the paradox that a pregnant woman may be sued for harming but not for aborting a fetus.

The consensus among legal commentators appears to be that the *Roe* decision does not preclude tort action for previable fetuses. Kadar argues that the *Roe* decision is irrelevant to the question of recovery for the wrongful death of a stillborn fetus (1980, 651). Because *Roe* v. *Wade* was not a wrongful death case, it did not directly address the question of recovery for such. He shows that, in fact, the courts have used *Roe* in three ways concerning recovery for wrongful deaths of fetuses.

First, in an attempt to *deny recovery,* the courts have used *Roe* to support the argument that there should be no recovery because the fetus is not a "person" within the fourteenth amendment. Second, in an effort to *limit recovery* to viable fetuses, the decision has been used to support the argument that recovery should be allowed only when the fetus is viable because that is when the state's interest in prenatal life becomes "compelling" according to *Roe.* Finally, in an effort to *expand recovery,* the decision has been used to support the argument that recovery should be allowed because according to *Roe* the state does have an interest in prenatal life [italics added] (Kader 1980, 663).

Simon agrees that *Roe* has little relevancy in medical treatment cases because, rather than asserting the mother's right to carry the fetus to term, the emphasis then shifts to her right to act in a particular manner during pregnancy (1978, 79).

The reactions of state courts to *Roe* in this area has been inconsistent at best. Although some courts rely heavily on various interpretations of *Roe,* others have virtually ignored *Roe,* and some do not even cite it. This is not surprising because the Court in *Roe* gave ambiguous signals but no specific guidance on the issue of fetal rights. A dissenting opinion in *Toth* v. *Goree* makes clear the irrelevancy of *Roe* v. *Wade* to the issue of prenatal injury.

In *Roe,* the Supreme Court considered how "important interests in safeguarding health, in maintaining medical standards, and in protecting potential life" restricted the privacy rights of a pregnant woman. . . . The balancing of the state's interest in regulating abortion with the right of privacy led to the Court's decision that the state interference in the abortion decision is sometimes impermissible. But the case at hand presents none of the interests found crucial in *Roe.* We are not concerned with the right of a mother to freely terminate her pregnancy at a certain stage. Rather we have the case of a wrongful and unwanted termination. Certainly a tortfeasor cannot invoke the mother's privacy rights to defend his wrongdoing. Nor is the issue of whether a fetus is a person within the meaning of the Fourteenth Amendment presented. If it were, *Roe* would settle the issue. But nothing in *Roe* precludes this Court from ruling that a fetus, viable or not, is a person within the meaning of our state's wrongful death act (1975, 305).

Another court in *Harman* v. *Daniels* (1981) concluded that the mere fact a fetus is not constitutionally entitled as a person to claim certain remedies or rights in no way prevents Congress from extending protection to unborn children by appropriate legislation. Likewise, in *Presley* v. *Newport* (1976), the court ruled that recovery for injuries resulting in stillbirth is allowable, even if the fetus is not viable at the time of injury.

In contrast, the majority of the Michigan Court of Appeals in *Toth* denied an action on behalf of a stillborn previable fetus injured in the third month of gestation. The court relied upon *Roe* and stated as follows:

If the mother can intentionally terminate the pregnancy at three months, without regard to the rights of the fetus, it becomes increasingly difficult to justify holding a third person liable to the fetus for unknowingly and unintentionally, but negligently, causing the pregnancy to end at the same stage. There would be an inherent conflict in giving the mother the right to terminate the pregnancy yet holding that an action may be brought on behalf of the same fetus under the wrongful death act (*Toth* v. *Goree* 1975, 301).

The New Hampshire Supreme Court (*Wallace* v. *Wallace* 1980) agreed with the *Toth* court, and argued that the presumption that a previable fetus injured and born dead has no standing was consistent with, if not required by, *Roe* v. *Wade*. According to the court, "It would be incongruous for a mother to have a federal constitutional right to deliberately destroy a nonviable fetus . . . and at the same time for a third person to be subject to liability to the fetus for his unintended but merely negligent acts."

Although most court decisions are consistent with *Toth* and *Wallace* and conclude that wrongful death torts for previable fetuses are not actionable, fetuses that suffer injury prior to viability, but that survive gestation and are born, often are viewed as entitled to the legal protection of the Constitution (*Abele* v. *Markle* 1972). As stated in Chapter 3, a cause of action must belong to a person or entity capable of enforcing the right violated. Although the previable fetus currently does not enjoy such a right under *Roe* v. *Wade,* if it survives and is born live, a cause of action can accrue. Again, however, confusion over viability and the status of the fetus results in conflicting decisions from one jurisdiction to the next. Because of the importance of clarifying the concept of viability prior to determining the status of the fetus as a person, some attention here is directed toward its medical and legal context.

Fetal Viability and Fetal Status: A Changing Concept

The preceding discussion illustrates that the question of fetal viability continues to be a key factor in determining the rights of the unborn. Although viability for the *Roe* Court is the pivotal constitutional point at which state interests in the fetus can contraindicate maternal rights to procreative autonomy, at its base it is a medical concept. "Throughout the opinion, the emphasis was on medical factors: Even the viability distinction, which supplied the dividing line between permissible and impermissible abortion, was based on medical knowledge" (Rubin 1982, 69). In writing the majority opinion, Justice Blackmun relied heavily on what he believed to be the consensus of the medical profession—that at least 40 to 50 percent of fetuses born at twenty-eight weeks of gestation would survive. Although acknowledging that viability could come as early as twenty-four weeks, twenty-eight weeks was emphasized as the pivotal point.

What the Court did not seem to realize is that medical viability is not biologically fixed at a permanent time. In light of rapid advances in medical technology and changing medical interpretation, the assumption that fetal legal rights are somehow based on a scientific, predetermined point of viability will undergo substantial re-evaluation. There are reports, for instance, of premature infants surviving at as early as twenty-two weeks gestation (Lenow 1983, 20). Although the majority in *City of Akron* v. *Akron Center for Reproductive Health, Inc.* (1983) reiterated its support for the trimester approach, Justice O'Connor in her dissent argued that advances in technology are moving the point of viability backward, and that the Court must re-evaluate its original *Roe* framework, which is "clearly on a collision course with itself" (p. 4778).

In addition to the impact of technology on the precarious definition of viability, there continues to be disagreement within the community as to what survival rates should be indicative of predicting viability: 5 percent, 10 percent, 50 percent, 80 percent? Obviously, the lower the survival rate one is content with, the earlier the viability cutoff point will be made. Conversely, defining viability later in gestation presumably would lead to a few abortions of fetuses that could have survived. The medical parameters of viability, therefore, are shrouded in value judgments as to criteria for fetal viability.

The National Commission for the Protection of Human Subjects in its report on fetal research surveyed changes in survival rates of premature infants, assessed the state of technology designed to sustain premature infants, and recommended guidelines for use by physicians in determining whether a fetus, delivered spontaneously or by induced abortion, is viable or nonviable (1975). Based on extensive data and expert testimony, the commission contends that a prematurely delivered fetus is viable when a "minimal number of independently sustained, basic, integrative physiologic functions are present" (1975, 55). Together, these functions must "support the inference" that the fetus will be able to increase in tissue mass (growth) and in the number, complexity, and coordination of basic physiologic functions (development as a self-sustaining organism). If these coordinated functions are absent, the fetus is nonviable, even though some other signs of life are apparent. According to the report, the functions detailed cannot be assessed separately in the fetus in a consistent, reliable, and precise manner, although they can be reasonably inferred by measurement of weight and estimation of gestational age. The commission concludes: "Thus, organisms of less than 601 grams at delivery and gestational age of 24 weeks or less are at present nonviable.... A weight of 601 grams or more and gestational age over 24 weeks may indicate that the minimal basic functions necessary for independent growth and development are present" (1975, 56).

Obviously, in abortion decisions measurement of viability cannot rely on direct measurement of weight and size. Moreover, in prenatal injury torts determination of the viability status at the time of injury is problematic. However, there are developing medical standards for estimating viability *in utero* despite continued controversy over which of the many variables has greatest relevance in determining viability. According to the commission, the best estimates available to date are based on measurement of head size through ultrasound, usually accurate within one week during the twenty- to twenty-six-week stage. Benirschke, however, contends that crown-rump measurement remains the most reliable estimate (1981, 53).

The commission concludes that an estimated gestational age of twenty-two weeks or less by ultrasound would "virtually eliminate" the possibility of viability by the weight and age criteria above. They add, however, that any reduction of the twenty-two-week limit would provide an additional safeguard. Kass argues that we should treat any fetus with an audible heartbeat as if it were viable, although some will not be (1975, 11). That normally would occur at about twenty weeks. According to Strong, "given current technology, that criterion (viability) would place the dividing line at somewhere around 500 grams" (1983, 15). The commission also warns, again demonstrating the crudeness of prediction and the variability among fetuses, that, whatever boundaries are established for viability, there is always a chance that a viable infant may be born after prediction of nonviability by gestational age. "Further," it notes, "these criteria for viability are based on current technology, which is subject to change." Therefore, any criteria established must be viewed as temporary and reviewed periodically for their continued appropriateness, something the courts until now have been less than willing to do as they generally remain tied to the twenty-eight-week limit established in *Roe*. According to Bentley Glass, "be sure, however, that advancing technology . . . will steadily move forward the age of fetal viability outside the womb" (1983, 350).

Social Recognition of Fetus as a Person

At the same time that technology is altering our definition of medical viability, changes in our perceptions of the fetus are undergoing drastic change. Reproductive innovations that humanize the fetus presumably will have an influence on one's acceptance or rejection of the prenatal liability of the mother at various stages in human development.

In discussing criteria of selfhood used by a society, Grobstein declares: "The social status of personhood is accorded through recognition and acceptance by others. Recognition and empathy registered by observers are especially important criteria for assessing levels of selfness when policy issues are at stake" (1981, 89). Even Baron, who suggests we are perfectly capable of refusing to grant personhood on the basis of empathy where that status would exact a result we are unwilling to accept, agrees that in close cases empathy may carry the day (1983, 122). Social recognition, in addition to behavioral manifestations and evidence of functional capabilities, is a critical sign that rudiments of personhood might be present.

Until the recent decade, the fetus *in utero* could not take on the social recognition of a human except conceptually. Hidden in the womb, the first evidence of life was the movement detectable to the mother at quickening, around the eighteenth week of pregnancy. Even here, however, the evidence was only of life, not of recognition of a human form. Since the late 1960s, a number of biomedical innovations have significantly altered the perception of the fetus. Ultimately, these innovations promise to result in the recognition of human qualities at progressively earlier stages of fetal development. One of the most critical qualities of recognition is viewing the fetus in the womb. Only in the last ten years has it been possible to view the fetus *in utero* through sophisticated electronic equipment. As ultrasound technology has advanced to produce more explicit visual images of the fetal limbs and movement, it is reasonable to expect a tendency to perceive the fetus as a small baby instead of an unseen organism residing in the womb. According to John C. Fletcher,

I think this technology itself has had a tendency to allow us to identify fetuses as persons much earlier if we decide to. My point is that there may be a sociobiological force working here. If you identify with a person when you see the fetus this imprints on you the idea that there is one of us here that we can't neglect. The technology itself has a powerful logical grip in terms of identifying personhood (1983, 96).

Ultrasound technology allows presentation of a humanlike form as early as fifteen weeks. Also, ultrasound observations give evidence of spontaneous fetal movements as early as nine weeks, at least two months before quickening. The most discernible impact of ultrasound on one's perception of the fetus, however, occurs during the second trimester, when the fetus exhibits miniature yet unmistakable human features. Apparently, it is not uncommon for women undergoing ultrasound monitoring to refer to their "baby" when discussing the fetus. Fletcher, Golbus, and Ryan discuss the more evident closeness of a pregnant woman to the fetus and her identity with the fetus as a person after seeing ultrasound pictures and prenatal diagnosis karyotypes (Doudera and Shaw 1983, 95ff.). The capability of determining the sex of the fetus through amniocentesis by the twentieth week or so introduces yet another human attribute to the fetal identity. The unborn "baby" now takes on the identity of "he" or "she," often with naming accompanying discovery of the sex.

Fetoscopy foretells even greater opportunities to humanize the fetus through direct observation of the fetal body. Although fetoscopy is limited currently by technical restrictions that enable viewing of only small sections of the fetus at a time, as its field of vision expands couples will be able to see minute details of the fetus. Without doubt, this capability will accentuate social or at least parental recognition of the fetus as an individual human entity. Although Glass questions at what precise time the gradual emergence of consciousness and awareness of the fetus will confer the status of personhood, the appearance of sensory activity and pain provided by technology is critical (1983, 349).

Perhaps the most consequential challenges to prevailing impressions of the fetus as something prehuman are the result of recent successes in fetal surgery (the legal implications of which are discussed later). Although corrective prenatal surgery promises renewed hope for many fetuses that otherwise would have been born with severe handicaps or not born at all, it is likely to produce conflict between the right of the woman to her privacy and the right of the fetus to whatever society deems to be proper medical care. King suggests "recent research has garnered so much knowledge about the fetus and its environment that we can view the fetus as a 'second patient'" (1980, 190). Should this view progress, it would represent a dramatic reversal of the notion that the woman is the only patient, with the fetus simply another maternal organ. If the fetus becomes a patient in its own right, it adopts characteristics that before were impossible and thus diminishes the corresponding rights of the mother. Under such circumstances, the fetus not only has a salient human form and a sexual identification, but also is a patient.

Despite the uncertainties as to whose rights ultimately will predominate, the rapidly evolving advances in a variety of *in utero* treatments, including fetal surgery, accentuate a subtle but real shift toward recognizing the independent self of the fetus. Technologies that enable one to view the growing organism as human; amniocentesis, which labels that entity as a "boy" or a "girl"; and prospects of a wide variety of direct surgical interventions certainly provide the developing fetus with recognition as a person. Although it does not seem feasible to speak of the fetus as a fully autonomous person, these technologies give the fetus broader human characteristics, leading to a redefinition of parental responsibility to the unborn patient.

Human Life Amendments: Impact on Fetal Status

There have been many attempts in Congress recently to pass a Human Life Amendment (HLA) or a Human Life Statute (HLS). Although no effort is made here to discuss the details of the various failed bills or their policy contexts, it is crucial to analyze what, if any, impact these actions, if successful, would have on fetal rights. With the certainty of oversimplification, it can be stated that most HLA and HLS efforts have redefined personhood as beginning at conception. Whatever strategy is used, the effect would be to extend constitutional protections to conceptuses throughout the entire gestation period.

Robertson (1983b) concludes that the medicolegal effects of an HLA would not be drastic or far-reaching because the HLA is not self-executing and would require further legislation to achieve full protection of fertilized eggs, embryos, and fetuses. Although an HLA could lead to state restrictions on pregnant women to benefit fetuses beyond prohibition of abortion, the states already have considerable power to intrude on the freedom and bodily integrity of a pregnant woman in order to protect the well-being of the fetus. In light of existing state power to protect unborn children, even under *Roe* v. *Wade,* the primary effect of an HLA on the health of fetuses would be to prohibit abortion. Westfall concurs that "tort law is an area where an HLA would be unlikely to do more than accelerate a trend, already well established in many states, toward full recognition of conceptuses as 'persons'" (1983, 187). The major result of HLA, if any, might be to impose more uniform standards in prenatal injury and wrongful death torts.

Pilpel, however, disagrees and contends that passage of an HLA would take away all rights of privacy from fertile women of childbearing age (1983). She fears that if the fetus is defined as a person from conception, prenatal injury torts would proliferate. This assumes that such actions cannot be recognized without an HLA, an assumption that seems flawed in light of current action in the courts.

AN EMERGING MATERNAL DUTY TO USE
PRENATAL TECHNOLOGIES

Despite many inconsistencies, recent case law clearly demonstrates a cause of action against third parties for negligence in informing the parents about available prenatal diagnostic technologies. Physicians have been held liable to substantial damage claims for wrongful birth of children born with defects that would have been identifiable by techniques recommended to the parents by the physician. Also, there is some evidence that parents will also be held liable for prenatal injury or death torts in the near future. As prenatal technologies move from primarily diagnostic to therapeutic in scope, the courts are even more likely to extend their notions of prenatal injury to include acts of omission as well as acts of commission. This may well place increased pressure on parents to exercise responsibility to the unborn child by availing themselves of the rapidly expanding selection of prenatal diagnostic and treatment technologies. This section describes some of the more prominent prenatal screening and diagnostic techniques and discusses how maternal responsibility might be shaped by each.

Prenatal Diagnosis

Prenatal diagnosis has become an important component of clinical prenatal care and is now a medical standard for certain women at risk for abnormal offspring (Verp and Simpson 1985). Of the 3.6 million infants delivered in the United States annually (Fuchs and Perrault 1986), about .5 percent will suffer from a chromosomal abnormality, 1 percent will have a dominant or X-linked disease, .25 percent will have a recessive disease, and about 9 percent will have an irregularly inherited disorder (Scriver 1985, 96). Although many genetic diseases are very rare, collectively they represent a significant cause of infant mortality. In addition, between 30 and 50 percent of hospitalized children have diseases of intrinsic origin, meaning birth defects, single gene, and gene-influenced disease. "Moreover, these patients have 'chronic' disease; their stay in the hospital is longer than average, and readmissions are more frequent than for patients of other types of disease" (Scriver 1985, 98).

In order to reduce the incidence of genetic disease, many prenatal diagnostic technologies are used currently in the United States. By far the most common technique for detection of genetic disorders *in utero* is amniocentesis. In this procedure a long thin needle attached to a syringe is inserted through the lower wall of the woman's abdomen, and approximately 20 cubic centimeters of the amniotic fluid that surrounds the fetus is withdrawn. This fluid contains some live body cells shed by the fetus. These cells are placed in the proper laboratory medium and cultured for approximately two weeks. At this time, karyotyping of the chromosomes is conducted to identify any abnormalities in the chromosomal complement as well as the sex of the fetus. If indicated, specific biochemical assays can be conducted to identify up to 120 separate metabolic disorders and approximately 90 percent of neural tube defects. If a fetus is prenatally diagnosed as having a severe chromosomal or metabolic disorder, therapeutic abortion is offered to the mother. Although amniocentesis has been conducted as early as the fourteenth week of pregnancy, some commentators have concluded that waiting until sixteen to eighteen weeks from the beginning of the last menstrual period produces the maximum number of viable cells and optimal safety because of the availability of a greater quantity of amniotic fluid (Golbus et al. 1979).

Initial concern over the potential medical risks of amniocentesis has largely dissipated. One older study conducted by the National Institute of Child Health and Human Development (NICHD) concluded that "midtrimester amniocentesis is a highly accurate and safe procedure that does not significantly increase the risk of fetal loss or injury" (NICHD Amniocentesis Registry 1976). In one analysis of over three thousand consecutive amniocenteses, the authors agreed that prenatal diagnosis is "safe, highly reliable, and extremely accurate" (Golbus et al. 1979, 157; see also Benacerraf, Gelman, and Frigoletto 1987). The overall accuracy of amniocentesis in assessing chromosomal constitution and establishing the presence or absence of a detectable inborn error of metabolism exceeds 99.4 percent (DHEW 1979, 61; see also Verp and Simpson 1985, 17).

The procedure is now regarded as a routine clinical procedure, and several successful lawsuits against physicians who failed to advise amniocentesis for patients over thirty-five have accelerated its use. By 1980, approximately forty thousand women per year were undergoing amniocentesis. Moreover, a 1982 article in the *Journal of the American Medical Association* on maternal age and births in the 1980s indicated that demand for amniocentesis is bound to increase because of the trend toward high maternal age in the population (Adams, Oakley, and Marks 1982, 493).

Approximately 85 percent of amniocenteses are conducted for chromosomal evaluation, about three-fourths for women over thirty-five years old (Verp and Simpson 1985, 22). The reason for the emphasis on amniocentesis for women over age thirty-five is that the frequency of chromosomal abnormalities, especially the most common one, Down syndrome, increases dramatically with maternal age (Verp and Simpson 1985, 23). Of women having live births in 1980, 29 percent of those aged thirty-five and older, and 4 percent of younger mothers, underwent amniocentesis (Fuchs and Perreault 1986, 77). Previous birth of a child afflicted with Down syndrome or other chromosomal abnormality, parental chromosome abnormality, and severe parental anxiety are other reasons for chromosomal evaluation. The remaining 15 percent of prenatal diagnoses are indicated by: previous offspring or close relatives with neural tube defects; the possibility of a sex-linked disorder; or, carrier status of both parents for an inborn metabolic disorder such as Tay-Sachs disease.

Amniocentesis also can be used to detect Rh incompatibility between the fetus and the mother. This condition results when the fetus inherits the gene for Rh$^+$ blood from the father and the mother is Rh$^-$. If some Rh$^+$ red blood cells cross the placenta into the Rh$^-$ blood of the mother, antibodies formed in the mother against the Rh$^+$ antigen can lead to severe anemia, brain damage, and possible death of the fetus (2,600 incidents per year in the past). The development of Rh immunoglobulin, however, makes it possible to prevent this process from occurring. Early diagnosis of Rh incompatibility coupled with treatment has successfully reduced the frequency of Rh hemolytic diseases caused by incompatible Rh factor pregnancies. This also represents one of the few current examples of amniocentesis used in conjunction with treatment of the disorder. In addition to its diagnostic applications, amniocentesis can be used in the third trimester to estimate fetal maturation and prevent premature delivery via Cesarian section. It can help in selecting the optimal time for intervention by providing valuable information as to the relative risk of delay in delivery versus premature deliver of the infant.

Chorionic villus sampling (CVS) is a procedure in which a biopsy is taken from the placenta, which has identical DNA as the fetus. Transabdominal CVS extracts a small amount of placental tissue from a needle that is put through the pregnant women's abdomen. Transcervical CVS uses a pump-type sampler to aspirate a specimen of placental tissue under direct view of a laparoscope. The advantage of CVS over amniocentesis is that CVS can be conducted as early as the ninth week of pregnancy, thus providing first trimester diagnosis (Elias, Simpson, and Shulman 1989). Although earlier studies found elevated miscarriage rates, improvements in technique have resulted in optimistic findings in recent studies making it just as safe as amniocentesis for mother and fetus (Clark et al. 1989; Ledbetter et al. 1990). If these data are confirmed, because of the ability to conduct CVS much earlier than amniocentesis, CVS undoubtedly will replace it as the preferred approach in the near future. The advantage for the pregnant woman is to give her the same information at a time when a much safer abortion is possible than the midterm abortions associated with amniocentesis (Evans et al. 1989).

A technology even more widely used than amniocentesis and CVS that has become indispensable in prenatal diagnosis is ultrasound or "pulse-echo" sonography. This procedure uses high-frequency, nonionizing, nonelectromagnetic sound waves directed into the abdomen of the pregnant woman to gain an echo-visual image of the fetus, uterus, placenta, and other inner structures. It is a noninvasive technology that is painless for the woman and reduces the need for X-ray scanning procedures. Studies to date have found no harmful long- or short-term hazards to the fetus from diagnostic ultrasound (Office of Medical Applications of Research 1984, 669). In addition to its use in conjunction with amniocentesis to determine fetal position, fetal age, and amniotic fluid volume, ultrasound can also be used to observe fetal development and movement as well as detect some skeletal-muscular malformations and major organ disorders (Warsof et al. 1986). More sophisticated devices can show images of fetal organs, such as the ventricles and intestines. Ultrasound use is also essential in conjunction with fetoscopy or placental aspiration and in fetal surgery (see later sections of this chapter). In conjunction with ultrasound, magnetic resonance imaging (MRI) has the potential to provide detailed diagnosis of nervous system abnormalities and other internal fetal problems (Williamson et al. 1989).

Although some observers have emphasized the "necessity for ultrasound examination of all pregnancies" (Rosendahl and Kivinen 1989, 947), a panel of medical and scientific experts, while recognizing the present value of ultrasound in obstetrics and identifying twenty-seven clinical indications where it can be of benefit, advised that "data on clinical efficacy and safety do not allow a recommendation for routine screening at this time" (Office of Medical Applications of Research 1984, 672). They further cautioned that ultrasound examinations performed solely to satisfy the family's desire to know fetal sex, view the fetus, or obtain a picture of the fetus should be discouraged. Despite this caution, some hospitals now provide patients with videotapes of their fetus on ultrasound. Given the broad medical applications of ultrasound, however, its use will continue to escalate. It appears that its fullest development and applications are yet to be realized.

Potentially, a wide variety of hereditary disorders, including hemophilia and possibly Duchenne muscular dystrophy, not approachable via amniotic samples, might be possible through fetoscopy (Perry 1985). Fetoscopy is an application of fiber optics technology that allows a direct view of the fetus *in utero*. The fetoscope is inserted in an incision through the woman's abdomen, usually under the direction of ultrasound. Although only small areas of the fetal surface can be examined at a time, the fetoscope can be maneuvered around in the uterus to examine the fetus section by section. Fetoscopy is also used for sampling fetal blood under direct observation from a fetal vessel on the surface of the placenta. This is accomplished by inserting a small tube into the uterus and aspirating a minute quantity of blood for diagnostic testing. Fetoscopy also has direct therapeutic use in the intrauterine transfusion of fetuses with hemolytic disease and considerable potential for introducing medicines, cell transplants, or genetic materials into fetal tissues in order to treat genetic diseases (DHEW 1979, 9).

Despite substantial progress in fetoscopy and fetoscopic aspiration in the last decade, they are still considered applied research because of the hazards they pose for the fetus. Escalated rates of premature birth as well as a miscarriage rate of between 3 and 5 percent accompany these procedures and must be reduced considerably before fetoscopy can be considered routine medical practice. There is no doubt, however, that fetoscopy is a van-guard technology for future efforts in *in utero* treatment of genetic disease and for fetal surgery.

Approximately six thousand infants are born each year in the United States with neural tube defects, the majority equally divided between anencephaly and spina bifida (Main and Mennuti 1986). Although there is a 2 to 3 percent risk of the defect recurring after one affected pregnancy, over 90 percent of neural tube defects occur without prior indication that prenatal testing is warranted (Macri and Weiss 1982). In 1973, however, an association between elevated levels of maternal serum alpha-fetoprotein (AFP) and open neural tube defect was reported. Since then, research on screening has proliferated.

The level of AFP is determined from either amniotic fluid or maternal serum collected between the fourteenth and twentieth week of pregnancy. At present, approximately 90 percent of neural tube defects can be diag-nosed through use of these tests. Because dynamic changes in AFP levels occur normally during this period of gestation, more critical control data and more advanced techniques for quantification are required. Also, be-cause there is some overlap in the distribution of AFP levels in amniotic and maternal serum AFP, both in pregnancies with neural tube defects and in normal pregnancies, there is still a false positive rate of approximately one in ten thousand cases.

Although measurement of AFP in amniotic fluid samples taken from women at known risk for fetal neural tube defects is recommended, mass serum AFP screening from unselected pregnant women is regarded as pre-mature. FDA approval of diagnostic kits to test for neural tube defects spurred controversy by consumer groups and scientists alike. Primary ob-jections focused on the high rate of false positives, the gross nature of the test, and the possibility that women will abort fetuses solely on the basis of this preliminary screening device when the actual probability of having an affected child is very low. The American Medical Association (AMA) Council on Scientific Affairs emphasizes the need for "intensive statewide pilot" projects to discover the appropriateness and efficacy of screening in the United States (1982). In contrast, Main and Mennuti concluded that "voluntary maternal serum screening should be offered to the general ob-stetric population in the United States" (1986, 16). Another observer cau-tions, however, that such screening must be coupled with ultrasound examination and is suitable only for certain parents (Simpson 1986, 222). Furthermore, Johnson et al. note that because of heightened levels of ma-ternal serum AFP in the pregnancies of black women not affected by open spina bifida compared to white women, an adjustment must be made in AFP values when used on black women (1990). This variation by race could mean that there might be differences in AFP among women of vari-ous ethnic backgrounds, thereby calling for more complex screening protocols. It appears the use of both maternal serum AFP screening and amniocentesis to identify neural tube defects will become more common in the near future.

There is continual expansion of the prenatal diagnostic techniques available to women to identify fetal defects. In the past few years many of these, including amniocentesis, CVS, and ultrasound, have become standard clinical procedures. In most instances, these technologies enhance a woman's reproductive freedom by providing information that helps her decide how to manage the pregnancy. However, as with all reproductive technologies, anything that can be done voluntary also can be coerced. If prenatal diagnosis were to become legally mandatory by imposing tort liability on those persons whose failure to use it results in the birth of a fetus with injury, then its very availability could limit the freedom of a woman who chooses not to use it. What if, after a physician recommends that a woman at high risk for a Down Syndrome infant has amniocentesis, she refuses and has a child with that chromosomal abnormality? Will she be legally liable for the wrongful life of the affected infant? Will her action be seen by the community as irresponsible? What if she undergoes amniocentesis, finds out the fetus is affected, but, because of religious objections, refuses to abort the fetus?

One dilemma surrounding current use of these techniques is that, while they give us the ability to reduce the incidence of genetic disease, they do so primarily by eliminating the affected fetus through selective abortion, not by treating the disease. Future developments in gene therapy might shift emphasis toward treatment, but prenatal diagnosis will continue largely to expand parental choice only to the extent it allows them to terminate pregnancies of affected fetuses. Thus, it will continue to be a policy issue congruent with abortion.

The dilemma becomes more immediate, however, if therapy is available in conjunction with the diagnosis, for instance in the case of Rh incompatibility. In *Grodin* v. *Grodin* (1980) the court recognized the right of a child to sue his mother for failure to obtain a pregnancy test. The logic of this ruling implies a child would also have legal recourse to sue his or her mother for failing to monitor the pregnancy and identify and correct threats to his or her health during gestation. As Robertson points out, "the issue in such a case would be whether the mother's failure to seek a test was negligent in light of the risks that the test posed to her and the fetus and the probability that the test would uncover a correctable defect" (1983a, 448). Of course, prenatal diagnosis could be directly mandated by state statute with criminal sanctions for women who fail to comply with the law. According to Robertson, state authorities could justify such a statute on public health grounds (1983a, 449). Despite constitutional questions of invasion of bodily integrity and privacy, Robertson feels it would probably meet a compelling state interest standard.

Carrier Screening

Even more problematic is the duty of prospective parents in high-risk groups to be screened for carrier status prior to having children. This involves screening for carriers of particular recessive genetic diseases. The primary clinical objective of this type of screening is to identify individuals who, if mated with another person with that same particular genetic trait, have a 25 percent chance of having offspring with the disease. Once identified, couples with carrier status can be offered prenatal diagnosis if it is available for that disease, or at least be educated as to the risk they take in having children.

Carrier screening programs have been in effect in many states and localities for Tay-Sachs disease and sickle-cell anemia since the early 1970s. Sickle-cell programs have been especially controversial because the trait is concentrated in the black population, and, unlike Tay-Sachs screening, which has always been voluntary, sickle-cell screening started out as mandatory in many states. Carrier screening tests for many recessive genetic diseases and even more precise genetic trait markings will be available in the near future. The most rapid developments have been in the area of DNA probes to identify polymorphisms (genetic variations) that mark a particular trait. Following the discovery of such a molecular probe for the Huntington's disease gene in 1983, efforts have been initiated to identify genetic markers for Alzheimer's disease, manic-depression, malignant melanoma, and a host of other conditions. In addition, considerable attention is being directed to the genetic bases of alcoholism, and research is proceeding at a rapid pace to provide techniques to identify persons susceptible to alcohol dependency.

Ironically, these new capabilities accentuate rather than reduce the political, legal, and ethical issues of genetic counseling and screening. When screening leads to aversion, or treatment, of genetic disease, the issues, though often controversial, are reasonably straightforward. However, when screening involves identifying heightened risk or susceptibility for particular conditions, it is considerably more problematic. As new diagnostic tests and genetic probes emerge, public expectations will intensify and the demand for accessibility to information derived from such efforts heightened. Once the tests become accepted as legitimate by policy makers, legislatures and courts likely will recognize professional standards of care that incorporate them. Recent legislation in California requiring physicians to inform pregnant patients of the availability of voluntary alpha-fetoprotein tests (Steinbrook 1986) and similar court pressure involving a variety of prenatal tests attest to the public policy dimensions inherent in these applications.

Do prospective parents have a responsibility to be familiar with and use tests warranted for their particular family background in order to avoid propagating offspring with the disease? Furthermore, if a testing program is available and they are advised by their doctor to use it but refuse, are they liable for a preconception injury tort or wrongful life tort for a child born with the disease? Although these questions seem distant now, rapid advances in genetic screening, combined with the legal trends discussed earlier, advise attention to the social and ethical issues they raise concerning parental duty to offspring.

Collaborative Conception

New knowledge concerning the transmission of genetic disease, along with the capability to identify carriers of a growing number of deleterious traits, raise another question. Do carriers of genetic disease or genes that make their children more susceptible to ill health have a duty to either refrain from procreating or use collaborative conception technologies such as artificial insemination or embryo transfer so that these deleterious genes are not transmitted to their offspring? If there is such a duty, where are the lines to be drawn? Will the line be drawn with genetic diseases like Huntington's or sickle-cell anemia, a heightened risk for manic-depression or alcoholism, or susceptibility to early heart disease?

With current techniques in artificial insemination, cryopreservation, and embryo transfer, these individuals no longer necessarily need to refrain from conception in order to protect their offspring. Now, for instance, if a husband is suspected of carrying a dominant gene for Huntington's disease, he can use the services of a sperm bank or donor. Although this process eliminates his biological contribution to the child, it also eliminates by 50 percent the risk of transmitting the disease to his progeny. Similarly, if both persons in a couple are identified as carriers of a recessive disease, they can: take a 25 percent chance that their child will have the disease and live with it; undergo prenatal diagnosis if available for that disease and abort the one-in-four fetus identified as having the disease; or use reproductive technology, such as artificial insemination, and be content with a healthy child, albeit one not genetically their own.

Although these options currently are open to couples, the key question here is whether or not they have a responsibility to take the latter two options and, thereby, reduce the chance of bearing a child with an avertable genetic disease? Does the child born with Tay-Sachs disease have a cause of action against a physician who fails to advise the use of artificial insemination in case of a disease that cannot be diagnosed prenatally? If the physician or genetic counselor recommends such action and the parents refuse, should the parents be liable for the wrongful life of their child? Again, the availability of technologies shapes the options available as well as the alternative perceived by the community as most responsible.

THE FETUS AS A PATIENT: *IN UTERO* SURGERY

Technologies in prenatal diagnostics have given us the capacity to discern an array of fetal defects *in utero*. The newer generation of prenatal technologies, however, is shifting emphasis to treatment and correction of these defects before birth. Fetal therapy and surgery, although still in the formative stages, promise to aggrandize concern for the fetus significantly. As we rapidly move from the sad choice between aborting and carrying to term an identified affected fetus toward surgical treatment of the defect, situations will arise where the benefits to the fetus may far outweigh negligible or minimal risks to the mother (Fletcher 1983, 307). Although the interests of the mother in having a healthy child and of the fetus are likely to be congruent, in some cases their interests will conflict.

One of the most difficult legal issues to be faced in the near future will be how to balance the rights of the mother and the medical needs of the fetus when they conflict. The basic issue here is whether the fetus is a patient separate from its mother in cases where the fetus can be treated either medically or surgically. Prior to recent developments in fetal surgery, the fetus was generally considered a medical patient and certain problems were treated with medicines administered to the mother or directly into the amniotic fluid. Although these procedures required the cooperation of the mother, they were not as physically intrusive as surgery. The difficulty with fetal surgery is that any treatment of the fetus can be accomplished only by invading the physical integrity and privacy of the mother. The mother must consent to surgery, not only for her unborn child, but also for herself.

Although many obstetricians prefer to view the mother and fetus as a single biological entity sharing interests furthered by proper maternal care during pregnancy, this perception is bound to be altered in light of advances in fetal care that clearly contrast the fetus with its mother for treatment purposes (Lenow 1983, 2). Moreover, as neonatology burgeons as a field, the fetus will gain more advocates within the medical community (Bolognese 1982). Due to this potential conflict between obstetricians representing maternal interests and neonatologists representing fetal interests, judicial deference to the medical profession's determination of viability may be problematic (Lenow 1983, 7). However these issues are resolved, the remarkable advances being made in fetal surgery are certain to accentuate potential conflict between mother and fetus.

Techniques of Fetal Surgery

Until the early 1980s, the only options offered by the prenatal diagnosis of a fetal disorder were to carry the affected fetus to term or abort it. About the only exception to this rule was blood transfusions to the fetus to treat Rh incompatibility, which have been conducted successfully since the early

1960s. Now, however, there are three basic approaches to treating the en-
dangered fetus. The first entails administering medication or other substances (i.e., biotin, digitalis, cortisone, or related hormone drugs)
indirectly to the fetus through the mother's bloodstream. Second, timely
delivery can be induced so that the infant's problem can be treated immediately outside the womb. The third and newest approach is direct treatment
of the fetus in the womb. *In utero* surgery has been made possible by new
developments in ultrasound, amniocentesis, and fetoscopy, and also by sophisticated surgical instrumentation designed specifically for these intri-
cate procedures on fetuses. As a result, a series of breakthroughs have been
made in rapid progression since 1981 (Ruddick and Wilcox 1982).

The first reported fetal surgery was performed in April 1981 on a thirty-
one-week-old fetus twin suffering from a severe urinary tract obstruction.
The procedure involved insertion of a polyethylene catheter into the blad-
der to drain off the urine build-up. Normally, the fetus voids urine into the
amniotic fluid about once an hour. If this flow is blocked, the build-up of
pressure can damage the kidneys and lungs and threaten life. In the first
case the surgery was successful, and these problems were averted (Golbus
et al. 1982). In a similar case, surgeons operating under ultrasound treated
a urinary tract obstruction in a twenty-two-week-old fetus by draining with
a needle an accumulation of fluid from a large cyst that threatened the life
of the fetus (Harrison, Golbus, and Filly 1981). Here again the procedure
was successful, and the unaffected kidney continued to perform normally.

Also under ultrasound, doctors at several locales have implanted miniature shunting devices in the brains of fetuses diagnosed as having hydrocephalus, a dangerous build-up of fluid in the brain (Rosenfeld 1982).
These shunts allow the fluid to be drained from the upper ventricles of the
brain into the amniotic sac. In one case, surgeons also inserted a four-inch-
long valve-control shunt to permit continued drainage during the remaining three months of pregnancy. The surgery was successful in reducing the
swollen head to its normal size and was culminated by an uncomplicated
Cesarian section. Related applications of fetal surgical methods have been
used to drain a collapsed lung that had become filled with fluid and to
drain excess fluid from the chest and abdomen of another fetus.

The most dramatic type of fetal surgery involves the actual removal of
the fetus from the uterus with its return upon completion of the surgery.
One recent application of this procedure was conducted to repair a
diaphragmatic hernia on a twenty-four-week-old fetus (Harrison et al.
1990). Approximately 75 percent of fetuses with this condition die despite
optimal neonatal care. In this case, the maternal abdomen was surgically
opened under ultrasound used to locate the placental position. The left
side of the fetus was brought outside of the uterus. Continual monitoring
of the fetal vital signs accompanied the fifty-four-minute surgery.
"Through a left subcostal incision in the fetus, the left lobe of the liver was

carefully retracted, the herniated viscera (stomach, large and small intestine, and spleen) were removed from the chest, and the large diaphragmatic defect was closed with a Gore-Tex patch" (Harrison et al. 1990, 1582).

Upon completion of the surgery on the fetus, the uterus was closed in three layers, with fibrin glue applied between them. The amniotic fluid volume was replenished with warm preserved amniotic fluid. Weekly follow-up ultrasound showed an active, growing fetus. At thirty-two weeks gestation, seven weeks after surgery, a healthy 1920 g male infant was delivered via Cesarian section. At eight months of age the baby was growing and developing normally at home. Harrison and associates also note that a female fetus with the same condition, repaired at twenty-five weeks gestation, was delivered at thirty-two weeks and is thriving (1990, 1584). A decade earlier a similar procedure was performed on a twenty-one-week-gestation fetus to correct a urinary tract obstruction (Harrison et al. 1982). In that case the surgery was termed a success, but the infant died of underdeveloped lungs following his birth three months after surgery.

Although puncturing the heart of a defective five-month-old fetus and letting it wither is hardly as impressive or appealing as the above cases, this procedure, performed on a twin fetus, did assure the continued existence of the remaining twin, which otherwise would have been aborted (Kerenyi and Chitkara 1981). In this well-publicized case, the forty-year-old woman had undergone amniocentesis and found that one twin had Down syndrome while the other was normal. She decided to abort them both rather than carry the Down syndrome fetus to term. Instead, the puncture procedure was performed in the twentieth week under ultrasound. The court acted as a guardian for the normal fetus and permitted the procedure. After confirming through a blood test that the correct fetus had been killed, the woman gave birth to a healthy infant four months later. At least nine cases have been published where selective feticide was performed on twins as a result of information gained through prenatal diagnosis (Philip and Bang 1985, 175). The frequency of twin pregnancies of women who had amniocentesis with information about twinning problems varied from 1 to 2 percent in seven studies (Philip and Bang 1985, 171). Accordingly, this procedure probably will be more common in the future, despite the furor it raised.

Notwithstanding these successes, it must be stressed that all *in utero* surgeries are presently high-risk procedures limited in use to fetuses in danger of dying before or soon after birth without the surgery. Also, for many disorders it is improbable that effective treatment will be developed in the foreseeable future. Furthermore, the threat of precipitating preterm delivery or abortion remains a severe constraint on all but the most routine *in utero* interventions, despite great strides in preventing those problems. Some risk also faces the mother any time fetal surgery is attempted. Another risk of fetal surgery is that in saving a fetus who otherwise would die, a seriously disabled newborn may survive. Certainly, fetal surgery also clearly demonstrates the gap between technical capacity and social law and values.

Rosenfeld declares that when the applause over successes in fetal surgery dies down, "one must quietly consider the consequences" (1982, 22). As fetal surgery becomes more commonplace, which it is certain to do, and as it is performed earlier in gestation, the status of all fetuses as potential patients will further complicate the issue of fetal rights. John C. Fletcher, the ethicist for the National Institutes of Health, feels that "improvements in fetal therapy will establish a stronger ground to protect the affected fetus' right to life," and that this will collide with established ground for the woman's right to choice concerning abortion (1983). Ruddick and Wilcox agree that "fetal therapy, especially lifesaving surgery, would seem to make it easier to respect" the fetal claim to the right to life (1982, 11). While Elias and Annas view forcible medical treatment as "brutish and horrible," they concede the following:

When fetal surgery becomes accepted medical practice, and if the procedure can be done with minimal invasiveness and risk to the mother and significant benefit to the fetus, there is an argument to be made that the woman should not be permitted to reject it. Such rejection of therapy could be considered "fetal abuse" and, at a late stage in pregnancy, "child abuse," and an appropriate court order sought to force treatment (1983, 811).

Fetal Surgery: The Legal Context

The concept that the fetus may be a patient, an individual whose maladies are a proper subject for medical treatment as well as scientific observation, is "alarmingly modern" (Harrison 1982, 19). As noted earlier, the unique feature of fetal surgery is that it requires violation of the mother's rights of personal autonomy if she does not consent. No new legal problems arise unless the mother refuses to consent, in which case the legal dilemma is agonizing, especially if she desires to carry the fetus to term. In our society, the status of patient usually carries with it the notion of autonomy. But in these cases, whose rights take precedence, those of the fetus or those of the mother whose body must be "invaded" in order to facilitate the surgery? Although case law is primitive in this area, some precedents exist in which the courts have ordered procedures over the objections of the mother solely to provide medical care for her unborn child.

An early case was *Raleigh Fitkin-Paul Morgan Memorial Hospital* v. *Anderson* (1964), in which the New Jersey Supreme Court granted a hospital authority to administer blood transfusions to a pregnant Jehovah's Witness, approximately seven months pregnant, who refused to consent to the procedure on religious grounds. The court extended its *parens patriae* power to protect the life of the unborn fetus by ordering the blood transfusions. In this case, the court stated it had no difficulty in ordering the procedure to save the life of the unborn child because the welfare of the child and the mother were so intertwined and inseparable that it would be impracticable to attempt to distinguish between them.

In a similar case, a New York superior court (*In re Jamaica Hospital* 1985) ordered a blood transfusion of a Jehovah's Witness for the benefit of her previable fetus, ruling that the state's interest in the fetus outweighed the woman's interest. In 1986, the District of Columbia Superior Court granted Georgetown University Hospital's request for a court order to perform a Cesarian section on a young woman who refused to consent (*In re Mayden* 1986). Moreover, she was required to attend the court hearing held in the hospital despite being in labor (Merrick 1990, 7).

Kolder and associates uncovered a pattern of such court-ordered treatment of pregnant women (1987). In a survey of obstetricians in forty-five states published in *The New England Journal of Medicine*, the authors found that court orders for Cesarian sections had been obtained in eleven states. Among the twenty-one cases in which court orders were sought, the orders were obtained in 86 percent. Significantly, the data indicate a greater likelihood of hospitals to seek court orders for minority women. Eighty percent of the women were black, Asian, or Hispanic, and 24 percent did not speak English as their primary language (Kolder et al. 1987, 1193).

One case that illustrates the extent to which a state is willing to force a woman to accept treatment on behalf of the viable fetus she is carrying is *Jefferson* v. *Griffin Spaulding County Hospital* (1981). In *Jefferson* the Georgia Supreme Court reaffirmed the principle of viability in *Roe* by determining that a fetus in the third trimester has a legal right to the preservation of its life that overrides the religious freedom of the mother. In this case, Jefferson refused to have a Cesarian section on religious grounds, despite the medical indications that, without it, the chance of survival of the infant would be less than 10 percent and the mother 50 percent (Poe 1981). The superior court found that, as a matter of fact, the child was viable and fully capable of sustaining life independent of the mother. For the court, there were two persons with separable lives. The court also ruled, however, that the mother could not be forced to present herself to the hospital.

On the following day, the Georgia Department of Human Resources petitioned the juvenile court for temporary custody of the unborn child, alleging the child was being deprived of proper prenatal care, and sought a court order requiring the mother to submit to a Cesarian section. The court found in favor of the Human Resources Department and gave it full authority to make all decisions concerning the child, including consent for surgery on the mother. The Georgia Supreme Court denied a motion filed by the Jeffersons to stay the superior court's edict, declaring that the state is the ultimate guardian of society's basic values and that the life of the unborn child takes precedence over the mother's religious beliefs. Ironically, Jefferson uneventfully delivered a healthy baby without surgical intervention, despite the high odds against it given by the physicians (Annas 1982, 16).

The ruling in *Jefferson* is critical for defining the legal right of the unborn to equal protection under the law. When maternal actions are judged detrimental to the health or life of a potential child, the court has shown little hesitancy to constrain the liberty of the mother. Although the court spoke in terms of a state interest, it actually weighed fetal rights against maternal rights, thus creating an enforceable legal duty on the part of the mother to safeguard the life of the fetus at the expense of her constitutional rights (Finamore 1983, 86). The *Jefferson* court relied on *Roe* v. *Wade* to establish a state interest in protecting a viable fetus. According to Finamore, however, this formulation "significantly transcends" the boundaries of *Roe* by enabling the state to compel medical treatment to save the life of the fetus (p. 87). "This result imputes rights to the fetus which are enforceable against the mother. It also creates a corollary duty on the part of the mother to safeguard the life and health of the fetus" (Finamore 1983, 87). The *Jefferson* decision also raises a serious question as to the extent to which the courts should defer to medical judgment in compelling medical care, since the prognosis given the court proved to be wrong.

Although *Jefferson* relied heavily on the *Roe* court's viability distinction and authorized surgery to protect a near-born fetus, as *in utero* treatment develops to the point that surgery is possible for previable fetuses, on what basis might the courts order a procedure? As long as *Roe* stands, the woman would appear able to evade a court order by having a legal abortion. What if she decides to carry the fetus to term, but refuses to consent to surgery for the health of the fetus?

In *Taft* v. *Taft* (1983) the court was faced with a dilemma relating to fetal welfare, although not to surgery on the fetus itself. The husband of a woman in her fourth month of pregnancy sought a court order granting him authority to force her to submit to a cerclage operation, which involves suturing so that the cervix will hold the pregnancy until later in gestation. Although the mother wanted the baby, she refused on religious grounds to consent, even though a physician testified she would miscarry without the procedure. The trial court granted the husband authority to consent, but this decision was reversed on appeal by the Massachusetts Supreme Judicial Court, which noted that "no case has been cited to us, nor have we found one, in which a court ordered a pregnant woman to submit to a surgical procedure in order to assist in carrying a child not then viable to term" (p. 397). The court, however, did not close the door to the possibility that the state possesses an interest in an unborn's life sufficiently compelling to restrict a person's constitutional right to privacy. According to the court:

We do not decide whether, in some circumstances, there would be justification for ordering a wife to submit to medical treatment in order to assist in carrying a child to term. Perhaps the State's interest, in some circumstances, might be sufficiently compelling . . . to justify such a restriction on a person's constitutional right of privacy (p. 397).

One of the most publicized cases involving coerced treatment of a pregnant woman for the alleged benefit of the fetus is that of Angela Carder, a twenty-seven-year-old patient terminally ill with cancer and twenty-six and a half weeks pregnant. In 1987 a superior court judge ordered Carder to undergo a Cesarian section against her wishes and those of her physician (*In re A.C.*). Attorneys for the hospital sought the court ruling to clarify whether the hospital had a duty to attempt to save the baby's life when it appeared Carder's death was imminent. The judge was informed that the operation could hasten Carder's death, but gave the baby a 50 to 60 percent chance of surviving. Carder's counsel immediately sought a stay from the District of Columbia Court of Appeals but was denied it by a hastily assembled panel of three judges. The surgery was performed, the baby died two hours later, and Carder died two days later.

After a review request by the American Civil Liberties Union, however, the new *en banc* decision was issued by the District of Columbia Court of Appeals in 1990. Three years after the original hearing (and Carder's death), the court strongly reversed the original decisions by a vote of 7 to 1. The court reiterated the right of all patients to make informed decisions regarding medical treatment and held that "in virtually all cases the question of what is to be done is to be decided by the patient—the pregnant woman—on behalf of herself and the fetus" (*In re A.C.* 1990, 1110). Furthermore, if the patient is incompetent, her decision must be ascertained through substituted judgment. This requires that the judge examine previous statements of the patient, the patient's value system, and what family members, loved ones, and family physicians think the patient would want. The court also found that the patient's quality of life cannot affect decision making.

The right of bodily integrity is not extinguished simply because someone is ill, or even at death's door. To protect that right against intrusion by others . . . we hold that a court must determine the patient's wishes by any means available, and must abide by those wishes unless there are truly extraordinary or compelling reasons to override them (p. 1130).

Although the court thus does not preclude the notion that the state

might in some cases prevail over the pregnant patient's interests, it emphasized repeatedly "that it would be an extraordinary case indeed in which a
court might ever be justified in overriding the patient's wishes and author-
izing a major surgical procedure such as a cesarean section" (p. 1142).
Legal scholar George J. Annas concludes that the *A. C.* opinion came as
close to saying that the decision of a pregnant woman, even in labor,
should never be overridden by a judge as any court can (1990, 29). According to Annas, "The conclusion thus seems inescapable: the use of the judi-
ciary to force women to undergo medical treatments against their will is
not only counterproductive, unprincipled, sexist, and repressive, it is also
lawless" (1990, 29). Despite Annas's conclusions, other legal commentators are less inclined to read *A.C.* as closing the door on the state's interest
in overriding a pregnant woman's choices to protect the fetus (Merrick
1990, 11).

Many questions are left unanswered by the decisions to date regarding
coerced surgery to protect the fetus. What standards of care will the courts
use, and where will they be willing to draw the boundaries? Would the
courts come to similar conclusions with a fetus twenty-eight weeks old, or
twenty-four, or twenty, if, medically speaking, they were viable? If the
court can order a woman to undergo a Cesarian section, can it not also
order her to allow corrective surgery on her unborn yet viable fetus of
twenty-four weeks? According to a 1982 report of the President's Commission for the Study of Ethical Problems in Medicine and Biomedical and Behavioral Research: "Future developments in gene surgery or gene therapy
may lead to further departures from the principle that a competent adult
may always refuse medical procedures in nonemergency situations and
from the assumption that parenting and reproduction are largely private
and autonomous activities" (1982, 66).

If the courts can intervene to the extent of ordering a surgical procedure
in the best interests of the fetus, can they, with much less difficulty, control
the behavior of women that is proven detrimental to the health of the
fetus, such as alcohol and drug consumption or working in a high-risk
environment? Such decisions constitute a framework for examining currently emerging potential alternations in societal views toward maternal
responsibility.

Clewell and associates suggest that one mechanism for protecting the
rights of the unborn when medical treatment is considered would be an advocate appointed by the court to represent the interests of the fetus (1982).
Although they believe parents bear prime responsibility for making such
medical decisions, it is best if a separate advocate can be identified for the
fetus. According to Clewell and associates, this person not only seeks the
best treatment for the fetus but also protects it from "unwarranted or unnecessary assaults" (1982, 1320). Because the advocate is separate from
the fetus and the parents, he or she is more able to view objectively the en-

tire situation and the whole range of options available. Under this system, the advocate would also stand between the fetus and the physicians to serve as an unbiased source of informed consent for the fetus. Despite the difficulty and expense of this advocacy system, something along these lines may be essential in the near future, as conflicts between parents and the unborn become more common.

CONCLUSION

Despite many inconsistencies among court decisions, there is a perceptible trend in tort law toward recognizing maternal responsibility for the well-being of the unborn child. Although viability remains a crucial distinction in some jurisdictions, the pattern clearly is to find a cause of action against third parties for fetal death or prenatal injury at the previable stage. The abrogation of intrafamily immunity and the willingness of some courts to hold parents liable for prenatal injury open the door for increased action in this area. In a short time, torts against parents for prenatal injury caused either by commission or omission have been recognized. A major reason for this shift has been recent advances in medical science.

Until recently, the courts were hesitant to recognize causes of action for prenatal injury because of the difficulty of demonstrating proximate cause and determining reasonable standards of care. Advances in medical technology and in knowledge of fetal development, however, are rapidly altering this situation. The availability of a broad array of prenatal diagnostic techniques, such as amniocentesis, ultrasound, and fetoscopy, along with advances in genetic screening and collaborative conception techniques, place increased pressure on parents to use them. The most intrusive of these developments, fetal surgery, potentially pits the right of a fetus to be born with a sound mind and body against the autonomy of the mother. In addition to increasing the social recognition of the fetus, these advances in medical science make prenatal injury cases similar to more conventional malpractice or injury torts.

Court action in this area must proceed with utmost caution. In the effort to protect the rights of the unborn child and to deter harmful behavior, there is a danger of compromising the autonomy and even the physical integrity of pregnant women. The rapid diffusion of these technologies and their acceptance by society is creating an environment in which the courts might be forced to adopt very stringent standards of care for pregnant women—standards that not only dictate life style choice during pregnancy but also mandate use of prenatal diagnostic tests, genetic screening, and any other appropriate medical innovations. The courts must be aware of the need for a delicate balance between the rights of the woman and the interests of the developing fetus and temper their judgments accordingly.

5

Selected Policy Issues in the Mother-Fetus Relationship

Chapter 4 illustrated some of the many dimensions of the maternal-fetal relationship often obscured in the oversimplified rhetoric of the abortion debate. It also demonstrated how greatly advances in medical science are altering the fragile balance between the rights of the mother and her unborn child, resulting in new and painful dilemmas. This chapter examines in detail some of the public policy ramifications arising from the shift toward greater concern for the well-being of the unborn. Particularly, it focuses on the extent to which the government ought to take an active role in defining responsible parental action.

If women are expected to avoid situations that are dangerous prenatally to their unborn children or preconceptionally to their potential children, do they have an obligation to avoid exposure to teratogenic substances by not working in high-risk industrial jobs? How does one reconcile concern for fetal vulnerability with the woman's right to work protection under various employment opportunity statutes? Also, increased rates of pregnancy among teenagers continue to represent a critical social problem. What steps ought governmental agencies take to reduce teenage pregnancy and protect the potential children of teenagers, who are at high risk for a variety of avoidable defects? Finally, new reproductive technologies are complicating significantly the notion of parenthood. The application that perhaps raises the most serious policy implications is surrogate motherhood, where one woman carries a fetus to term for another woman. To what extent ought the government become involved in defining the boundaries of this new concept of motherhood, and what implications do surrogate contracts that strictly regulate the surrogate mother's life style have on maternal responsibility in general? In their own way, each of these three issues raises

125

considerable debate over the roles of women and of the state in childbearing. As such, they warrant special attention.

WORK PLACE HAZARDS: FETAL VULNERABILITY
AND MATERNAL RESPONSIBILITY

A policy issue that promises to be highly controversial in the coming decades centers on fetal vulnerability to work place hazards. It explicitly contrasts the right of the mother to control her life against the need of the fetus for as risk-free an environment as possible. Does a fetus have an independent right, superior to that of the mother, requiring a work place free from environmental hazards? Conversely, should a fertile woman be allowed to work in an environment that might endanger the health of her offspring? If so, how much and what type of risk is allowable, if any, before precluding such employment? Furthermore, work place hazards directly bring the government into the issue. The strong societal interest in preventing fetal deformity demands that some accommodation be made to remove the mother from dangerous work environments. But society has also made a commitment to remove barriers preventing women from choosing their own careers. When these two goals conflict, which they do in this area, the issue becomes a critical public one.

Although the U.S. Department of Labor as early as 1942 recommended that pregnant women should avoid work place exposure to certain known toxic substances, the problem first came to public prominence with the publication of a U.S. Department of Health, Education, and Welfare (DHEW)-sponsored report on the occupational health problems of pregnant women (Hunt 1975). This report acknowledged the growing scientific evidence that occupational exposure to some chemicals can affect a worker's capacity to produce normal children. In response, some major U.S. companies removed women of childbearing age from their jobs and refused to hire women with childbearing capacity. One survey found that spokespersons for every major chemical company maintained that no woman biologically capable of bearing children should be exposed to substances that pose a direct risk to the health and viability of the unborn child (Rawls 1980). An estimated 100,000 jobs have already been closed to women on grounds of reproductive hazards, with the ultimate potential closure of twenty million positions (Becker 1986, 1226). Moreover, Bayer suggests that any effort to extend exclusionary policies to those sectors of the economy where females represent a major segment of the labor force, such as health care, would be disruptive as well as harmful to the well-being of women workers (1982, 15).

This issue of employment policies and pregnancy is becoming more consequential as more women of childbearing age join the labor force, especially in traditionally male-dominated occupations in heavy industry where there is a substantial probability of exposure to toxins. According to Furnish, the size of the population potentially at special risk is enormous (1980, 122). Of the twenty-five million women of childbearing age in 1985, approximately 70 percent were working. The Occupational Safety and Health Administration (OSHA) estimated that one million of these women were working in occupations where there was potential exposure to chemical substances that might cause birth defects, miscarriages, or both. Moreover, over a million babies a year are born to women who worked while they were pregnant. Although most of these women had healthy babies, the population at risk is large and continually expanding.

Importantly, this controversy has to be viewed within the context of the long struggle of women to overcome overt job discrimination, much of it rationalized by their pregnancy status (Huckle 1982). Only within the last several decades have women made serious inroads into discriminatory hiring practices excluding them from previously male-dominated jobs for which they were otherwise qualified. Concern for fetal health threatens to reverse these significant gains in equal opportunity.

In contrast, representatives of the industries with exclusionary policies have attempted to justify their action as a means of protecting the health of the developing fetus. They argue that the potential fetus has a right to be protected from injuries that might result if the mother is exposed to work place toxins. Certainly, employers are also attempting to protect themselves from potential future tort liability in cases of children harmed by fetal exposure to hazardous material (Moelis 1985, 369). As we learn more about the teratogenic and mutagenic effects of agents toxic for the fetus, but not necessarily for the mother, it is increasingly likely that such large damage suits will be successful. Therefore, the companies do have a reasonable economic interest in protecting themselves from that eventuality.

Fetal Vulnerability or Protection Policies

In order to protect the fetus for economic as well as moral reasons, a number of companies have established fetal protection policies that exclude all fertile women from positions where workers are exposed to high levels of potential toxins. This action is reasonable from a fetal development perspective because the effects of teratogens are often most severe early in the pregnancy, especially during the first month when the woman often is unaware of her pregnancy. The result of such a class action approach, however, is overcompensation, because many women of reproductive age do not plan to have any children or have already completed their family. The reaction of some industries to this possibility have been even more controversial, because what they have proposed is to permit a woman to continue employment in the high-risk job if she agrees to be sterilized. Another option often available to the woman is to accept a lesser assignment outside the high-risk environment, but usually at considerably lower pay.

It is critical to note that fetal protection policies are much more prevalent in traditionally male, blue-collar jobs, despite significant evidence that some of the most high-risk settings are in female-dominated work places. As Table 5.1 illustrates, hospital employees, office workers, hairdressers, and clothing and textile workers are exposed to many potential risk factors. Some recent data also suggest a slightly increased risk of miscarriage, preterm birth, and low birth weight babies among women who work the rotating shifts or irregular hours common in hospitals (Axelsson, Rylander, and Molin 1989; Armstrong, Nolin, and McDonald 1989). The conspicuous absence of fetal vulnerability policies in occupations highly dependent on women to supply relatively low-cost labor raises serious questions concerning the motivation for such policies. If society's concern for fetal welfare is serious, why are any women allowed to work in low-paid, dangerous jobs? It appears that fetal well-being depends on how expendable women of childbearing age are to the work force in each industry. The argument that fetal protection is but another pretext for excluding women from high-paying industrial jobs gains credence under these circumstances. Exclusionary policies to protect fetal health are certainly suspect if this inconsistent pattern continues.

Table 5.1
Potential Health Hazards to Fetus in Selected Occupations

Occupation	Potential Risk Factors
Health Care (nurses, aids, dental assistants, laboratory technicians)	Ionizing radiation Infection (i.e., hepatitis) Mercury vapor Anesthetic gases Disinfectants and sterilizing agents Phenolic compounds
Clothing and Textile	Benzidene-type dyes Formaldehyde Solvents Carbon Disulfide

Office Workers	Benzene in rubber cement, cleaning
	  compounds and solvents
	Ozone or methanol and ammonia from
	  duplicating machines
	Air contaminants (i.e., tobacco smoke)

Hairdressers and Cosmetologists	Bleaches Hair dyes Nail varnishes (acetone, toluene, xylene, plasticizers)

Source: Furnish, 1980:123-124.

Not surprisingly, these exclusionary policies have been attacked by civil libertarians and feminists. Rosiland Petchesky contends that the recent focus on fetal rights brings us back "to the Victorian notion that a woman's childbearing capacity . . . should determine where and whether she may work" (1980). Mary Becker (1986) sees acceptance of fetal vulnerability policies as a throwback to the protective policies of *Muller* v. *Oregon* (1908). By viewing women as a class in terms of their reproductive function, these policies fail to treat women as individuals (Accurso 1985). Allyson Duncan feels excluding women from employment under fetal protection programs should be severely limited, as it threatens basic rights to privacy (1989). Another author concludes that emphasizing positive social programs stressing prenatal care are more appropriate (Katz 1989). Lawrence Moelis supports strengthened measures to lessen overall toxin levels in high-risk industries and continued job security for women in such positions, despite some potential risk to the progeny of these women (1985). He also provides evidence that the dangers of work place hazards to fetuses have been exaggerated by many of these industries in framing their exclusionary policies.

Despite the obvious constraints that concern for fetal vulnerability to work place hazards puts on advances of women and its conflict with trends toward equality in the work place, concern for fetal welfare is growing. "The fetal protection programs that exist today are evidence that the balance between women's privacy rights and fetal health is moving toward the interest in preserving fetal health" (Clement et al. 1987, 524). Supporters of fetal protection policies emphasize the state interest in protecting the health of the fetus. Attorneys Nothstein and Ayres, for instance, assert that the state "probably has the right to promulgate safety standards in order to preclude women with reproductive capacity from exposing themselves to workplace hazards that significantly increase the risk of birth defects, even before a child is conceived" (1981, 316).

Although many observers emphasize the option of making the work place environment safe for all employees and, therefore, having no need to discriminate by status or sex, there is little chance of much headway in that direction for many years, especially in industries such as health care, where the hazards are largely unavoidable. However, even though working conditions cannot be risk free, some observers feel that a system of incentives created by the acceptance of fetal protection policies will strongly influence the quality of work place conditions for many years (see Buss 1986, 590). By allowing exclusion of women from a teratogenic work place, we send the message that as long as toxins are only teratogenic, they are marketable.

Although Linda Howard rejects the idea of "romantic paternalism" in the attempts of industry to protect women by not allowing them to work in high-risk positions, she argues that these objections do not demonstrate satisfactorily that any employee has the right to assume the risk of fetal as well as personal injury.

But when fetal health is implicated, sex-based discrimination may well be excusable. Given the social and economic costs of producing and caring for defective children and the substantial likelihood that the employment of workers in unhealthful environments will result in the birth of such children, it is justifiable to exclude some members of one sex from a very narrow class of industries in order to prevent this outcome—as long as the exclusion is in fact narrowly tailored, objectively applied, and based upon credible scientific evidence (1981, 836).

What constitutes "credible scientific evidence" and "objectively applied" exclusion? And, most importantly, who decides: the woman, the employer, the government?

The Mounting Scientific Evidence of Fetal Harm

As noted in Chapter 2, it is extremely difficult to link environmental factors with harm to the fetus. One reason is that a combination and interaction of two or more agents is often critical but very difficult to isolate. Also, much of the data necessarily is based on epidemiological studies, which result in statistical but not causal evidence. Statistical data are amenable to varying interpretation, depending on the perspective of the user, thereby resulting in conflicting conclusions. In spite of the difficulties of proof, however, a growing body of evidence has confirmed the hypothesis that toxic environmental factors give rise to fetal harm. According to Eula Bingham, then director of OSHA,

the more we learn about the effects of environmental toxic exposures on reproduction, the more we suspect that it is a substantial burden. The list of chemicals and other toxic substances such as radio frequency/microwaves grows almost daily as our research efforts expand. NIOSH now lists 56 substances which are mutagenic in animal tests and 471 teratogens (1980, 5).

An increasing number of research studies have evaluated and found ties between selected chemical and physical agents in the work place and fetal injury or death (Valentine and Plough 1982, 147).

Although the precise manner in which many chemicals affect the fetus is unknown, evidence of the devastating impact of a number of substances on the fetus is accumulating (see Table 5.2). The National Institute for Occupational Safety and Health (NIOSH) registry on the toxic effects of chemical substances contains entries for over seventy-nine thousand chemicals. Although only thirty to forty of these agents are proven human teratogens, over one thousand exhibit some teratogenic potential in ani-

Table 5.2
Selected Environmental Chemicals that May Be
Potentially Teratogenic in Humans

Chemical Agent	Effects
Carbon disulfide	Increased frequency of spontaneous abortions and premature births
Carbon monoxide	Increased frequency of spontaneous abortions and stillbirths; low birth weight; brain damage (microcephaly, spasticity, retarded psychomotor development)
Dichloro-diphenyl-trichloroethane (DDT)	Increased frequency of premature deliveries
Inhalation anesthetics	Increased frequency of spontaneous abortions in women chronically exposed; no evidence for increased risk of malformations in offspring
Lead	Increased frequency of spontaneous abortions and stillbirths, neurologic defects, intrauterine growth retardation, and postnatal failure to thrive
Methyl mercury	Cerebal palsy, chorea, ataxia, tremors, seizures, mental retardation, polyneuritis, and blindness
Polychlorinated biphenyls (PCBs)	Dark ("cola" colored) skin, eye defects, premature tooth eruption, gingival hypertrophy, hypotonia and severe acne
Vinyl chloride	Increased frequency of spontaneous abortions, central nervous system defects, craniofacial anomalies, genital organ defects

Source: Elias and Annas (1987:215)

mal studies (NIOSH 1988, 2). Toxic substances can harm the fetus either indirectly by altering the parents' genetic material or reproductive system, or directly by affecting the developing fetus *in utero*. Agents with mutagenic effects alter the chromosomal structure of the parents' germ plasm, while teratogens operate directly on the fetus to cause malformations. In addition, carcinogenic agents have been identified that are capable of acting on the cells of the fetus, eventually leading to cancer in their offspring. Obviously, determination of these long-term intergenerational effects are very difficult to ascertain.

Another problem in attempting to establish "safe" levels of exposure to potentially harmful agents is that tolerance varies substantially from one fetus to the next and by the timing of the exposure. The fetus is considerably more susceptible than the mother to toxic environmental agents because of the high rate of cell division and the ongoing process of cell differentiation. Also, the fetus, unlike the mother, is often unable to metabolize and excrete the substance and, thus, bears the entire effect while the mother may suffer no ill effects. Many teratogens pose their greatest danger to the developing embryo during the first several months of pregnancy, when the mother is not likely to know that she is pregnant. Moreover, there is some evidence that women may absorb some toxins faster than men and in greater quantities when pregnant (Buss 1986, 580). As a result, it will be difficult to design a policy that responds adequately both to the woman's employment rights and to the danger of harm to the fetus.

Out of the four million or so chemicals and substances in use in the United States, lead is the most well-documented link to fetal damage. The incidence of abortions and stillbirths among female workers exposed to excessive lead levels is abnormally high, and the children of such workers have been found to be susceptible to convulsions after birth. Maternal exposure to elevated environmental lead levels during pregnancy has been correlated with mental retardation and neurological disorders in the offspring (Rom 1980). Mercury, too, is known to pass through the placental barrier and cause damage to the central nervous system of the fetus, resulting in retardation, palsy, and seizures, as well as heightened rates of stillbirths (Smith 1977).

Many other substances widely used in industry are known or suspected to have adverse effects on the reproductive systems of exposed workers. Chromosomal damage has been reported in workers exposed to the solvent benzene, an element in paint strippers, rubber cement, nylon, and detergents. Anesthetic gases produce miscarriages and birth defects in the progeny of both male and female operating room and dental personnel (Cohen 1980). Exposure to pesticides and chlorinated hydrocarbons, used to manufacture dry cleaning fluid and other general solvents, causes serious fetal damage (Howard 1981). Workers exposed to vinyl chloride risk severe impairment to their reproductive system, and exposure has been tied to abnormal rates of miscarriage and the chromosomal damage of fetuses. Moreover,

among pregnant women working in a biological media preparation laboratory, a high abortion rate and the birth of a child with clubfeet have been related to high selenium levels. Industrial exposure of pregnant women to fat solvents such as xylene, trichloroethylene, methylechloroethylene, and acetone has been related to the birth of children with vertebral defects (Furnish 1980, 127).

In addition to these substances, other agents have been linked to fetal harm. Ionizing radiation, especially for women in the health industry, can cause substantial fetal damage. Infections that might cross the placental barrier can cause spontaneous abortion, fetal infection, or fetal abnormalities. Among these, hepatitis is most common. The incidence of neonatal hepatitis rises to nearly 77 percent when the mother becomes infected during the third trimester or shortly after delivery, while incidence is only 10 percent when the mother is infected in the first or second trimester. It also has been pointed out that infants in nurseries transmit the virus of rubella, a teratogenic virus, to nurses and attendants (Hunt 1978, 76).

The Paternal Contribution to Fetal Damage

Although it is generally agreed that the most direct harm to the developing fetus comes through exposure of the pregnant woman to toxic work place agents, there is growing evidence that fertile males also might contribute to fetal damage. This is critical for public policy, because if predicated on the assumption that the prime or only source of harm for the fetus is through the mother, then policies that discriminate against women of childbearing age might be justified under some circumstances to protect the health of the unborn. If, however, the effect of these agents on the male reproductive system also harms the fetus, then the current policy focus on women and work place hazards is misplaced (Williams 1981, 704). To date, corporate policies have centered on the maternal contribution to fetal health and have failed to consider the male role, which is finally receiving attention in reproductive research.

Although research only recently has been directed toward the male, a few extensive studies suggest that reproductive harm to fertile males can manifest itself in birth defects in the worker's offspring. For instance, there is evidence that exposure to lead in males leads, among other things, to a decreased ability to produce normal sperm. This condition might produce abnormal pregnancies in their mates (Howard 1981). Moreover, wives of males exposed to vinyl chloride experience a significantly higher than normal rate of fetal death (Infante et al. 1976). Heightened rates of chromosomal aberrations in males who work with vinyl chloride have led medical experts to conclude that occupational exposure causes germ cell damage in the father. Children of male vinyl chloride workers, and even children born in communities near vinyl chloride processing facilities, have an increased incidence of congenital birth defects (Infante et al. 1976). Similarly, there is evidence that males occupationally exposed to chloroprene suffer decreased motility of sperm. Other studies report that wives of workers exposed to chloroprene suffered three times the expected number of miscarriages (Infante et al. 1980).

In one case involving parental actions against an employer (*Coley* v.

Commonwealth Edison Co. 1989), a U.S. district court granted Commonwealth Edison summary judgment. Two male employees, whose work included cleaning up chemical and nuclear spills, alleged that conditions of their job caused their two children to be born with severe and permanent injuries; one child later died. Although the *Coley* ruling was based on the grounds that a wrongful birth tort had nothing to do with the facts of the case, it is interesting in that it illustrates potential novel suits of preconception injury from exposure of a male to work place hazards.

Despite the evidence in these areas, most research continues to focus on the pregnant worker. According to the Council on Environmental Quality, there is at best limited scientific basis for treating men and women differently because of potential adverse effects on the fetus. It is crucial that more research be done on the potential contribution to fetal damage caused by male worker exposure to teratogens or mutagens if we are to analyze the justness of employer policy. When an employer excludes women of childbearing age from employment because of possible effects of toxins on the fetus, that policy will in part be judged by the factual evidence of harm. Clearly, if a substance harms both men and women and their offspring, any policy that excludes only women discriminates on the basis of sex. According to Clement and associates, when a work place toxin puts both female and male employees at risk, and only women are excluded, the men are also discriminated against because they are allowed to work in jobs that endanger their reproductive capacity (1987, 522). Although attention is bound to continue to be directed at women, especially concerning teratogenic agents, the issue of work place hazards necessitates considerably more research for males as well as females.

Government Response: The Courts

Discrimination against women in the work place was for a long time rationalized on paternalistic grounds or on the basis of pregnancy. In 1905, the Supreme Court in *Lochner* v. *New York* struck down protective legislation that applied to both men and women. Three years later, however, in *Muller* v. *Oregon* (1908), the Court upheld protective legislation that applied only to women on the grounds of a woman's special maternal role. According to the Court:

That a woman's physical structure and the performance of maternal functions place her at a disadvantage in the struggle for subsistence is obvious. This is especially true when the burdens of motherhood are upon her . . . . As healthy mothers are essential to vigorous offspring, the physical well-being of women becomes an object of public interest and care in order to preserve the strength and rigor of the race (p. 421).

Women's biological role in procreation, therefore, justified discriminatory policy in the work place, according to the Court.

By the 1970s, women had made great strides in removing the most ostensible forms of discrimination in the work place through a series of equal opportunity acts. Title VII of the 1964 Civil Rights Act included a prohibition against discrimination in employment "because of" or "on the basis of" sex. Several Court decisions reinforced Title VII. In *Rosenfeld* v. *Southern Pacific Co.* (1971), for instance, the Ninth Circuit ruled that a California law prohibiting the employment of women for more than ten hours per day or to lift weights over fifty pounds was in violation of Title VII. In *Cleveland Board of Education* v. *La Fleur* (1974), the Supreme Court held that mandatory maternity leaves for teachers were unconstitutional under the Due Process Clause of the Fourteenth Amendment. The Court held that the arbitrary cutoff dates (five months before expected childbirth to three months after birth) violate due process because they create a conclusive presumption that every teacher who is four or five months pregnant is incapable of continuing her duties, whereas any such teacher's ability to continue past a fixed pregnancy period is an individual matter.

In *Geduldig* v. *Aiello* (1974), however, the Supreme Court determined that the exclusion of pregnancy from disability insurance plans was not in violation of the Equal Protection Clause of the Fourteenth Amendment because pregnancy is a "condition," and the issue is not one of gender discrimination. The Court ruled that the state is not required by the Equal Protection Clause to sacrifice the self-supporting nature of the program, reduce the benefits payable for covered disabilities, or increase the maximum employee contribution rate just to provide protection against another risk of disability, such as normal pregnancy. According to the Court, the plan

does not exclude anyone from benefit eligibility because of gender but merely removes one physical condition—pregnancy—from the list of compensational disabilities. . . . Absent a showing that distinctions involving pregnancy are mere pretexts designed to effect an invidious discrimination against the members of one sex or the other, lawmakers are constitutionally free to include or exclude pregnancy from the coverage of legislation such as this on any reasonable basis, just with respect to any other physical condition (p. 496–97).

In two other controversial decisions, the Supreme Court accepted the *Geduldig* rationale that disparate treatment of pregnant women did not always constitute sex discrimination. In *General Electric Co.* v. *Gilbert* (1976), the Court ruled that the exclusion of pregnancy benefits from otherwise comprehensive medical plans did not constitute disparate treatment because pregnancy is not a gender-based classification, since not all women become pregnant. In *Nashville Gas Co.* v. *Satty* (1977), however, the Court held that the petitioner's policy of forfeiting accumulated seniority for female employees during unpaid, mandatory pregnancy leave, although it did not constitute disparate treatment, did have a disparate effect on women and, therefore, did violate Title VII.

By 1977 confusion about the boundaries of *Gilbert,* and the fact that the Court was willing to permit some disparate treatment of pregnant women without identifying this treatment as sex discrimination under the 1964 Title VII provision, led to pressure on Congress to clarify Title VII. Reaction of Congress to a well-organized lobbying effort on the part of feminists and labor, as well as dramatic media coverage of purported violations, was swift (Huckle 1982). In October 1978, Congress passed the Pregnancy Discrimination Act, which included the Pregnancy Amendment to Title VII of the Civil Rights Act. This amendment left no doubt that the intent of Congress was to include discrimination on the basis of pregnancy as a clear case of sex discrimination. The act stated that "women affected by pregnancy, childbirth, or related medical conditions shall be treated the same for all employment-related purposes . . . as other persons not so affected." This amendment ensured a clash between the law and two interest groups: employers intent on excluding pregnant women from particular jobs, and pregnant employees who wished to be excused from particular jobs temporarily. Mattson criticizes the act for disregarding "the potential for harm to the unborn in certain working environments" (1981, 33). The Pregnancy Discrimination Act extended the scope of Title VII to the whole range of matters concerning the childbearing process, but it gave virtually no consideration to the issue of fetal vulnerability to work place hazards.

There are two defenses available to employers in Title VII challenges. The Bona Fide Occupational Qualification (BFOQ) can be met only under two conditions: the qualification invoked must be reasonably necessary to the essence of the employer's business, and the employer has a reasonable factual basis for believing that substantially all women would be unable to safely and efficiently perform the duties of the job. The second defense for making such employment distinctions is the judicially defined defense of "business necessity" (*Robinson* v. *Lorillard* 1971). Under this defense, the business purpose must be "sufficiently compelling" to override any discriminatory impact.

In *Harriss* v. *Pan American World Airways* (1980), the Ninth Circuit Court read the act to transform all pregnancy distinctions into disparate treatment violations. It also allowed only the more difficult BFOQ defense for disparate treatment. Because fetal injuries do not ordinarily hamper the employee's job performance, however, employers would have a very difficult time using the BFOQ defense of discriminatory treatment of pregnant women to protect the fetus. The *Harriss* ruling therefore presents serious difficulties in the fetal vulnerability context ("Life with Mother" 1983, 331).

In *Wright* v. *Olin Corp.* (1982), the Fourth Circuit Court became the first appellate court since the 1978 amendment to hear a Title VII sex discrimination suit grounded on the pregnancy-based distinction. The court clearly made an effort to reconcile Title VII and fetal vulnerability to work place hazards. It attempted to answer the question: under what circumstances and on what basis can employment practices avowedly designed to protect the unborn fetuses of women from work place dangers be justified despite their "disproportionate adverse impact upon women's employment opportunities?" In this case, the plaintiffs brought a class action suit charging that certain practices and policies of the employer were in violation of Title VII. Prominent among these alleged violations was the defendant's "female employment and fetal vulnerability program," which excluded women from some jobs and restricted access to others based solely on pregnancy or fertility.

Olin's "fetal vulnerability" program created three job classifications: Restricted jobs were those requiring contact with or exposure to chemicals known or suspected to be harmful to fetuses. Only women over sixty-three years of age or medically diagnosed as infertile could be placed in restricted jobs. Controlled jobs were those requiring very limited contact with harmful chemicals. Pregnant women could work in controlled jobs only after case-by-case evaluation. Nonpregnant women could work in controlled jobs after signing a form stating that they recognized the existence of risk. Finally, unrestricted jobs were those presenting no hazard to a pregnant woman or her fetus. These jobs were open to all women (p. 1182).

The trial court concluded that the program did not violate Title VII. The central finding was that the policy was instituted for "sound medical and humane reasons," not with the intent to discriminate against females because of their sex but to protect the unborn fetus. Reversing the district court, the appellate court conceded that the situation before them did not "fit with absolute precision" into any of the developed theories of Title VII claims and defenses. While the court agreed the plaintiffs had established a prima facie case of Title VII violation that could only be rebutted by a business necessity defense, it rejected the argument that all classifications based on pregnancy constitute disparate treatment for women. The court of appeals held that an employer may impose otherwise impermissible restrictions on employment opportunities for women if the restrictions are reasonably necessary to protect the health of the unborn children of female employees against work place hazards (p. 1189–90). However, in remanding the claim to the district court to allow Olin Corporation an opportunity to assert the affirmative defense of business necessity in a manner consistent with the court's guidelines, Olin must prove that protecting the fetus from exposure to toxic substances requires restrictions on female, but not male, employees.

The burden of persuasion is upon the employer to prove that significant risks of harm to the unborn children of women workers from their exposure during pregnancy to toxic hazards in the workplace make necessary, for the safety of the unborn children, that fertile women workers, though not men workers, be appropriately restricted from exposure to those hazards and that its program of restriction is effective for that purpose (p. 1190).

As discussed earlier, based on current scientific knowledge, that is not an easy task.

In establishing a case for the possible protection of the unborn by limiting maternal employment opportunities, the *Olin* court placed fetuses in a larger classification of business licensees and invitees, whose safety as a proper matter of business concern lies somewhere between the two established classes of workers and customers. Unwilling to believe that Congress intended to strip all protection from licensees and invitees, the court concluded that this class of individuals, including unborn children, qualifies as a class whose safety might be the subject of business necessity ("Life with Mother" 1983, 335). Although Phillips concedes that this opinion "strikes a needed balance between the employment rights of women and the moral responsibility of self interest of employees," he concludes:

Unfortunately, because of the complexity and novelty of the cases presented and the absence of clear congressional intent concerning the tension between employment rights and the social and economic concerns surrounding fetal health, the Fourth Circuit's decision in *Wright* v. *Olin Corp.* may prove no sturdier than a house of cards. The court's opinion rests on three conclusions: (1) that the Pregnancy Discrimination Act did not transform all pregnancy-based distinctions into instances of disparate treatment; (2) that each established Title VII defense is not limited to one corresponding type of Title VII claim; and (3) that the defense of business necessity is sufficiently elastic to include concern for fetal vulnerability within its scope. Should the Supreme Court reject any of these findings, *Wright*'s effect would be seriously undermined (Phillips 1983, 337).

The Eleventh Circuit applied its own interpretation of how fetal protection policies should be treated under Title VII (*Hayes* v. *Shelby Memorial Hospital* 1984). In this case a certified X-ray technician was fired upon informing her supervisor she was pregnant. In light of scientific evidence of the risk to the fetus of nonionizing radiation, the radiology department recommended that Hayes be removed from all areas where radiation was used. The hospital claimed that it fired Hayes because it was unable to find alternative employment for her. The court found the hospital's policy in violation of Title VII and stated that in order "to avoid Title VII liability for a fetal protection policy, an employer must adopt the most effective policy available, with the least discriminatory impact possible" (p. 1553). Like *Olin*, however, the *Hayes* court intimated that a more exhaustive consideration of scientific information and more carefully crafted language could make exclusionary policies legally acceptable (Buss 1986, 583). According to *Hayes,* a fetal vulnerability policy that applies to only one sex is in violation of Title VII unless the employer demonstrates: "(1) that a substantial risk of harm exists; (2) that the risk is borne only by members of one sex; and (3) the employee fails to show that there are acceptable alternative policies that would have a lesser impact on the affected sex" (p. 1554). In an almost identical case, the Fifth Circuit also rejected the business necessity defense for the hospital's exclusionary policy (*Zuniga* v. *Kleberg County Hospital* 1982).

Contradictory opinions were rendered by two U.S. circuit courts in very similar cases involving women flight attendants. In *Levin* v. *Delta Air Lines, Inc.* (1984), the Fifth Circuit held that the airline's policy of removing pregnant flight attendants from flight duty was not in violation of Title VII. The court ruled that the discriminatory policy was justified by business necessity and was a reasonable response to the airline's safety concerns.

In contrast, the Fourth Circuit refused to consider Eastern's concern for the health of the employee or her fetus a valid business necessity and held that its policy grounding pregnant flight attendants out of concern for the health of the fetus was in violation of Title VII (*Burwell* v. *Eastern Air Lines, Inc.* 1980).

Eastern's contention that an element of business necessity is its consideration for the safety of the pregnant flight attendant and her unborn child is not persuasive. If this personal compassion can be attributed to corporate policy it is commendable, but in the area of civil rights, personal risk decisions not affecting business operations are best left to individuals who are the targets of discrimination (p. 371).

Interestingly, unlike the *Hayes* or *Olin* courts, the *Burwell* court refused to limit its rejection of protective exclusionary policies to those that could not be objectively justified. Regardless of how commendable the employer's motives, excluding women from the work place denies them their civil right to equal opportunity in employment (Buss 1986, 587).

A U.S. Supreme Court decision on fetal protection policies was handed down in March 1991. It came in the wake of two separate and conflicting rulings—one federal, one state—involving Johnson Controls, Inc., policy. In *International Union, UAW* v. *Johnson Controls, Inc.* (1989), the case the Supreme Court agreed to review, unions and employees brought suit claiming that Johnson Control's fetal protection policy precluding fertile women from working in high lead exposure positions in its battery manufacturing operation violated Title VII.

In 1988, the U.S. District Court for the Eastern District of Wisconsin granted the employer's motion for a summary judgment. Upon reargument of the case, the U.S. Court of Appeals, Seventh Circuit, affirmed the trial court's ruling. After citing a long history of concern for employee health by Johnson Controls (previously Globe Union), the appellate court found that the fetal protection policy was reasonably necessary to industrial safety and, thus, should be recognized as a BFOQ protection against claims of sex discrimination. According to the court, available scientific data indicates that the risk of transmission of harm to the fetus as a result of lead is confined to fertile female employees (p. 889). Therefore, the employer's fetal protection policy was based upon real physical differences between men and women relating to childbearing capacity and was consistent with Title VII. The court also held that the union failed to show that less discriminatory alternatives would be equally effective to achieve the firm's purpose of protecting fetuses from substantial risk of harm created by lead exposure (p. 901).

In a conflicting state ruling, the California Court of Appeals, Fourth District, reversed a superior court decision that found that Johnson Controls's fetal protection policy did not violate the California Fair Employment and Housing Commission (*Johnson Controls, Inc.* v. *California Fair Employment and Housing Commission* 1990). The appellate court held that the fetal protection program "unquestionably discriminates against women" because only women are affected by its terms (p. 160). Although the court admitted that the dispute is "fraught with public policy considerations" and pits state interests in protecting the health of employees and their families against state interests in safeguarding equal employment opportunities for women, it concluded that categorical discrimination against a subclass of women, such as all women of childbearing capacity except those proven to be sterile, violates the California statute prohibiting discrimination on the basis of sex. "However laudable the concern by businesses such as the Company [Johnson Controls] for the safety of the unborn, they may not effectuate their goals in that regard at the expense of a woman's ability to obtain work for which she is otherwise qualified" (p. 178).

Moreover, even though Johnson Controls counseled against sterilization, the fetal protection program that precluded hiring women capable of childbearing in certain high-paying jobs was an invitation to women to have themselves sterilized if they had a great enough need for the job. The program thus violated the statute precluding employers from requiring employees to become sterilized as a condition of employment (p. 165). Contrary to the U.S. Court of Appeals in *International Union,* the California court held that Johnson Controls could not defend its fetal protection program as a BFOQ.

In a surprising 9-0 decision, the Supreme Court on March 20, 1991, reversed *International Union,* declaring that employers may not exclude women from jobs through fetal protection policies. Although the Court was divided on whether such policies could ever be justified under BFOQ defense (in concurring opinions White, Rehnquist, Kennedy, and Scalia did not rule this out), all nine justices agreed that Johnson Controls's fetal protection policy is facially discriminatory and violates Title VII of the Pregnancy Discrimination Act. Furthermore, five members led by Justice Harry A. Blackmun, who authored the majority opinion, left no room for a BFOQ defense of any fetal protection policy. For Blackmun, "decisions about the welfare of future children must be left to the parents who conceive, bear, support and raise them rather than the employers who hire those parents. . . . Women as capable of doing their jobs as their male counterparts may not be forced to choose between having a child and having a job" (p. 17).

Blackmun said that the Court had no difficulty concluding that Johnson Controls cannot establish a BFOQ, because there is no evidence that fertile women are any less efficient than anyone else in the manufacture of batteries (p. 17). Nor can concerns about the welfare of the next generation be considered part of the essence of Johnson Controls's business. Furthermore, the absence of a malevolent motive does not convert a facially discriminatory policy into a neutral policy with a discriminatory effect (p. 10). No matter how sincere Johnson Controls's fear of prenatal injury, it does not "begin to show that substantially all of its fertile women employees are incapable of doing their jobs" (p. 18). Finally, regarding the issue of liability, the Court concluded that the prospect of legal liability for employers in the absence of fetal protection policies "seems remote at best," implying that compliance with federal civil rights law would shelter employers from damage suits. Should this transpire, what was perceived by women's rights groups as a decisive victory might be a bittersweet one. The ultimate impact of *Johnson Controls* will be how employers respond in the absence of fetal protection policies, and how the courts deal with future work place liability cases that arise.

Regulatory Action on Work Place Hazards

Some observers have argued that a more fruitful solution is to be found in government regulation of work place hazards. "As workplace pollutants, fetal hazards are more appropriately controlled through regulation than through judicial action. Courts, confined by the particular facts of a case and lacking administrative powers and scientific expertise, provide inadequate protection against environmental hazards" (Buss 1986, 591). Ashford and Caldart agree that industrial control of reproductive hazards will come about, not by court applications, but rather by industry response to economic constraints or compliance with government regulations (1983, 562). In contrast, however, other observers doubt that regulation itself is capable of reconciling the conflicting interests through political mechanisms (Furnish 1980).

Reproductive hazards potentially can be regulated by a variety of federal agencies. Part of the regulatory confusion today results from jurisdictional conflict among these agencies. There are two likely sources of regulation: the 1970 Occupational Safety and Health Act and the Toxic Substances Control Act (TSCA). The purpose of the Occupational Safety and Health Act is "to assure so far as possible every working man and woman in the Nation safe and healthful working conditions" (29 U.S.C. §6516, 970). It gives the secretary of labor various mechanisms for regulating workplace safety and health, including a broad general duty clause providing that each employer "shall furnish to each of his employees employment and a place of employment which are free from recognized hazards that are caus-ing or are likely to cause death or serious physical harm to his employees (29 U.S.C. §654[1]).

In 1980, OSHA concluded that exclusionary policies such as those im-posed against pregnant women undermine the principle that the work place should be a safe environment for all persons. Instead of discriminat-ing against women of childbearing age or coercing them into ending their fertility, exposure standards should be set that recognize such vulnerabil-ity. In other words, OSHA argued that high-risk industries should not be able to reduce their liability for damage awards by excluding classes of workers. Moreover, no worker should be forced to sacrifice her reproduc-tive right to privacy in order to hold her job. OSHA became embroiled in the case involving American Cyanamid's exclusionary policy, which re-sulted in five women being sterilized at the Willow Island, West Virginia, plant in order to keep their jobs. After considerable administrative litiga-tion, in April 1981 the Occupational Safety and Health Review Commis-sion dismissed OSHA's citation against American Cyanamid's fetus protection policy, concluding that as a matter of law, the hazard alleged by the secretary was not intended by Congress to be included under OSHA. Furthermore, the commission declared that the choice of sterilization is not the product of corporate policy but rather "grows out of economic and social factors which operate primarily outside the workplace."

The case eventually ended up in federal court (*Oil, Chemical and Atomic Workers* v. *American Cyanamid Co.,* 1984) and was heard by the circuit court for the District of Columbia. Although the court admitted that the women who were sterilized in order to keep their jobs at the Willow Island plant "were put to a most unhappy choice" (p. 450), it held that the "lan-guage of [OSHA] cannot be stretched so far as to hold that the sterilization option of the fetus protection policy is a 'hazard' of 'employment' under the general duty clause" (p. 445). Furthermore, it stated that "the general duty clause does not apply to a policy as contrasted with a physical condi-tion of the workplace" (p. 448). In light of this decision, it is questionable whether fetal protection policies would fall within the regulatory powers of the secretary of labor under OSHA.

Perhaps in anticipation of this response by the courts, late in the Carter administration guidelines were drawn up by OSHA, the Equal Employment Opportunity Commission (EEOC), and the Office of Federal Contract Compliance Programs that would specifically regulate these corporate policies. These guidelines, which focused on the right of a woman to control her reproductive capacity and employment, would have tolerated exclusionary policies for pregnant women only as a last resort. Also, such protective actions would be temporary, pending full examination of systematic research as to the contribution of the male to fetal harm. Due to opposition from a broad variety of business groups concerned with governmental intrusion and feminist and trade union groups that argued the guidelines were not stringent enough, the proposed regulations were politically vulnerable. The decision on the part of the Reagan administration to withdraw the proposed guidelines was no surprise (Bayer 1982, 18).

In 1988, the EEOC issued its first policy guidance on reproductive and fetal hazards. The policy guidance declares that any practice denying employment opportunities to one sex because of reproductive or fetal hazard, without similarly barring the other sex, is unlawful under Title VII. The EEOC recognized the application of the business necessity defense in fetal liability cases, but stated that employers invoking the defense must demonstrate that there is a substantial risk of harm to the fetus, that the risk is transmitted only through women, and that there are no less restrictive alternatives to excluding women from the work place. Any such denial of employment must be justified by objective, scientific evidence, which the EEOC recognizes is difficult given the inconclusiveness of much of the research on fetal hazards. Although the 1988 policy guidance does not attempt to declare unlawful every fetal protection policy, it is designed to prevent unnecessary restrictions on women's employment opportunities.

In January 1990, the EEOC published additional policy guidance in reaction to the Seventh Circuit Court's decision in *Johnson Controls*. The EEOC rejected the court's finding for placing the burden of proof on the employee. Because fetal protection cases involve facially discriminatory policies, the burden of proof must be on the employer to prove that its policy is a business necessity, rather than on the plaintiff to prove that it is not. Moreover, the commission found that the significantly more narrow BFOQ is a better approach than business necessity to fetal protection policies. Therefore, in cases it handles, the EEOC will require employers to prove that protection of fetuses from risk is reasonably necessary to the normal operation of their businesses, and that the exclusionary policy is reasonably necessary to implement the protections. Again, the emphasis is on objective evidence of substantial harm in order to restrict access to jobs. A subjective or good-faith belief that an exclusionary policy is necessary to protect employees or to minimize liability is not a valid defense of exclusionary policies.

Another regulatory strategy would be to use Environmental Protection Agency (EPA) powers under TSCA to regulate fetal hazards in the work place. TSCA is a comprehensive statute that deals exclusively with toxins. It requires chemical producers, processors, and distributors to report to the EPA all information that indicates a substance presents a substantial risk. Moreover, the statutory threshold for triggering EPA action is low in that the information need only indicate that there "may be a reasonable basis" to conclude the toxin is hazardous (15 U.S.C. §2603 [f2]).

It seems reasonable, as Buss suggests, that any employer who concludes on the basis of scientific evidence that its work place is not safe for the developing fetus should be considered in possession of information required under TSCA to be reported immediately to EPA (1986, 595). Any evidence of work place toxins deemed hazardous enough to women employees and their fetuses to justify an exclusionary employment policy should trigger a regulatory response. As logical as this approach appears, however, there seems to have been little initiative in this direction by the Reagan or Bush administrations, despite their stated concern for protecting the health of the unborn. Also, the economic ramifications of this strategy could be significant and are likely to instead increase pressures for fetal protection policies implemented at the expense of women's employment rights.

Torts for Fetal Injury Due to Work Place Hazards

If we assume that work place hazards will not soon disappear and make all occupations risk free; that regulation, at least in the near future, will not resolve the problem; and that Title VII will limit severely concern for fetal welfare when it abrogates women's rights, there seem to be few preventive measures open. This brings us back to the remedial option of torts for prenatal injury. Although remedial action is no substitute for prevention, there must be some mechanism at least for the child so harmed to recover damages. Although proof of duty and causation might be difficult to prove, they are no more problematic in some cases (e.g., lead or vinyl chloride) than in other prenatal torts.

Should successful damage claims against employers for fetal damage emerge (none have to date), employers are likely to require waivers from workers where the work environment might contribute to the birth of defective children. If such waivers are effective in protecting the employer from the claims of parents, the mother might be held legally responsible for placing the welfare of her unborn in jeopardy if she intentionally chooses to work in a high-risk environment, despite her knowledge of fetal vulnerability. This is especially relevant where the employer offers to transfer all pregnant employees with wage-level maintenance. The economics and morality of this scenario bothers Furnish:

It is not seemly that society condone or encourage the malformation of the fetus as a result of exposure to a toxic work environment by first enacting laws that forbid taking the fetus' susceptibility into account and then "compensating" for the ensuing damage by requiring employers to assume the risk of such births and to insure against it. This in turn predictably results in the suggestion that the rights of the unborn be waived by parents who will be under intense financial pressure to do just that (1980, 87).

Despite such concern, it has been reported that such waivers are already in use.

Work Place Hazards: Balancing Competing Claims

The ongoing controversy over protection of the fetus from work place hazards cogently illustrates the conflict between women's right to employment and reproductive autonomy and the re-emergence of a concern for the rights of the yet unborn. Does the state have an overriding interest to protect future generations by allowing employers the right to exclude females of reproductive age from the work place if there is sufficient medical evidence that fetal harm is possible from exposure? If so, what constitutes sufficient medical evidence? Conversely, should the civil rights laws be enforced to protect women from such exclusionary practices? Who ought to bear the burden of protecting the potential children of workers from work place toxins—all potential mothers by losing their jobs, or industry by either reducing toxins to safe levels for the potential unborn or assuming liability for children born defective because of work place teratogens?

Some balance must be struck between these competing claims. Although Valentine and Plough are correct in their conclusion that present scientific uncertainty about reproductive hazards casts doubt on the wisdom of strong regulation at this point, considerable effort is needed to make it easier for women to protect their unborn while at the same time not have to sacrifice their jobs (1982, 154). Assurances of job security, seniority, and wages must be given women during pregnancy, along with temporary transfers to lower-risk positions. The present either-or mentality must be overcome. Title VII, while attempting to eliminate discrimination based upon pregnancy, does create a very real dilemma both for employers and for pregnant women. Furnish is correct in her conclusion that the most direct means of achieving the goal of accommodation is to amend Section 701(k) of Title VII to allow temporary removal of a mother at her request or pursuant to evenly applied employer rules. Although such exclusions in the interests of fetal health are not permissible under Title VII as currently written and construed, if applied with care the interests of women, the employer, and the fetus would be met. A slower and more cumbersome route to the same end would be the judicial one along the lines of *Wright,* where the court offered guidelines for the reconciliation of interests.

The controversy over exclusionary policies in the work place designed to protect fetal rights not only will continue, but also will intensify in the near future. Also, as noted in Chapter 3, torts for wrongful birth and life are increasing in frequency and in success as evidence of the teratogenic and mutagenic effects of a variety of toxins mounts. Industry will heighten its effort to protect itself from such torts by instituting policies to minimize its liability. Exclusionary policies are a ready means of accomplishing this goal.

TEENAGE PREGNANCY

A second troublesome policy area concerning mother and fetus centers on teenage pregnancy. Although the potential conflict between mother and fetus transcends age boundaries, teenage mothers raise unique problems. Special problems center on the question of consent (particularly for girls under sixteen), the capacity to understand the responsibilities of motherhood, the lack of adequate prenatal care, and a heightened risk of behavior potentially harmful to the developing fetus.

In 1985, over one million teenagers became pregnant resulting in over 400,000 abortions and nearly 500,000 pregnancies. Of these pregnancies, more than 31,000 were born to females fourteen years of age and younger (Henshaw and Van Vort 1989, 85). Nationally, teenagers account for 26 percent of all abortions and 13 percent of all births, but in some urban areas the majority of abortions and births are to teenagers. Moreover, teenagers account for nearly one-third of all unintended pregnancies (Westoff 1988, 7). Although pregnancy rates of teenagers have actually declined very slightly since 1980, they remain the highest among Western nations. Also, the heightened concern about fetal rights is certain to intensify debate over the teenage pregnancy problem.

The costs of teenage pregnancy, both personal and societal, are high and affect not only the girl and her baby, but also society. Since almost half of those who give birth will bear their child out of wedlock (83 percent among nonwhite teenagers), many will require public support. The public cost of teenage childbearing in 1985, including welfare, medical care, and food stamps, has been estimated at $16.65 billion (Burt 1986). The public will pay an average cost of $13,902 over the next twenty years for the family begun by each first birth to a teenager in 1985, for a total of $5.16 billion. The cumulative economic costs of caring for teenage mothers and their children is significant. Personal costs accompanying these public ones include incomplete educations, reduced employment opportunities, the imposition of childrearing responsibilities on teenagers unable to handle them, greater possibilities that the resulting poverty and frustration will undermine the development of their babies, and heightened medical risk for mother and child. (For different interpretations, see Upchurch and McCarthy 1990, who found that most young mothers dropped out of school first and then became pregnant; Hofferth 1987, who concluded that early childbearing had no independent impact on wages; and Edwards 1990, who argued that "predictions about teenage mothers being sentenced to a life in the underclass are dramatically overstated.") Without diminishing the personal and public costs of others involved, attention here is directed toward the welfare of the developing fetus. (See Dash 1989; Furstenberg, Brooks-Gunn, and Morgan 1987; and Vinovskis 1988 for valuable discussions of these other dimensions of teen pregnancy.)

Within the enormous field of preventive medicine one area seems particularly important, that involving the "complex of overlapping problems associated with teenage pregnancies, illegitimacy, prematurity, low birthweight, low IQ, deficient prenatal and infant care, and high mortality rates, not only for these children in infancy but also later on in life and also for the mothers" (Vaupel 1980, 113). Mothers under age fifteen experience a rate of maternal deaths two-and-one-half times that of mothers aged twenty to twenty-four (Alan Guttmacher Institute 1981). The younger the mother, the higher the risk of complications in pregnancy resulting in increased risk to the fetus. Teenage mothers are 92 percent more likely to have anemia and 23 percent more likely to experience a premature birth than women over twenty. Furthermore, young maternal age has been found to be a predictor of health problems in the first year of an infant's life, particularly with regard to the incidence of sudden infant death, accidents, and gastrointestinal problems (Makinson 1985, 132). These exaggerated rates of stillbirths, miscarriages, and infant death in the first year of life among pregnant teenage women result from a combination of physical immaturity, poor nutritional habits, and inadequate prenatal care.

A frequent result of teenage pregnancy, especially to girls under fifteen, is low birth weight and premature birth. As discussed earlier, low birth weight is a major cause of infant mortality and contributes to serious long-term conditions, including mental retardation, retarded growth development, cerebral palsy, epilepsy, and other birth injuries and neurological defects. These conditions often necessitate expensive medical care for the infant in intensive neonatal care units. Despite remarkable advances in medicine's capacity to aggressively treat VLBW babies, their survival rates and quality of life, should they survive, remain on average poor (Lantos et al. 1989; Shankaran et al. 1988). Although the medical risks of teenage pregnancy can be reduced with proper health care, the risks to young mothers and their fetuses cannot be eliminated (Baldwin and Cain 1980).

In addition to the heightened risks for both the young mother and the fetus solely because of the mother's physical underdevelopment, the pregnant teenager often confounds the problem by partaking in habits detrimental to her health such as poor nutrition. Cigarette smoking among teenage women is alarmingly high. Crack use is increasing among teenagers most likely to become pregnant; further complications include the abuse of alcohol and other drugs, lack of adequate prenatal care, and the frequent presence of sexually transmitted diseases in this population. Even if the teenager consciously maintains a proper diet during pregnancy and does not participate in other high-risk activities, it might not be sufficient because, as discussed earlier, the lifelong nutritional status of the adolescent is critical. Megadoses of vitamins and other nutrients administered to a pregnant woman can be harmful to the fetus, while their insufficiency in the mother might also be deleterious to the fetus. Denial of pregnancy, late confirmation, ignorance of the need for health care, and financial burdens also contribute to the medical problems of pregnant teenagers. Moreover, many teenage mothers have great difficulty caring for and raising their children, particularly if they are from a low-income family (Annis 1978, 73). The burdens of poverty and poor education stay with these women and their children throughout their lives, thereby exacerbating the problems and passing them on to the next generation.

The issue of teenage pregnancy clearly illustrates the conflict between the well-being of the fetus and maternal autonomy. If left to make her own decisions, the teenage mother might cause harm to the developing fetus, but how do we protect the fetus without inextricably violating the privacy of the mother? The issue is complicated further when the mother is herself legally a minor. Reproduction as a basic right is often viewed simply in biological terms: if a female is capable biologically of becoming pregnant, she has the right to have the child, have an abortion, and have the state support her if need be. It is ironic that while a physician needs parental consent before conducting even the most routine medical procedure on a minor, in procreation-related matters, including abortion, parental approval or even notification is not necessary constitutionally. Although fourteen-year-old girls cannot drink, drive, marry, or sign legal documents, they can and do have babies in large numbers. Again, the emphasis when dealing with reproductive decisions of minors is on biology. However, as demonstrated here, many teenagers are neither emotionally nor physically capable of providing a safe fetal environment or of adequately raising a child.

Primary emphasis in reducing fetal loss and damage due to teenage motherhood must be on education, not only sex education, but also on the responsibility owed the potential child. It must be made clear that the baby is not a plaything, a way to get out on one's own, or a means of obtaining public assistance. It is, instead, the largest commitment a woman will make in her entire life, especially during the prenatal period, when the entire well-being of the developing fetus depends on maternal behavior. It should be impressed upon young teenagers that such responsibility is possible only after the potential mother has demonstrated the capacity to exercise responsible and informed autonomy. Rather than a means of avoiding problems, having a baby compounds them severely.

A variety of private foundations are working on multifaceted programs in the area of teenage pregnancy. They include the Pew Memorial Trust, the Lilly Endowment, and the Andrew W. Mellon, Robert Wood Johnson, Rockefeller, Ford, Mott, Joyce, Danforth, Hewlett, and William Penn foundations. Although these specific programs have met with some success in reducing teenage pregnancy or alleviating accompanying problems, the scope of the problems remains a national tragedy in epidemic proportions, as new generations are brought into the cycle and the medical problems and costs of teenage pregnancy escalate.

I have stated elsewhere that a hard question in light of the general failure of traditional social programs to stem the problems significantly, is whether more explicit control of teenager's procreative prerogatives is warranted to benefit both potential teenage mothers and their progeny (Blank 1991a). Ought technological solutions, such as the imposition of long-term subdermal implants on sexually active teenagers, be used? Although technically feasible, does protection of unborn fetuses warrant coercing, by any degree, a young teenage girl to have this five- or six-year reversible contraceptive surgically implanted in her body when she becomes sexually active, to be removed only when she becomes physically and emotionally mature? Is there a compelling state interest to abrogate the autonomy of potential mothers in order to protect the unborn? In addition to the serious moral questions raised by such an approach, there are many constitutional questions and challenges to strongly held values in the liberal tradition. Who is to judge who is responsible enough to have a child: the parents, a birth control counselor, a physician, a representative of the public health service? Why target only young women for forced life-style changes, when older pregnant women are at high risk as well? Why direct intrusive methods only at the female?

The strategy to reduce the problems associated with unwanted pregnancy for young teenagers requires a multifaceted approach that includes, where appropriate, technological innovations in fertility control. It would be a mistake, however, to assume that there is any single, or simple, technological fix to a complex social problem. This is especially true in light of recent findings that the relatively poor pregnancy outcomes of young mothers are related to negative environmental and health factors common among poor women of all ages (Geronimus 1987). According to Mary G. Edwards, "there is no reason to assume that those young women having children as teenagers would have more positive pregnancy outcomes if they waited five, ten or fifteen years to bear children unless there were a significant improvement in the general health and improved access to good nutrition and prenatal health care" (1990, 4).

Likewise, in a study of five Western countries, Makinson concludes that the major problems of teenage pregnancy are associated more with socioeconomic factors than with the biological effects of age. "Some evidence indicates that if maternal age has an effect, it is only among very young teenage mothers. However, socioeconomic factors, including inadequate prenatal care, also manifest themselves most severely at the youngest ages" (Makinson 1985, 138). Policy strategies to deal with the problems of pregnancy by young teenagers, then, cannot focus only on fertility control. Clearly many such pregnancies are neither unplanned nor unwanted, raising severe questions concerning any attempt to coerce the use of subdermal implants by young females. Although sexually active teenagers should be strongly encouraged to use long-term reversible methods of fertility control as they become generally available, mandated use is neither an attractive policy option nor a feasible, practical approach at this time.

SURROGATE MOTHERHOOD AND MATERNAL RESPONSIBILITY

Although the discussion of maternal responsibility here has assumed that the women carrying the fetus to term is the biological and legal mother of the fetus, recent reproductive technologies have altered the facts and added considerable complexity to the issue. Artificial insemination in combination with cryopreservation techniques for freezing germ material, *in vitro* fertilization, and an array of innovations in embryo transfer mean that, with increased frequency, the woman carrying the fetus is not necessarily the genetic or biological mother. More critical, however, are the accompanying applications of these technologies, where a couple or single person will contract with a woman to carry a child to term for them. These surrogate mother contracts have proliferated since 1980 as many couples with fertility problems attempt to have children through surrogacy contracts. The first publicized surrogate birth via artificial insemination occurred in Kentucky in 1980. Since that time, an estimated one thousand births have resulted from the use of surrogate mothers in the United States (New York State Task Force on Life and the Law 1988, 25).

Under the most straightforward surrogate motherhood (SM) procedure, an infertile woman and her husband enter into an agreement with the surrogate by which she will be artificially inseminated with the sperm of the husband. After fertilization, the surrogate carries the fetus to term. When the baby is born she relinquishes her rights to it and surrenders it to the couple. Usually, but not always, this agreement is a detailed legal contract stipulating that the surrogate will receive compensation for her service. The result of this procedure is a child for a couple that otherwise would have to undergo lengthy and possibly unsuccessful adoption proceedings. SM also has an added attractiveness to some couples because the child is biologically the husband's. However, SM is not without substantial risk for the couple entering such an agreement. Although SM includes the use of a clinical procedure, it is primarily a legal procedure carried out under the auspices of lawyer brokers.

At a time when the courts, legislators, and legal profession are grappling with SM in conjunction with artificial insemination technology, new reproductive options are emerging that complicate the problem considerably. These innovations include *in vitro* fertilization (IVF), embryo transfer, and embryo adoption. Under an IVF approach, the egg of the wife, fertilized *in vitro* with the husband's sperm, is transferred to the uterus of a surrogate mother to carry to term. This alters the legal status because all the genetic material has come from the couple. "All" that the surrogate provides here is the womb for nine months. Already one such application has resulted in a case where the surrogate mother has gone to court to obtain custody of "her" child. Similarly, the embryo lavage procedure, by which an embryo is literally flushed from a donor woman (usually after artificial insemination with the husband's sperm) about five days after fertilization, gives new meaning to the term "rent a womb" and raises critical policy issues (see Blank 1990).

The Legal Context of Surrogate Motherhood

The legal problems surrounding surrogate motherhood are troubling because of the heavy physical and emotional commitment required of the surrogate. Unlike artificial insemination, where a donor anonymously sells his semen, SM takes nine months out of a woman's life. In addition to the normal risks of pregnancy, her privacy is bound to be invaded by the prospective legal parents, who might also be the genetic parents. The surrogate mother must be willing to be inseminated by the sperm of a stranger—or implanted with the embryo of strangers—carry the fetus to term, often under careful scrutiny of the couple or their legal agent, and turn over the baby to the couple immediately after birth.

The legal risk to the couple is also high because they must rely totally on the good faith of the surrogate to deliver a healthy baby as promised. A couple involved with SM must proceed only with the utmost caution because there is no assurance that any rights they might have in the child are guaranteed. Contracts to bear a child place most of the legal risks on the prospective adoptive parents, because, in the end, the decision to give up the legal rights to custody of the child rest upon the surrogate mother's informed consent and willingness to honor the agreement after the child is born. A court should be reluctant to hold a surrogate to the specific performance of such a contract, no matter how sound legally, should she refuse to give the child to the biological father and his wife. What if she decides to abort the child against the wishes of the couple, or if they attempt to prevent her from smoking or drinking during pregnancy? Also, what should be done if a surrogate who willingly turns over the child at birth has a change of heart later and demands the return of "her" child? Must the couple go through formal adoption proceedings in order to legitimize the child and protect their custody rights? Or, what if the child is born with a congenital defect and the couple refuses to take custody as stipulated in the agreement? These are but a few of a myriad of questions raised by SM that must be addressed by case law, statutory law, and extensive legal and ethical analysis. (Of the many books published on SM in the late 1980s, Martha A. Field's 1988 work is a most valuable overview of the legal and ethical issues.)

Most analysis on this issue so far has centered on whether or not SM contracts are legally permissible and, if so, legally binding. It should be noted that even if such contracts are not declared illegal, they might be judged contrary to public policy and thus be invalid. Furthermore, even if they are legally valid, they might not be enforceable in light of the variety of issues posited above. As with all applications of reproductive technologies, the legality of surrogate agreements must be interpreted within the constitutional guarantees of the right to bear a child. As noted earlier, childbearing ought to be free from unwarranted or unjustified government intrusion. The basic question is whether or not the government has a compelling interest to intervene in surrogacy contracts. Does a woman's right to privacy in matters of reproduction include a right to be a surrogate mother and, if so, under what conditions? (See Andrews [1989] and Rothman [1989] for conflicting views on this point.)

Despite the many concerns surrounding SM, payment has emerged as a key issue. In *Doe* v. *Kelly* (1981) the Michigan Court of Appeals ruled that while a husband and wife could adopt a child via the SM procedure, it would be illegal for them to pay a fee to the surrogate mother. The court held that there was no fundamental right to buy and sell children, and that such action violated baby-selling statutes, which in thirty-six states prohibit monetary inducement for adoption (Office of Technology Assessment 1988, 281). The Kentucky Supreme Court, however, held that surrogate parenting contracts do not violate the state's prohibition against purchasing a child for adoption (*Surrogate Parenting Associates, Inc.* v. *Commonwealth ex rel Armstrong* 1986). While the court concluded that surrogacy was analogous to artificial insemination, it emphasized that the contract, although not unlawful, was voidable by the surrogate mother.

In the most authoritative decision to date, the New Jersey Supreme Court declared surrogate contracts in that state unenforceable (*In re Baby M,* 1988). Although the court granted custody of baby Melissa to William Stern, the genetic father who had contracted with Mary Beth Whitehead to

be a surrogate mother of his child, it invalidated surrogate mother contracts. Such contracts violate state adoption laws because of payment and
constitute a form of baby selling. A less-known fact about the *Baby M* case
is that Mary Beth Whitehead and her former husband Richard Whitehead
reached an out-of-court settlement with the Infertility Center of New York,
which had brokered the contract. They charged the clinic with fraud and
negligence in arranging the contract that ended in this prolonged and bit-
ter custody dispute.

Although the New Jersey ruling affects directly only that state, in reaction to *Baby M* many state legislatures moved toward passing statutory
provisions to prohibit or regulate SM. One study found seventy-three bills
on SM in twenty-seven states: twenty-five of the bills would have forbidden
SM, twenty-six would regulate it, twenty-two would create commissions to
study it (Isaacs and Holt 1987, 28). In 1987, Louisiana became the first
state to enact a statute that makes SM contracts unenforceable. In 1988,
Michigan became the first state to make it a criminal offense to enter or
arrange a surrogacy contract and impose substantial penalties of fines or
imprisonment. In contrast, Arkansas passed legislation endorsing SM,
Kansas exempts SM from prohibitions on adoption agency advertising,
and Nevada has legalized SM contracts.

Legal analysts disagree on whether or not criminal statutes affecting prohibitions of payment ought to be changed. Van Hoften, for instance, concludes that the penal code provisions prohibiting payment for the transfer
of custody and adoption should not be modified, at least at this stage
(1981, 385). Attorney William J. Winslade, however, disagrees, contend-
ing that baby-selling statutes were intended to protect poor women from
selling their children as well as to prevent economic exploitation of such
babies and adoptive parents (1981, 154). SM, however, is at variance with
the intention of these laws because the woman is not selling a baby already
conceived or born, but rather entering into an agreement to have a baby
with the purpose of giving it up for adoption.

Winslade sees payment of expenses and a nominal (ten-thousand-dollar)
fee to a woman for the inconvenience and risk of childbirth as at best "a
modest" compensation (1981, 154). Field argues that the most oppressive
result of all would be to allow surrogacy but to prohibit the payment of any
fee (1988, 26). However, Noel Keane, pioneer SM broker, contends that if a
woman has a basic constitutional right to procreate, there is a question of
whether any state interest in preventing the buying and selling of surrogate
services overrides that fundamental right (1980, 160). Additionally, the surrogate mother would seem to have similar constitutional protection to bear,
but not raise, the child. Evidence suggests that while economic motives
alone are seldom sufficient reason for a woman to enter a surrogacy agreement, 85 percent of actual applicants to be a surrogate mother would require a fee if they were to go through with the procedure (Miller 1983, 18).

When the incentive is monetary, not one of compassion for the infertile couple, SM raises several potential problems: First, it might result in the exploitation of women who find the money attractive and who are willing under a contract to submit to severe restrictions on their privacy for a year or so and to give up the babies they carry to term in their bodies. One study found that all thirty women who had babies as surrogates experienced some grief, some so much that they sought therapeutic counseling (Parker 1983, 117). Although there is no evidence to date of the emergence of a class bias to SM (i.e., middle-class couples contracting with economically vulnerable women), this danger will heighten as SM becomes more commonplace. In most cases on record, some fee has been paid to the surrogate mother. The usual method of payment is for the couple to cover prenatal expenses as they come due and place the major portion of the fee in escrow until delivery of the baby. There is at least one report of a blackmail attempt by a surrogate mother who threatened to have an abortion unless the couple paid her $7,500 (Keane and Breo 1981).

Proponents of SM contend that monetary problems can be reduced substantially with an adequate contract. Katie Brophy, a lawyer from Kentucky involved in SM through Surrogate Family Services, Inc., proposed a basic contract that has been used by all surrogate mothers thus far in that state. The major purposes of this contract are to protect the confidentiality of all parties, protect the parties against the medical and emotional risks, and make appropriate use of expert opinion and guidance at every step along the way. Brophy admits that many provisions of the contract are unenforceable and might be considered void because of a statute or a particular court's view of public policy, but this contract serves at least to appraise the parties to it of the various problems that might arise and to provide contingencies in case they do (1982, 264). The contract presented by Brophy is twenty-five pages long and very detailed. Included are specifications concerning provisions for amniocentesis, behavior of the surrogate during pregnancy, and conditions under which abortion is permitted or required. It also spells out the fees and expenses to be paid, who will have custody of the child, contingency in case of miscarriage, and contingency suits should either the surrogate mother or the couple breach the contract. Even when a contract is used, many legal observers recommend that at birth of the child, with the consent of the surrogate, the couple should go through formal adoption proceedings.

The question of whether the surrogate is being compensated for the inconvenience and risks of pregnancy and the out-of-pocket expenses paid for her baby is certain to remain at the core of the legal controversy over SM. It is unlikely that a woman can be stopped from having a baby for another party if she so desires; the problem comes when she is compensated for that action. It is argued that she who takes the risk and bears the discomfort of pregnancy is the one to make the decision. This argument also assumes that she has a right to be compensated for her trouble. In effect, she is providing a service by renting her womb for nine months, and a just compensation is warranted.

As surrogate contracts become commonplace, competition among providers conceivably could lower the cost. It is more likely, however, that as demand escalates the cost of surrogacy will escalate. Unless some consumer protection is provided, exploitation of this demand from less trustworthy surrogate businesses will be manifest in high charges for inadequate service. Most likely, these firms will maximize their profit by reducing needed psychological counseling and screening of all parties to the contract and cutting other less tangible costs, to the detriment of both the couple and the surrogate mother. The question of exploitation of the surrogate by bargaining for lower fees must also be examined carefully by lawmakers in states where surrogate contracts involving payment are allowed. Whatever emerges policywise, it is clear that motherhood under these circumstances becomes a business proposition. Procreation here is a commercial endeavor where the various parties (couple, surrogate mother, attorneys, and so forth) are related through legal contracts. Barbara Katz Rothman warns that this practice will encourage "production standards" in pregnancy and will result in viewing pregnancy as a service rather than a relationship between mother and fetus (1987, 4).

Surrogate Mother Responsibility for Prenatal Care

SM provides an excellent opportunity to see how successful intense pressures for responsible maternal behavior during pregnancy might be. As noted above, SM contracts often specify in great detail what standard of behavior is expected of the woman during pregnancy, including proper nutrition, prenatal medical care, no smoking, and no drinking. Presumably, if commercial surrogacy contracts become more common, the interests of a couple in having a healthy baby might intrude severely on the personal autonomy of the surrogate mother. Assuming SM contracts are recognized in some jurisdictions as binding, what will preclude a cause of action against a surrogate mother who breaches the contract by negligently harming the fetus through her failure to provide agreed-upon care during gestation? Also, it is possible, though less likely, that the child upon birth could initiate tort action for prenatal injury against the surrogate mother who carried him or her to term under the contract. Conceivably, the adoptive (and possibly genetic) parents would be parties to such a suit against the woman.

Ironically then, children born via SM might be the first class of persons with a legal claim emanating from the contract for adequate maternal behavior during their prenatal life. Unlike conventionally conceived and carried children, the surrogate mother of these children could be legally bound to provide the best of prenatal care and a safe environment for the fetus. If she did not, not only might she not collect the fee, but she also might face a lawsuit by other parties to the contract or by the injured child for negligence during pregnancy.

CONCLUSION

The three seemingly disparate topics discussed in this chapter extend considerably the emerging debate over reproductive autonomy of women. Fetal protection policies that pit a woman's right to employment against social concern for fetal health, policies to reduce the social problem of teenage pregnancy by controlling the behavior of young women, and surrogacy contracts that introduce a new legal dimension to maternal responsibility in producing a healthy baby for a third party each represent a potentially explosive policy issue. Together, they have significant consequences for redefining the relationship between mother and fetus and escalating the political debate over reproductive rights. In each instance, women's rights during pregnancy are being challenged out of concern for the unborn, potential unborn, or some third parties. Along with the legal trends and developments in medical technology and knowledge reviewed in earlier chapters, these issues promise to transform conventional notions of gestational motherhood and expand the already acrimonious debate over reproduction.

6

Defining Responsibility for Fetal Health

Thus far this book has focused attention on the extent to which rapid advances in medical knowledge and technology are altering the political and legal framework of the relationship between mother and fetus. It has analyzed trends in case law and legislation surrounding these changes and concluded that the courts have moved toward recognizing a broadening array of state interests in the welfare of the fetus, often at the expense of the mother. Although these patterns do not seem to represent a conscious effort to abrogate maternal rights, cumulatively they contribute to a climate that frequently pits mother against fetus. The approach of the book until now has been largely descriptive, demonstrating what is transpiring and what policy problems are emerging.

In this chapter, I move from this description of case law patterns, the state of technology, and the intensifying debate to present my own views on the policy issues raised in previous chapters and on preferred strategies for dealing with the issues. My major premise is that the relationship between the pregnant woman and the developing fetus is special, culturally as well as biologically unique. Although there are strong pressures to make this relationship potentially adversarial, generally this approach serves neither party well. The fetus more than a born child needs the mother for its health and life, and many acts of commission and omission by the woman can be injurious to the fetus. Any feasible strategy for dealing with the problems raised here must, therefore, place emphasis on the common, shared interests of the mother and fetus, not on the conflicts. Unfortunately, the dominant emphasis on individual rights in our society continues to exaggerate the potential conflict between mother and fetus.

The problems in the mother-fetus relationship, then, cannot be separated from the broader social context. Drastic socioeconomic inequities and the resulting lack of adequate primary care for a large segment of the population continue to contribute to the risk for women and the fetuses they carry. Although large numbers of women lacking proper health care and education live in isolated rural areas, paradoxically, the most vulnerable women are congregated in urban areas, often within sight of the most impressive concentrations of medical technology in the world.

In addition to the macrosocial context is knowledge of the individual pregnant woman's personal experiences, without which one cannot explain her behavior. The emphasis on punishing a pregnant woman diverts attention from the root causes of the woman's often self-destructive behavior that also threatens the fetus. How many of these women were victims of sexual abuse, incest, and other attacks on their self-esteem? In the long run, a policy can succeed only by understanding why particular women act in ways dangerous to the health of their fetuses and by treating these causes.

Although I argue that no individual can escape some responsibility for their actions, the social and personal plight of an increasing number of young women makes rational choice problematic and illusive. The birth of addicted, very premature, or otherwise ill babies to these women, however, only extenuates the problem and continues the dreadful cycle into another generation. For all the stated concern of elected officials for the health of children and their right to be born with a sound mind and body, they have consistently come up short on action. Unless we are willing to expend considerable resources to overcome the problems of poverty, illiteracy, housing, and lack of access to good prenatal care and meaningful employment for women of childbearing age, the future looks bleak for many children.

THE TECHNOLOGICAL IMPERATIVE AND WOMEN

We must also realize that the issue of maternal responsibility for fetal health is itself framed by the broader social value system in the United States. Our great faith in technology and medical knowledge and overdependence on the technological fix has not only medicalized pregnancy, but created a perfect child mentality. This clearly is reflected in the courts' acceptance of medical "fact" in cases of forced Cesarians, even when this supposed fact is uncertain and probabilistic. Significantly, the public's view of responsible maternal behavior is shaped by the rapidly changing technological context, which in the last decade has shifted emphasis to fetal health.

As a result of society's reliance on medical technology, when new choices become available to women they rapidly become obligations to make the so-called right choice by accepting the socially approved alternative (Hubbard 1990, 156).

The "right to choose" means very little when women are powerless. . . . Women make their own reproductive choices, but they do not make them just as they please; they do not make them under conditions which they themselves create but under social conditions and constraints which they, as mere individuals, are powerless to change (Petchesky 1980, 685).

Furthermore, these technologies contribute to the medicalization of reproduction, which threatens the freedom and dignity of women in general. By requiring third-party involvement and dependence on medical expertise, new technologies force women to surrender control over procreation. Ruth Hubbard decries the practice of making every pregnancy a medical event and sees it as a result of the economic incentive for physicians to stimulate a new need for their services during pregnancy in light of declining birth rates and increasing interest in midwives and home birth (1985, 567). Rothman adds that the new images of the fetus resulting from prenatal technologies are making us aware of the unborn as people, "but they do so at the cost of making transparent the mother" (1986, 114). Furthermore, diagnostic technologies that pronounce judgments halfway through the pregnancy make extraordinary demands on women to separate themselves from the fetus within.

The medical status of the fetus *as distinct from the woman who is pregnant* is becoming a star criterion to judge a woman's behavior before, during, and after pregnancy. It is no longer only our sexuality or marital status which defines us as good woman-mothers; now, we must not smoke or drink or deny medical intervention when we are pregnant, or else we are not acting in the "best interests of the fetus." Meanwhile, obstetricians have authorized themselves to act against the wishes of the pregnant woman if necessary to "protect" the interests of the fetus (Spallone 1989, 40).

Some feminists rightly argue that women bear most of the risks of any reproductive research and technological application. The history of human reproduction has been, in large measure, a story of the control of women, their fertility, and their fecundity by society. This control, whether self-imposed or inflicted by others in a given society, has resulted in a significant loss of the freedom of women and their exclusion from many activities, including intellectual creativity, waged work, and training for self-support (Oakley 1984, 84). Women, it is alleged, have been held hostage to the reproductive needs of society throughout history. The new prenatal technologies in many ways reinforce this condition. As persons whose self-identity and social role have been defined historically in relation to their procreative capacities, then, women have a great deal at stake in questions of reproductive freedom (Ryan 1990, 6).

Many feminists assert that the problem is exacerbated by the fact that the majority of researchers and clinicians are male (Corea 1985). Once again, it is alleged that women are being excluded from the debate in society about human reproduction. Despite the fact that she is most affected by these technologies, she is virtually absent from the legal, scientific, and governmental bodies that design the research, development, and delivery of the technologies. For instance, there is a major difference between a woman who would be a surrogate for a friend and a corporation formed by lawyers and gynecologists "for the purpose of selling women's reproductive powers to strangers" (Arditti 1985, 580). The skepticism of feminists toward prenatal technologies certainly is warranted, although there is disagreement even among feminists as to what is the best policy to surmount the problems.

There is little doubt that the status of women is intimately related to prenatal technologies. Technology is never neutral; it both reflects and shapes social values. Because of woman's critical biological role as the bearer of children, any technology that deals with reproduction affects her social role directly. Moreover, because these technologies focus on the role of women as mothers, they could lead to diminution of other roles. Some feminists argue that too much emphasis already is placed on women as only mothers in this society. Robin Rowland insists that women must re-evaluate this social overstatement of the role of motherhood. "The catchcry 'but women want it' has been sounded over and over again by the medical profession to justify continuing medical advances in this field. Women need to reevaluate just what it is they want and question this justification for turning women into living laboratories" (1985, 39).

While prenatal diagnosis, genetic screening, gene therapy, and new knowledge of fetal development expand options and will be used by women, as argued earlier, their existence carries with it a causal logic that could label as "socially irresponsible" women who fail to make use of them under certain circumstances. As Ruth Hubbard cogently states: "The point is that once such a test is available and a woman decides not to use it, if her baby is born with a disability that could have been diagnosed, it is no longer an act of fate but has become her fault" (1985, 567). Mies adds that the emphasis on quality control means for most women a loss of confidence in their own bodies and their childbearing competence (1987, 334). She argues that the social pressure on women to produce perfect children is already enormous today.

Although the technologies that allow for the conscious design of children do not necessarily result in the denigration of the role of women or the restriction of their reproductive rights, the danger clearly exists within the context of a social value system sympathetic to that end. A full policy assessment of these technologies, therefore, requires close attention to their cumulative impact on women as well as to women's actual experience as reproductive beings (Overall 1987). This, again, requires a widened commitment of policy makers to fund extensive behavioral research on women who are parties to these reproductive applications or who are contemplating using these services.

However, those who firmly reject any notion of fetal interests and, thus, any constraint on pregnant women are in a losing battle with advances in medical technology. Social recognition of the fetus as a human form is present even in first-trimester ultrasound monitoring. Identification of the sex of the fetus and an expanding array of genetic characteristics by chorionic villus sampling as early as nine weeks gestation adds to social recognition and empathy by bestowing boyhood or girlhood on the fetus. Most dramatically, the move toward routine medical and surgical intervention in the fetus *in utero* gives the fetus some degree of patient status.

Moreover, the data presented in Chapter 2 illustrate that many actions by the pregnant woman can be devastating to the developing fetus. These data become increasingly convincing evidence of proximate cause in prenatal injury or wrongful death torts and of negligence or even abuse in criminal cases. Unless legislatures act to protect women from liability or prosecution for alleged injury to the fetus, case law with its emphasis on the facts presented by the parties to each particular case is likely to further constrain or punish high-risk actions of pregnant women. To date, legislatures have been hesitant to take such policy initiatives.

SOCIAL RESPONSIBILITY: PREVENTIVE STRATEGIES FOR FETAL HEALTH

As I have argued in detail elsewhere, society must place a much higher priority on prevention of health problems (Blank 1988). Nowhere is this strategy more essential than in the protection of fetal health. Health promotion activities, including education starting in the early grades; counseling, particularly of women in high-risk populations; and pre-emptive treatment programs are critical societal responsibilities for reducing the occurrence of ill babies. Until society makes a concerted effort to carry out these responsibilities, efforts to protect fetal health by constraining women are premature. The current low priority put on prevention in the United States has, unfortunately, focused attention on problems after they occur.

Coercive governmental action charging a woman who gives birth to a cocaine-addicted baby with a criminal offense, and the use of the tort process to recover damages from a woman for injury done to the fetus she is carrying indicate the failure of society to address the problem of high-risk behavior before the damage is done. Field is correct when she concludes that, if the real goal is not control of women but "protection of the child to be and creation of as healthy a newborn population as possible, then appropriate means are education and persuasion, free prenatal care, and good substance abuse rehabilitation programs, available free of charge to pregnant women" (1989, 125). Although this approach is more expensive in the short run and requires considerably more effort to implement than ex post facto coercive measures, in the long run it is more fair and cost effective, both monetarily and for the national psyche.

A growing realization of these facts was reflected in the reports of many panels in the late 1980s. The Institute of Medicine (1985, 1988), the Public Health Service Expert Panel on the Content of Prenatal Care (1989), and Congress's Office of Technology Assessment (1988) all called for universal access to prenatal care for pregnant women as the critical strategy to improve the health of infants. For instance, the Institute of Medicine concluded that the nation should adopt as a new social norm the principle that all pregnant women should be provided access to prenatal, labor and delivery, and postpartum services appropriate to their needs. It admits considerable resources will be required to reorganize the entire maternity care system, including removal of all personal and cultural barriers to such care; to launch a vigorous education effort in schools, media, family planning clinics, social service networks, and work places; and to research how to motivate women to seek this care.

Although it is useful to argue that women should have access to these types of care, current barriers to pregnant drug abusers seeking care are significant. In addition to the lack of programs willing to accept them (Chavkin and Kandall 1990), pregnant women often face long waiting lists and the critical attitudes of practitioners. Furthermore, because a large number of these women are uninsured, they are dependent on public health programs. Unfortunately, neither federal nor state programs guarantee the prenatal, substance abuse, and other delivery services needed to maximize the chances of a healthy baby. At the same time demand for these services is increasing, the capacity of public clinics is actually declining in light of budget cutbacks (McNulty 1988, 297).

The most comprehensive discussion of how to implement prenatal care to deal with the problems raised in this book is found in the report of the Public Health Service Expert Panel on the Content of Prenatal Care (1989). This report demonstrates that the objectives of prenatal care, instead of pitting mother against fetus, are designed to serve the interests of the woman, the fetus and infant, and the family (Table 6.1). Importantly, the panel places considerable emphasis on the need for preconception care to prepare for pregnancy, because often it is too late to ensure a healthy pregnancy after it has begun. In fact, the preconception visit "may be the single most important health care visit when viewed in the context of its effect on the pregnancy" (Public Health Service Expert Panel on the Content of Prenatal Care 1989, 26). The birth of a healthy baby, then, depends in part on the woman's general health and well-being before conception, as well as on the amount and quality of prenatal care. Health care before preg-

Table 6.1
Objectives of Prenatal Care

The objectives of prenatal care for the pregnant woman are:

*   to increase her well-being before, during, and after pregnancy
        and to improve her self-image and self-care;

*   to reduce maternal mortality and morbidity, fetal loss, and
        unnecessary pregnancy interventions;

*   to reduce the risks to her health prior to subsequent
        pregnancies and beyond childbearing years; and

*   to promote the development of parenting skills.

The objectives of prenatal care for the fetus and the infant are:

*   to increase well-being;

*   to reduce preterm birth, intrauterine growth retardation,
        congenital anomalies, and failure to thrive;

*   to promote healthy growth and development, immunization, and
        health supervision;

*   to reduce neurologic, developmental, and other morbidities;
        and

*   to reduce child abuse and neglect, injuries, preventable acute
        and chronic illness, and the need for extended hospitalization
        after birth.

The objectives of prenatal care for the family during pregnancy and
the first year of the infant's life are:

*   to promote family development, and positive parental-infant
        interaction;

*   to reduce unintended pregnancies; and

*   to identify for treatment behavior disorders leading to child
        neglect and family violence.

Sources: Jack and Culpepper (1990:1148)

nancy can ameliorate disease, improve risk status, and help prepare the woman for childbearing (Jack and Culpepper 1990, 1147).

Table 6.2 illustrates the multifaceted aspect of preconception care. In addition to providing a baseline assessment of the woman's general health, risk assessment can identify specific psychological, social, and economic factors that pose a particularly high risk. Adverse health behaviors of the kind emphasized here, plus environmental factors such as domestic violence, psychiatric illness, and stress or depression can be identified prior to pregnancy.

Table 6.2
Components of Preconception Care

Risk Assessment

Individual and social conditions (extreme obesity, advanced maternal age, special diets, education, housing, and economic status);

Adverse health behaviors (use of tobacco, alcohol, and illicit drug abuse);

Medical conditions (immune status, medications taken, genetic status, acute and chronic illnesses, prior obstetric history);

Psychological conditions (stress, anxiety, depression, personal and family readiness for pregnancy);

Environmental conditions (workplace hazards, toxic chemicals, radiation contamination); and

Barriers to family planning, prenatal care, and primary health care.

Health Promotion

Promotion of healthy behaviors (proper nutrition, avoidance of smoking, alcohol, illicit drugs, and practice of safe sex);

Counseling about the availability of social, financial, and vocational assistance programs;

Advice on family planning, pregnancy spacing, and contraception;

Counseling about the importance of early registration and compliance with prenatal care, including high-risk programs if warranted;

Information on environmental hazards;

Advice on over-the-counter medications; and

Arrangements for ongoing care.

Intervention to Reduce Risk

Treatment of medical conditions and referral to high-risk pregnancy programs;

Referral for treatment of adverse health behaviors including substance abuse counseling;

Rubella and hepatitis immunization;

Nutrition counseling, supplementation, or referral to improve adequacy of diet;

Reduction of psychosocial risks that may involve counseling or referral to home health agencies, community mental health centers, safe shelters, or assistance with housing;

Home visits to further assess and intervene in the home environment; and

Provision of family planning services.

Sources: Public Health Service (1989:27-28).

In addition to the risk assessment component, preconception care emphasizes health promotion. Promotion of healthy life-style choices, counseling about the availability of services, and education on the importance of ongoing prenatal care are critical to the success of this component. Finally, the preconception visit provides an opportunity to intervene in specific risks identified in the assessment phase. The panel correctly argues that it is "imperative that women who enter pregnancy at risk or develop medical or psychosocial risk during pregnancy receive an augmented program of care" (Public Health Service Expert Panel on the Content of Prenatal Care 1989, 91), and the report suggests what this might entail for specific risk factors such as substance abuse.

Unfortunately, however, the report does not satisfactorily answer how those very women most at risk will be recruited into preconception care. Although the case for such care is persuasive and would appear to be the strategy of choice, how likely is it that the most vulnerable women would be included, even if additional funds were made available? Evidence suggests that even when prenatal care is available, many pregnant women, particularly those at high risk, avoid it. Before preconception care can be assumed effective with adequate funding, considerable behavioral research is necessary to understand more fully how to convince these women to seek prenatal care.

Society, then, has a responsibility to ensure adequate prenatal care to all pregnant women. Even under the best of circumstances (expanded funding, universal availability, and effective outreach), however, there will be some situations where a pregnant woman will clearly disregard all attempts to minimize her high-risk behavior and refuse to comply with counseling, referral, and treatment attempts. Reported cases of women who have given birth to two or more addicted babies, despite intensive efforts to encourage responsible behavior (including placement in substance abuse programs), necessitate consideration of more coercive intervention strategies. These extreme cases, although infrequent, may warrant more severe constraints on the woman's capacity to injure additional children, including methods such as surgical implantation of long-term reversible subdermal contraceptives (Blank 1991a).

THE RIGHTS CONTEXT:
A FORMULA FOR CONFLICT

Although the primacy given individual rights in U.S. political culture has worked to protect the interests of the most vulnerable groups in the past, it creates inexorable dilemmas when strictly applied to the mother-fetus relationship. The problem is heightened by the fact that proponents both of women's rights and fetal rights often try to optimize their positions by insisting that the rights must be absolute. Often the arguments are framed in either-or terms: either the woman's right to privacy or the fetus's right to a sound mind and body. Moreover, the specter of abortion underlies any discussion of this conflict.

Figure 6.1 demonstrates how the rights of the pregnant woman and the fetus can be distributed on two continuums, each ranging from no rights to full or absolute rights. In quadrant I the woman's rights to privacy are predominant and the fetus has no claim to rights. In contrast, quadrant IV recognizes a claim to fetal rights and the legitimacy of constraining maternal behavior by limiting the scope of her rights. In quadrant II, where both the mother and fetus have full human rights, there is no problem as long as the rights are congruent. However, when conflict arises between the interests of the mother and fetus, this concept of rights does not allow for reso-

Figure 6.1
The Rights Context: Mother versus Fetus

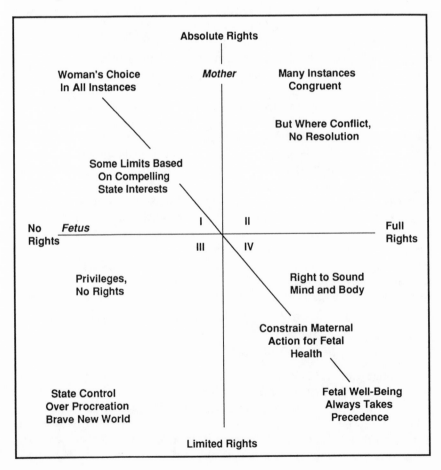

lution. Quadrant III at the extreme represents a Brave New World scenario where neither woman nor fetus has significant rights, and control of procreation is fully in the hands of the state.

Although much of the ethical debate in the literature is actually centered in quadrant II, with advocates on either side arguing for full unfettered rights, the diagonal line through quadrants I and IV largely defines the policy options feasible within this context. In the upper left area the woman's freedom to choose in all the matters discussed in this book would be unquestioned. Conversely, in the lower right extreme the fetal right to life and health would be the major criterion. Obviously, this position would negate abortions and force the woman not only to carry the fetus to term but also to ensure fetal health even at the risk of her own life. I argue here that the most feasible and fair policy options rest in the middle ranges of this diagonal.

Even this typology is flawed, however, because the term "fetal rights" is a distortion of the real issue and obscures what ought to be the primary concern—the health of the child when born. It is not the fetus that has rights; rather, it is the child once born that must be protected from avertable harm during gestation. The goal of any policies designed to make the fetal environment as safe as possible should be to maximize the birth of healthy children. The unfortunate but conscious focus on fetal rights instead of on the rights of the newborn intensifies opposition without contributing to resolution of the problem. Although the fetus may have interests to be protected that will materialize after birth, it is clear under *Roe* v. *Wade* that fetuses do not even have a right to be born.

Just as the concept of fetal rights is flawed, so is the argument for a pregnant woman's absolute right to privacy unwarranted in light of our current knowledge of fetal development. Unless we are willing to give a woman license to practice infanticide, some constraints will always be imposed. That is precisely why the Court in *Roe* tried to reach a compromise by establishing a trimester approach. The Court specifically allowed for constraints on the woman's choice to terminate the pregnancy after viability.

Although the woman's procreative rights are now well established in U.S. law, they are neither absolute vis-à-vis the fetus, nor are they unalterable. As described in this book, new technologies and medical knowledge are challenging constantly conventional notions of maternal rights and placing increasing emphasis on correlative responsibilities to the fetus. As noted earlier, the good news is that in most instances the interests of the mother and fetus are compatible. The bad news, around which this book centers, is that they are in conflict with increasing frequency. Although in most cases the woman's right to procreative freedom ought to take precedence, in some instances state intervention not only is warranted but also obligatory to protect the interests of the future child by defining the woman's choices more narrowly. The major policy problem, then, is one of deciding how and where to set these limits.

THE POLICY PROBLEM: HOW TO PROPERLY
BALANCE MATERNAL AND FETAL INTERESTS

Clearly, the issue of how to provide a fair and reasonable balance between the interests of the pregnant woman and the fetus in cases of conflict
is one of the most sensitive and volatile issues of the 1990s. In a pluralist
society there is seldom consensus on any important matter dealing with the
actions of individuals. In the matter of the maternal-fetal relationship, the
conflict between the various stakeholders is intense and not amenable to
compromise. There remains vehement disagreement over whether a fetus
ought to have status of a person, what, if any, duty a pregnant woman has
to the fetus she is carrying, and what role the state ought to play in this
highly intimate relationship?

Even if it was agreed that a pregnant woman who chooses to carry her
pregnancy to term has a moral responsibility to make reasonable efforts toward preserving fetal health, this does not necessarily translate into a legal
duty to do so. By moving from a moral duty to a legal duty, we opt to permit state intervention to force the woman to make a particular moral
choice. This may require, in some instances, the creation of a legal duty to
accept medical procedures or treatments that benefit the fetus, even when
it puts the woman at risk and requires invasion of her bodily integrity. But
why should the pregnant woman be singled out for such a duty, when
other persons are not legally required to undergo medical risk for the benefit of someone other than themselves?

Notwithstanding a hesitancy to move too readily to impose a legal duty
on a pregnant woman, as I have argued earlier, there seem to be some instances where state intervention is not only acceptable but warranted. The
problem still remains as to what specific criteria should be used to determine when and how best to constrain maternal action to protect fetal interests. Table 6.3 illustrates the difficulty of setting boundaries on maternal
responsibility. It lists many maternal actions where there is evidence of at
least some risk to the developing fetus. It certainly would be ridiculous to
develop a policy that restrains the pregnant woman's behavioral choices for
all of the items listed. To do so would make the woman a slave of the fetus.
Moreover, it would be impossible to implement and enforce and, in most
cases, would do little to protect the interests of the fetus. As noted elsewhere in this book, it is most unlikely that any mother consciously behaves
in a manner designed to cause harm to her future baby. Although she
might engage in behavior that entails a risk to the child she will bear, no rational woman purposely acts to do harm. Although education, counseling,
and other services are essential to reduce the risk, to require a woman to
comply with the complete list would be foolish and even counterproductive because it would divert attention from the few most critical factors.

It is unfortunate that, due to legislative inaction, the courts have taken

Table 6.3
Actions of Pregnant Women that Might Affect Normal Fetal Development

```
Abuse of illegal substances
Use of any alcohol
Smoking or breathing secondary smoke
Drinking coffee
Not eating balanced diet
Use of over-the-counter and prescription drugs
Working in hazardous workplace
Living in high-risk environment
Exercising too much, or too little
Travelling late in pregnancy
Not obtaining adequate prenatal care
Suffering physical harm through accident or illness
Not following medical advice to:
        -       avoid sexual intercourse
        -       stay in bed for duration of pregnancy
        -       agree to cesarean section
        -       agree   to   stay   on   life-support   system   in
                        interests of the fetus
        -       agree to surgery
Being overweight, or underweight
Not entering treatment program or counseling
Not using collaborative conception, if advised
Not using prenatal diagnosis, if warranted
Not aborting a defective fetus diagnosed by prenatal diagnosis
```

on the major policy-making role in this area. Although the courts are well suited for adjudicating on the specific acts relevant to a particular case, court precedents often have broader social implications. The legal penalties available to influence the behavior of pregnant women fall into one of several categories. During pregnancy the courts might order incarceration or detention of the woman to physically constrain her behavior out of concern for fetal health. Legal penalties after birth include various civil tort actions or criminal sanctions. All legal approaches have problems.

As discussed in Chapter 3, part of the problem now facing pregnant women in tort liability cases stems from the acceptance of prenatal injury causes of action against third parties. The rapidly expanding torts for wrongful birth, wrongful death, and prenatal injury against third parties for commissions or omissions that result in the birth of affected children have been made out of concern for the individual party to the case. However, they have produced a legal context where it seems logically inconsistent to argue that the fetus has a cause of action against a third party, but not against the pregnant woman who might be the proximate cause of the injury. By their nature, the courts find it difficult to draw lines that exclude the culpability of the mother.

Criminal sanctions (premeditated, gross negligence, or negligence) for maternal behavior also have inherent problems. Although a major argument for legal sanctions is deterrence, there is no evidence that prosecution

of pregnant drug abusers has any deterrent affect on other women. For instance, a report to the American Medical Association (1990, 14) concludes
that criminal penalties are unlikely to influence behavior because:

the use of illegal substances already incurs criminal penalties. Pregnant women who
ingest illegal substances are obviously not deterred by existing sanctions; the reasons which prompt them to ignore existing penalties might very well also prompt
disregard for any additional penalties. Also, in ordinary instances, concern for fetal
health prompts the great majority of women to refrain from potentially harmful behavior. If that concern, generally a strong impetus for avoiding certain actions, is
not sufficient to prevent harmful behavior, then it is questionable that criminal
sanctions would provide the additional motivation needed to avoid behaviors that
may cause fetal harm (1990, 14).

There is some evidence to the contrary that a major effect of such highly
publicized cases is to discourage other pregnant women from obtaining
proper prenatal care out of fear of criminal prosecution, thus potentially
exacerbating the problem. It is reasonable that pregnant substance abusers
would avoid medical treatment for fear that their physician's knowledge of
their abuse could result in a jail sentence. Moreover, imposing criminal
sanctions on pregnant women for potentially harmful behavior could encourage other women to seek abortions in order to avoid legal repercus-
sions. Finally, evidence to date demonstrates that criminal prosecution of
pregnant women has a clear bias against minority and low-income women.
Although criminal sanctions might successfully punish a few women, the
lack of deterrence and its likely inequitable application make it unattractive
as a policy for assuring the birth of healthy children.

Although judicial intervention is warranted in exceptional cases, particularly when a pregnant woman refuses to undergo, with minimal risk to herself, lifesaving treatment for the fetus she is carrying, any such attempts
should require a strict standard of review. Only with clear and convincing
evidence, and a presupposition that the pregnant woman is to be given any
benefit of doubt, should the case proceed. A close reading of the trends in
case law reviewed here demonstrates that, until now, the courts, in their
understandable desire to recognize the interests of children born with injury, have created precedents threatening to the rights of pregnant women.

Based on the evidence presented in this book, the following concluding
statements, I feel, are meaningful starting points for a vigorous national dialogue on how to frame a workable and fair policy to deal with the mother-
fetus relationship.

The well-being of specific unborn children, as well as future generations, demands
that pregnant women be educated about the potential danger of their actions to the
developing fetus.

The well-being of specific unborn children requires the widespread use of emerging technologies for prenatal diagnosis, monitoring, and therapy.

The provision of universal prenatal and preconception care for all pregnant women, along with adequate counseling and substance abuse treatment programs, is essential and would reduce drastically problems leading to unhealthy maternal behavior.

In instances where preventive approaches fail and a pregnant woman refuses to modify her behavior and thus minimize the risk of damage to her offspring, society, primarily through its courts and legislatures, has a duty to intervene to protect the interests of the defenseless fetus.

Intervention by the state in the maternal-fetal relationship should always take the least intrusive yet effective means possible. Healthy children, not punishment of the mother, should be the primary objective of any intervention.

The balance between maternal autonomy and the interests of a child to be born with a sound mind and body is delicate and elusive, but all efforts must be made to arrive at this balance by fully taking into account these intertwined sets of rights and responsibilities.

It is imperative that the debate move beyond the frequently oversimplified rhetoric common in high stakes issues of this type. This is an area where a sort of national commission is urgently needed to fully assess the problem before technological advances fully outstrip our capacity to deal with it. Although we will never eliminate all cases of avoidable prenatal injury, we must make a strong commitment to reversing the heightened rate of such cases. The search for a simple solution has proven unworkable; now the difficult task begins to frame a fair, workable, and consistent national policy to protect the interests of both mother and fetus.

Appendix: Court Cases

Abdelaziz v. *A.M.I.S.U.B. of Florida, Inc.,* 515 So.2d 269 (Fla. App. 3 Dist. 1987)

Abele v. *Markle,* 351 F. Supp. 224 (1972)

Albala v. *City of New York,* 78 A.D.2d 389, 434 N.Y.S.2d 400 (1981)

Allaire v. *St. Luke's Hospital,* 184 Ill. 359, 56 N.E. 638 (1900)

Alquijay v. *St. Luke's-Roosevelt Hospital Center,* 9 A.D.2d 704, 471 N.Y.S. 2d 1 (A.D.1 Dept. 1984).

Ard v. *Ard,* 414 So.2d 1066 (Fla. 1982)

Band v. *Livonia Associates,* 439 N.W.2d 285 (Mich. App. 1989)

Becker v. *Schwartz,* 46 N.Y.2d 895, 413 N.Y.S.2d 895, 386 N.E.2d 807 (1978)

Bennett v. *Hymers,* 101 N.H. 483, 147 A.2d 108 (1958)

Bergstresser v. *Mitchell,* 577 F.2d 22 (8th Cir. 1978)

Bonbrest v. *Kotz,* 65 F. Supp. 138 (D.D.C. 1946)

Bouvia v. *Superior Court,* 179 Cal. App. 3d 1127 (1986)

Brennecke v. *Kilpatrick,* 336 S.W.2d 68 (Mo. 1960)

Briere v. *Briere,* 107 N.H. 432, 224 A.2d 588 (1966)

Burwell v. *Eastern Air Lines, Inc.,* 633 F.2d 361 (4th Cir., 1980), cert. denied, 450 U.S. 965 (1981)

Call v. *Kezirian,* 135 Ca. A.3d 189, 185 Cal. Rptr. 103 (1982)

Canterbury v. *Spence,* 292 A.2d 404 (N.J. 1972)

Carr v. *Wittingen,* 451 N.W.2d 584 (Mich. App. 1990)

Carroll v. *Skloff,* 202 A.2d 9 (Pa. 1964)

Chamness v. *Fairtrace,* 511 N.E.2d 839 (Ill. App. 5 Dist. 1987)

Childers v. *Hoffman-LaRoche, Inc.,* 540 So.2d 102 (Fla. 1989)

Chrisafogeorgis v. *Brandenberg,* 55 Ill.2d 368, 304 N.E.2d 88 (1973)

City of Akron v. *Akron Center for Reproductive Health, Inc.,* 51 LW 4767 (1983)

Cleveland Board of Education v. *La Fleur,* 414 U.S. 632 (1974)

173

Coley v. *Commonwealth Edison Co.,* 703 F.Supp. 748 (N.D.Ill. 1989)

Commonwealth v. *Lawrence,* 536 N.E.2d 571 (Mass. 1989)

Coveleski v. *Bubnis,* 571 A.2d 433 (Pa.Super. 1990)

Curlender v. *Bio-Science Laboratories,* 165 Cal. Rptr. 477 (1980)

Danos v. *St. Pierre,* 402 So.2d 633 (La. 1981)

Denham v. *Burlington Northern Railroad Co.,* 699 F.Supp. 1253 (N.D.Ill. 1988)

DiDonato v. *Wortman,* 358 S.E.2d 489 (N.C. 1987)

Dietrich v. *Inhabitants of Northampton,* 138 Mass. 14 (1884)

DiNatale v. *Lieberman,* 409 So.2d 512 (Fla. 1982)

Doe v. *Kelly,* 106 Mich. App. 169, 307 N.W.2d 438 (1981)

Doe v. *Smith,* 108 S. Ct. 2136 (1988)

Dorlin v. *Providence Hospital,* 118 Mich. App. 831, 325 N.W.2d 600 (1982)

Douglas v. *Town of Hartford,* 542 F. Supp. 1267 (D. Conn. 1982)

Downs v. *Poulin,* 216 A.2d 29 (Me. 1966)

Dumer v. *St. Michael's Hospital,* 69 Wis.2d 766, 233 N.W.2d 372 (1975)

Duncan v. *Flynn,* 358 So.2d 178 (Fla. 1978)

Dunlap v. *Dunlap,* 84 N.H. 352 (1930)

Dunn v. *Rose Way,* 333 N.W.2d 830 (Iowa 1983)

Egbert v. *Wenzl,* 199 Neb. 573, 260 N.W.2d 480 (1977)

Eich v. *Town of Gulf Shores,* 300 So.2d 354 (Ala. 1974)

Eisbrenner v. *Stanley,* 106 M.A. 357, 308 N.W.2d 209 (1981)

Eisenstadt v. *Baird,* 405 U.S. 438 (1972)

Ellis v. *Sherman,* 515 A.2d 314 (Pa. 1986)

Evans v. *Olson,* 550 P.2d 924 (Ok. 1976)

Florida v. *Johnson,* Case No. E89-890-CFA (Seminole Cty. Cir. Ct. July 13, 1989)

Fryover v. *Forbes,* 439 N.W.2d 284 (Mich. App. 1989)

Geduldig v. *Aiello,* 417 U.S. 484 (1974)

General Electric Co. v. *Gilbert,* 429 U.S. 125 (1976)

Giardina v. *Bennett,* 545 A.2d 139 (N.J. 1988)

Gleitman v. *Cosgrove,* 49 N.J. 22, 227 A.2d 689 (1967)

Goller v. *White,* 122 N.W.2d 193 (Wis. 1963)

Graham v. *Pima Cty,* Pima Cty. Super. Ct., No. 190297 (Jan. 18, 1983)

Green v. *Smith,* 71 Ill.2d 501, 377 N.E.2d 37 (1978)

Griswold v. *Connecticut,* 381 U.S. 479 (1965)

Grodin v. *Grodin,* 102 Mich. App. 396, 301 N.W.2d 869 (1980)

Group Health Association v. *Blumenthal,* 295 Md. 104, 453 A.2d 1198 (1983)

Hall v. *Murphy,* 236 S.C. 257, 113 S.E.2d 790 (1960)

Hamby v. *McDaniel,* 559 S.W.2d 774(Tn. 1977)

Harbeson v. *Parke-Davis,* 98 Wash.2d 460, 656 P.2d 483 (1983)

Harman v. *Daniels,* 525 F. Supp. 798 (W.D. Va. 1981)

Harris v. *McRae,* 448 U.S. 197 (1980)

Harriss v. *Pan American World Airways,* 649 F.2d 690 (9th Cir. 1980)

Hastings v. *Hastings,* 33 N.J. 247, 163 A.2d 147 (1960)

Hayes v. *Shelby Memorial Hospital,* 726 F.2d 1543 (11th Cir. 1984)

Hebel v. *Hebel,* 435 P.2d 8, 14 (Alaska 1967)

Henderson v. *North,* 545 So.2d 486 (Fla. App. 1 Dist. 1989)

Hewlett v. *George,* 68 Miss. 703, 9 So. 885 (1891)

Hoffman v. *Tracy,* 406 P.2d 323 (Wash. 1965)

Hornbuckle v. *Plantation Pipe Line Co.,* 212 Ga. 504, 93 S.E.2d 727 (1956)

Hudak v. *Georgy,* 567 A.2d 1095 (Pa. Super. Ct. 1989)

Hughson v. *St. Francis Hospital of Port Jervis,* 92 A.D.2d 131, 459 N.Y.S.2d 814 (1983)

Huskey v. *Smith,* 189 Ala. 52, 265 S.2d 596 (1972)

In re A.C., 533 A.2d 611 (D.C. App. 1987), vacated and rehearing granted, 539 A.2d 203 (1988), en banc, D.C. Ct. App. (April 26, 1990), reversed

In re Baby M, 537 A.2d 1227 (N.J. 1988)

In re Baby X, 97 Mich. App. 111 (1980)

In re Farrell, 464 F.2d 772 (D.C. Cir.), cert. denied, 409 U.S. 1064 (1972)

In re Jamaica Hospital, 128 Misc.2d 1006, 491 N.Y.S.2d 898 (Super. Ct., 1985)

In re Mayden, 114 Daily Wash. L. Rptr. 2233 (D.C. Super. Ct. July 26, 1986)

In re Phillip B., 156 Cal. Rptr. 48 (1979), cert. denied 455 U.S. 949 (1980)

In re President and Directors of Georgetown College, Inc., 331 F.2d 1000 (D.C. Cir.), cert. denied 377 U.S. 978 (1964)

In re Sampson, 178 N.E.2d 918, 328 N.Y.S.2d 686 (1972)

In re Troy D., 263 Cal. Rptr. 869 (Cal. App. 4 Dist. 1989)

International Union, UAW v. *Johnson Controls, Inc.,* 680 F.Supp.309, rehearing en banc, 886 F.2d 871 (7th Cir. 1989), reversed No. 89-1215 (U.S.S. Ct., 1991)

Jacobs v. *Theimer,* 519 S.W.2d 846 (Tex. 1975)

Jacobson v. *Massachusetts,* 197 U.S. 11 (1905)

Jarvis v. *Providence Hospital,* 444 N.W. 2d 236 (Mich. App. 1989)

Jefferson v. *Griffin Spaulding County Memorial Hospital,* 274 S.E. 2d 457 (Ga. 1981)

Jehovah's Witnesses in State of Washington v. *King's County Hospital,* 278 F. Supp. 488 (W.D. Wash. 1967)

Johnson v. *Superior Court,* 123 Ca. A.3d 1002, 177 Cal. Rptr. 63 (1981)

Johnson Controls, Inc. v. *California Fair Employment and Housing Commission,* 267 Cal. Rptr. 158 (Cal. App. 4 Dist. 1990).

Jones v. *Karraker,* 109 Ill. A.3d 363, 440 N.E.2d 420 (1982), affd, 10 FLR 1043 (Ill. 1983)

Justus v. *Atchison,* 19 Cal.3d 564, 139 Cal. Rptr. 97, 565 P.2d 122 (1977)

Keeler v. *Superior Court,* 2 Cal.3d 619, 470 P.2d 617, 87 Cal. Rptr. 481 (1970)

Lacesse v. *McDonough,* 279 N.E.2d 339 (Mass. 1972)

Levin v. *Delta Air Lines, Inc.,* 730 F.2d 994 (5th Cir. 1984)

Light v. *Proctor Community Hospital,* 538 N.E.2d 828 (Ill. App. 3 Dist. 1989)

Lochner v. *New York,* 198 U.S. 45 (1905)

Logan v. *Reeves,* 209 Tenn. 631, 354 S.W.2d 789 (1962)

McBride v. *Jacobs,* 274 F.2d 595 (D.C. Cir. 1957)

McKelvey v. *McKelvey,* 111 Tenn. 388, 77 S.W. 644 (1903)

Matter of Danielle Smith, 492 N.Y.S.2d 331 (Fam. Ct. Monroe Co. 1985)

Matter of Fletcher, 533 N.Y.S.2d 241 (Fam. Ct. 1988)

Matter of Gloria C. v. *William C.,* 476 N.Y.S.2d 991 (Fam. Ct. Richmond Co. 1984)

Matter of Klein, 538 N.Y.S.2d 274 (A.D. 2 Dept. 1989)

Matter of Milland, 548 N.Y.S.2d 995 (Fam. Ct. 1989)

Matter of Steven S., 126 Cal. App. 3d 23, 178 Cal. Rptr. 525 (1981)

Miller v. *Highlands Insurance Co.,* 336 So.2d 636 (Fla. 1976)

Milton v. *Cary Medical Center,* 538 A.2d 252 (Me. 1988)

Muhlenberg Hospital v. *Patterson,* 329 A.2d 518 (N.J. Super Ct. L. Div. 1974)

Muller v. *Oregon,* 208 U.S. 412 (1908)

Nashville Gas Co. v. *Satty,* 434 U.S. 136 (1977)

Nelson v. *Krusen,* 635 S.W.2d 582 (Tex. 1982)

O'Grady v. *Brown,* 645 S.W.2d 904 (Mo. 1983)

Oil, Chemical and Atomic Workers v. *American Cyanamid Co.,* 741 F.2d 444 (D.C. Cir. 1984)

Parham v. *J.R.,* 442 U.S. 584 (1979)

Park v. *Chessin,* 60 App. Div. 2d 80, 400 N.Y.S.2d 110 (1977), modified N.Y.L.J., Dec. 29, 1978, at 1 (N.Y. Ct. App.)

Parks v. *Parks,* 390 Pa. 287, 135 A.2d 65 (1957)

Payton v. *Abbott Labs,* 512 F. Supp. 1031 (Mass. 1981)

People v. *Apodoca,* 76 Cal. App. 3d 479, 142 Cal. Rptr. 830 (1978)

People v. *Bunyard,* 756 P.2d 795 (Cal. 1988)

People v. *Greer,* 79 Ill.2d 103, 402 N.E.2d 203 (1980)

People v. *Guthrie,* 97 Mich. App. 226, 293 N.W.2d 775 (1980)

People v. *Hamilton,* 774 P.2d 730 (Cal. 1989)

People v. *Sianes,* 134 Cal. App. 355, 25 P.2d 487 (1933)

People v. *Smith,* 59 Cal. App. 3d 751, 129 Cal. Rptr. 498 (1976)

People v. *Stewart,* Civ. No. 575396 (Mun. Ct. Cal., San Diego County, 1987)

Peterson v. *Honolulu,* 262 P.2d 1007 (Ha. 1969)

Plumley v. *Klein,* 388 Minn. 1, 199 N.W.2d 169 (1972)

Prado v. *Catholic Medical Center,* 536 N.Y.S.2d 474 (A.D. 2 Dept. 1988)

Presley v. *Newport Hospital,* 365 A.2d 748 (R.I. 1976)

Prince v. *Massachusetts,* 321 U.S. 158 (1944)

Procanik v. *Cillo,* N.J. Sup. Ct. No. A-89 (1984)

Raleigh Fitkin-Paul Morgan Memorial Hospital v. *Anderson,* 201 A.2d 537 (N.J. 1964), cert. denied, 377 U.S. 985 (1964)

Raymond v. *Bartsch,* 84 A.D.2d 60, 447 N.Y.S.2d 32 (1981)

Renslow v. *Mennonite Hospital,* 67 Ill.2d 348, 367 N.E.2d 1250 (1977)

Reyes v. *Superior Court,* 75 Cal. App. 3d 214, 141 Cal. Rptr. 912 (1977)

Robinson v. *Lorillard,* 444 F.2d 791 (4th Cir.), cert. dismissed, 404 U.S. 1006 (1971)

Roe v. *Wade,* 410 U.S. 113 (1973)

Roller v. *Roller,* 37 Wash. 242 (1905)

Rosenfeld v. *Southern Pacific Co.,* 444 F.2d 1219 (9th Cir. 1971)

Salazar v. *St. Vincent Hospital,* 95 N.M. 150, 619 P.2d 826 (1980)

Schloendorff v. *Society of New York Hospitals,* 105 N.E. 92 (1914)

Schroeder v. *Ear, Nose, and Throat Associates of Lehigh Valley,* 557 A.2d 21 (Pa. Super. Ct. 1989)

Schroeder v. *Perkel,* 87 N.J. 53 (S.C.N.J. July 15, 1981)

Scott v. *Kopp,* 494 Pa. 487, 431 A.2d 959 (1981)

Secretary of Labor v. *American Cyanamid,* OSHRC No. 79-5762 (1981)

Shirley v. *Bacon*, 267 S.E.2d 809 (Ga. App. 1980)

Siemieniec v. *Lutheran General Hospital*, 512 N.E.2d 691 (Ill. 1987)

Silesky v. *Kelman*, 161 N.W.2d 631 (Minn. 1968)

Singleton v. *Ranz*, 534 So.2d 847 (Fla. App. 5 Dist. 1988)

Skinner v. *Oklahoma*, 316 U.S. 535 (1942)

Small v. *Morrison*, 185 N.C. 577, 118 S.E. 12 (1923)

Smith v. *Brennan*, 31 N.J. 353, 157 A.2d 497 (1960)

Smith v. *Newsome*, 815 F.2d 1386 (11th Cir. 1987)

Sorensen v. *Sorensen*, 339 N.E.2d 907 (Mass. 1975)

Stallman v. *Youngquist*, 504 N.E.2d 920 (Ill. App. 1 Dist. 1987), reversed 531 N.E.2d 355 (Ill. 1988)

State v. *Anderson*, 135 N.J. Super. Ct. 423, 343 A.2d 505 (Law Div. 1975)

State v. *Brown*, 378 So.2d 916 (La. 1979)

State v. *Cornelius*, 448 N.W.2d 434 (Wis. App. 1989)

State v. *Evans*, 745 S.W.2d 880 (Tenn. Cr. App. 1987)

State v. *Green*, 781 P.2d 678 (Kan. 1989)

State v. *Hammett*, 384 S.E.2d 220 (Ga. App. 1989)

State v. *Harbert*, 758 P.2d 826 (Okla. Cr. 1988)

State v. *Merrill*, 450 N.W.2d 318 (Minn. 1990)

State v. *Murphy*, 570 P.2d 1070 (1977)

State v. *Oliver*, 563 A.2d 1002 (Vt. 1989)

State v. *Perricone*, 37 N.J. 463, 181 A.2d 751 (1962)

State v. *Trudell*, 755 P.2d 511 (Kan. 1988)

Streenz v. *Streenz*, 471 P.2d 282 (Ariz. 1970)

Strohmaier v. *Associates in Obstetrics and Gynecology*, 122 Mich. App. 116, 332 N.W.2d 432 (1982)

Surrogate Parenting Associates, Inc. v. *Commonwealth ex rel Armstrong*, 704 S.W.2d 209 (Ky. 1986)

Sylvia v. *Gobeille*, 101 R.I. 76, 220 A.2d 222 (1966)

Taft v. *Taft*, 388 Mass. 331, 146 N.E.2d 395 (1983)

Teramano v. *Teramano*, 216 N.E.2d 375 (Ohio 1966)

Thornburgh v. *American College of Obstetricians and Gynecologists*, 476 U.S. 747 (1986)

Toth v. *Goree*, 65 Mich. App. 296, 237 N.W.2d 297 (1975)

Trevarton v. *Trevarton*, 151 Colo. 418, 378 P.2d 640 (1963)

Tucker v. *Tucker*, 395 P.2d 67 (Okla., 1964)

Turpin v. *Sortini*, 31 Cal. 3d 220, 643 P.2d 954, 182 Cal. Rptr. 337 (1982)

Union Pacific Railway v. *Botsford*, 141 U.S. 250 (1891)

United States v. *Spencer*, 839 F. Supp. 1341 (9th Cir. 1988)

United States v. *Vaughn*, 117 Daily Wash. L. Rep. 441 (D.C. Super. Ct. March 7, 1989)

Vaillancourt v. *Medical Center Hospital of Vermont*, 425 A.2d 92 (Vt. 1980)

Verkennes v. *Corniea*, 38 N.W.2d 838 (Minn. 1949)

Volk v. *Baldazo*, 103 Idaho 570, 651 P.2d 11 (1982)

Walker v. *Railway Co.*, 28 L.R.Ir. 69 (1891)

Wallace v. *Wallace*, 421 A.2d 134 (N.H. 1980)

Webster v. *Reproductive Health Services*, 57 U.S.L.W 5023 (1989)

Wheeler v. *Yettie Kersting Memorial Hospital,* 761 S.W.2d 785 (Tex. App. Houston 1 Dist. 1988)

Williams v. *Marion Rapid Transit, Inc.,* 87 N.E.2d 334 (Ohio 1949)

Williams v. *State,* 561 A.2d 216 (Md. 1988)

Willis v. *State,* 518 So.2d 667 (Miss. 1988)

Wilson v. *Kaiser Foundation Hospital,* 141 Ca.A.3d 891, 190 Cal. Rptr. 649 (1983)

Woods v. *Lancet,* 303 N.Y. 349, 102 N.E.2d 691 (1951)

Wright v. *Olin Corp.,* 697 F.2d 1172 (4th Cir. 1982)

Wyoming v. *Pfannenstiel,* Criminal Complaint (Albany Cty. Filed January 5, 1990)

Zepeda v. *Zepeda,* 41 Ill. App. 2d 240, 190 N.E.2d 849 (1963)

Zuniga v. *Kleberg County Hospital,* 692 F.2d 986 (5th Cir. 1982)

Bibliography

Abel, E. L., ed. 1982. *Fetal Alcohol Syndrome.* Vol. 3, *Human Studies.* Boca Raton: CRC Press.

Abraham, L. 1988. Pregnant Women Face AIDS Dilemma. *American Medical News* (July 22):3, 34.

Accurso, A. E. 1985. Title VII and Exclusionary Practices: Fertile and Pregnant Women Need Not Apply. *Rutgers Law Journal* 17 (1):95-134.

Accutane Alert: Birth Defects. 1986. *The Harvard Medical School Health Letter* 3:1.

Adams, M. M., G. P. Oakley, and J. M. Marks. 1982. Maternal Age and Births in the 1980s. *Journal of the American Medical Association* 247:493-98.

Alan Guttmacher Institute. 1981. *Teenage Pregnancy: The Problem that Hasn't Gone Away.* New York: Alan Guttmacher Institute.

American Medical Association. 1990. Legal Interventions during Pregnancy. Report of the Board of Trustees, Report 00.

Anderson, R. L., and M. S. Golbus. 1989. Social and Environmental Risks of Pregnancy. In *Fetal Diagnosis and Therapy: Science, Ethics and the Law,* edited by M. I. Evans, A. O. Dixler, J. C. Fletcher, and J. D. Schulman. Philadelphia: J. B. Lippincott.

Andrews, L. B. 1989. *Between Strangers: Surrogate Mothers, Expectant Fathers, and Brave New Babies.* New York: Harper & Row.

Annas, G. J. 1981. Righting the Wrong of "Wrongful Life." *Hastings Center Report* 11 (1):8.

―――. 1982. Forced Cesareans: The Most Unkindest Cut of All. *Hastings Center Report* 12 (3):16-17, 45.

―――. 1987. The Impact of Medical Technology on the Pregnant Woman's Right to Privacy. *American Journal of Law and Medicine* 13 (2–3):213-32.

―――. 1989. Predicting the Future of Privacy in Pregnancy: How Medical Technology Affects the Legal Rights of Pregnant Women. *Nova Law Review* 13 (2):329-54.

_____. 1990. Foreclosing the Use of Force: *A. C.* Reversed. *Hastings Center Report* 20 (4):27-29.

Annegers, J. F. et al. 1974. Do Anticonvulsants Have a Teratogenic Effect? *Neurology* 31:364-73.

Annis, L. F. 1978. *The Child before Birth.* Ithaca, N.Y.: Cornell University Press.

Antonov, A. N. 1947. "Children Born during the Siege of Leningrad in 1942." *Journal of Pediatrics* 30:250-59.

Arditti, R. 1985. Review Essay: Reducing Women to Matter. *Women's Studies International Forum* 8 (6):577-82.

Armstrong, B. G., A. D. Nolin, and A. D. McDonald. 1989. Work in Pregnancy and Birthweight for Gestational Age. *British Journal of Industrial Medicine* 46:196-99.

Ashford, N. A., and C. C. Caldart. 1983. The Control of Reproductive Hazards in the Workplace: A Prescription for Prevention. *Industrial Relations Law Journal* 5:523-63.

Atchison, C. J. 1983. *Ard* v. *Ard:* Limiting the Parent-Child Immunity Doctrine. *University of Pittsburgh Law Review* 44:977-1003.

Axelsson, G., R. Rylander, and I. Molin. 1989. Outcome of Pregnancy in Relation to Irregular and Inconvenient Work Schedules. *British Journal of Industrial Medicine* 46:393-98.

Baldwin, W. H., and V. S. Cain. 1980. The Children of Teenage Parents. *Family Planning Perspectives* 12 (January-February):34-43.

Balisy, S. S. 1987. Maternal Substance Abuse: The Need to Provide Legal Protection for the Fetus. *Southern California Law Review* 60:1209-38.

Baron, C. H. 1983. The Concept of Person in the Law. In *Defining Human Life,* edited by A. E. Doudera and M. W. Shaw. Ann Arbor: Health Administration Press.

Bayer, R. 1982. Women, Work, and Reproductive Hazards. *Hastings Center Report* 12 (5):14-19.

Bayles, M. 1976. Harm to the Unconceived. *Philosophy and Public Affairs* 5 (3):292-304.

Beal, R. 1984. "Can I Sue Mommy?" An Analysis of a Woman's Tort Liability for Prenatal Injuries to Her Child Born Alive. *San Diego Law Review* 21:325-70.

Beauchamp, T. L. 1976. On Justifications for Coercive Genetic Control. In *Biomedical Ethics and the Law,* edited by J. M. Humber and R. F. Almeder. New York: Plenum Press.

Becker, M. E. 1986. From *Muller* v. *Oregon* to Fetal Vulnerability Policies. *University of Chicago Law Review* 53:1219-73.

Benacerraf, B. R., R. Gelman, and F. D. Frigoletto. 1987. Sonographic Identification of Second-Trimester Fetuses with Down's Syndrome. *Journal of the American Medical Association* 317 (22):1371-76.

Benirschke, K. 1981. Anatomy. In *Second-Trimester Abortion: Perspectives after a Decade of Experience,* edited by G. S. Berger, W. E. Brenner, and L. G. Keith. Boston: John Wright-PSG.

Berg, K. 1979. *Genetic Damage in Man Caused by Environmental Agents.* New York: Academic Press.

Berlin, C. M., and C. B. Jacobson. 1970. Link between LSD and Birth Defects Reported. *Journal of the American Medical Association* 212:1447-48.

Biggers, J. D. 1983. Generation of the Human Life Cycle. In *Abortion and the Status of the Fetus,* edited by W. B. Bondeson et al. Dordrecht, Holland: D. Reidel.

Bingham, E. 1980. Some Scientific and Social Hazards of Identifying Reproductive Hazards in the Workplace. In *Proceedings of a Workshop on Methodology for Assessing Reproductive Hazards in the Workplace,* edited by Peter F. Infante and Marvin S. Legator. Washington, D.C.: National Institute for Occupational Safety and Health.

Blank, R. H. 1983. Torts for Wrongful Life: Individual and Eugenic Implications. *Original Paper Series* No. 1, Social Philosophy and Policy Center.

———. 1984. *Redefining Human Life: Reproductive Technologies and Social Policy.* Boulder: Westview Press.

———. 1988. *Rationing Medicine.* New York: Columbia University Press.

———. 1990. *Regulating Reproduction.* New York: Columbia University Press.

———. 1991a. *Fertility Control: New Techniques, New Policy Issues.* Westport, Conn.: Greenwood Press.

———. 1991b. The Limits of Biomedical Technology Assessment: Values, Time Frame, and Public Expectations. In *Science, Technology, and Politics: Policy Analysis in Congress,* edited by G. Bryner. Boulder: Westview Press.

Bolognese, R. 1982. Medico-Legal Aspects of a Human Life Amendment. *Pennsylvania Law Journal Reporter* 5:13.

Botkin, J. R. 1988. The Legal Concept of Wrongful Life. *Journal of the American Medical Association* 259 (10):1541-45.

Bowes, W. A., and B. Selgestad. 1981. Fetal versus Maternal Rights: Medical and Legal Perspectives. *Obstetrics and Gynecology* 58 (2):209-14.

Brandt, E. N. 1982. Testimony, Hearing before the Subcommittee on Alcohol and Drug Abuse, U.S. Senate Committee on Labor and Human Resources. Washington, D.C.: U.S. Government Printing Office.

Brent, R. L. 1980. Radiation-Induced Embryonic and Fetal Loss from Conception to Birth. In *Human Embryonic and Fetal Death,* edited by I. H. Porter and Ernest B. Hook. New York: Academic Press.

Briggs, G. G., R. K. Freeman, and S. J. Yaffe. 1986. *Drugs in Pregnancy and Lactation.* Baltimore: Williams and Wilkins.

Brophy, K. M. 1982. A Surrogate Mother Contract to Bear a Child. *Journal of Family Law* 20:263-81.

Burt, M. R. 1986. Estimating the Public Costs of Teenage Childbearing. *Family Planning Perspectives* 18 (5):221-26.

Buss, E. 1986. Getting beyond Discrimination: A Regulatory Solution to the Problem of Fetal Hazards in the Workplace. *The Yale Law Journal* 95:554-77.

Callahan, D. 1973. *The Tyranny of Survival: And Other Pathologies of Civilized Life.* New York: Macmillan.

Capron, A. M. 1979. Tort Liability in Genetic Counseling. *Columbia Law Review* 79:681.

———. 1980. The Wrong of "Wrongful Life." In *Genetics and the Law II,* edited by A. Milunsky and G. J. Annas. New York: Plenum Press.

Carroll, D. E. 1986. Parental Liability for Preconception Negligence: Do Parents Owe a Legal Duty to Their Potential Children? *California Western Law Review* 22:289-316.

A Cause of Action for "Wrongful Life": [A Suggested Analysis]. 1970. *Minnesota Law Review* 55:67-91.

Chapman, J. 1979. What Are Your Odds in the Prenatal Gamble? *Legal Aspects of Medical Practice* 31:34.

Chase, H. P. et al. 1972. Alterations in Human Brain Biochemistry Following Intrauterine Growth Retardation. *Pediatrics* 50:403.

Chasnoff, I. J. 1988. Drug Use in Pregnancy: Parameters of Risk. *Pediatric Clinics of North America* 35 (6):1403-12.

Chavkin, W., and S. R. Kandall. 1990. Between a "Rock" and a Hard Place: Perinatal Drug Abuse. *Pediatrics* 85 (2):223-25.

Chernaik, B. I. 1976. Recovery for Prenatal Injuries: The Right of a Child against Its Mother. *Suffolk University Law Review* 10:582-609.

Chernoff, G. 1980. The Fetal Alcohol Syndrome: Clinical Studies and Strategies of Prevention. In *Prevention of Mental Retardation and Other Developmental Disabilities,* edited by M. K. McCormack. New York: Marcel Dekker.

The Child's Right to "Life, Liberty, and the Pursuit of Happiness": Suits by Children against Parents for Abuse, Neglect and Abandonment. 1981. *Rutgers Law Review* 34:154-86.

Clark, B. A., J. M. Bissonnette, S. B. Olson, and R. E. Magenis. 1989. Pregnancy Loss in a Small Chorionic Villus Sampling Series. *American Journal of Obstetrics and Gynecology* 161 (2):301-02.

Clarren, S. K., and D. W. Smith. 1978. The Fetal Alcohol Syndrome. *New England Journal of Medicine* 298:1060-67.

Clement, S., L. Goldstein, L. B. Krauss et al. 1987. The Evolution of the Right to Privacy after *Roe* v. *Wade. American Journal of Law and Medicine* 13 (2–3):368-525.

Clewell, W. H. et al. 1982. A Surgical Approach to the Treatment of Fetal Hydrocephalus. *New England Journal of Medicine* 306:1320-25.

Coffey, V. P., and W. J. E. Jessop. 1959. Maternal Influenza and Congenital Deformities. *Lancet* 2:935-38.

Cohen, E. N. 1980. Waste Anesthetic Gases and Reproductive Health in Operating Room Personnel. In *Proceedings of a Workshop on Methodology for Assessing Reproductive Hazards in the Workplace,* edited by P. F. Infante and M. S. Legator. Washington, D.C.: National Institute for Occupational Safety and Health.

Cohen, M. E. 1978. *Park* v. *Chessin:* The Continuing Judicial Development of the Theory of "Wrongful Life." *American Journal of Law and Medicine* 4:217.

"Coke Baby" 1990. Actions Increasing. *American Medical News* (June 8):2.

Coleman, S. et al. 1979. Tobacco—Hazards to Health and Human Reproduction. *Population Reports* L-1:L1–L37.

Constitutional Limitations on State Intervention in Prenatal Care. 1981. *Virginia Law Review* 67:1051-67.

Corea, G. 1985. *The Hidden Malpractice: How American Medicine Mistreats Women.* 2d ed. New York: Harper & Row.

Corey, L. 1982. Dx and Rx Changes in Primary Care for Genital Herpes. *Illustrated Medicine* 1 (2):1-8.

Council on Scientific Affairs. 1982. Maternal Serum Alpha-Fetoprotein Monitoring. *Journal of the American Medical Association* 247:1478.

——. 1983. Fetal Effects of Maternal Alcohol Use. *Journal of the American Medical Association* 249:2517-21.

Cowen, M., D. Hellmann, D. Chudwin et al. 1984. Maternal Transmission of Acquired Immunodeficiency Syndrome. *Journal of Pediatrics* 73:382-86.

Curran, W. J. 1990. Court-Ordered Cesarean Sections Receive Judicial Defeat. *New England Journal of Medicine* 323 (7):489-92.

Dash, L. 1989. *When Children Want Children: The Urban Crisis of Teenage Childbearing.* New York: William Morrow and Company.

Davis, J. A. 1976. Teratogenic and Subtler Effects of Drugs in Pregnancy. In *Prevention of Handicap through Antenatal Care,* edited by A. C. Turnbull and F. P. Woodford. New York: Elsevier.

Devore, N. E., V. M. Jackson, and S. L. Piening. 1983. TORCH Infections. *American Journal of Nursing* December: 1660-65.

DHEW (Department of Health and Human Services). 1979. *Antenatal Diagnosis: Predictors of Hereditary Disease or Congenital Defects.* Washington, D.C.: U.S. Government Printing Office.

Dickens, B. M. 1983. Comparative Legal Abortion Policies and Attitudes toward Abortion. In *Defining Human Life,* edited by A. E. Doudera and M. W. Shaw. Ann Arbor: Health Administration Press.

Dillon, W. P. et al. 1982. Life Support and Maternal Brain Death during Pregnancy. *Journal of the American Medical Association* 248:1089-91.

Dinsdale, C. E. 1982. Child v. Parent: A Viable New Tort of Wrongful Life? *Arizona Law Review* 24:391-420.

Dodge, P. R., A. L. Prensky, and R. D. Feigin. 1975. *Nutrition and the Developing Nervous System.* St. Louis: C. V. Mosby Company.

Doudera, A. E. 1982. Fetal Rights? It Depends. *Trial* 18 (4):38-44.

Doudera, A. E., and M. W. Shaw, eds. 1983. *Defining Human Life.* Ann Arbor: Health Administration Press.

Duncan, A. K. 1989. Fetal Protection and the Exclusion of Women from the Toxic Workplace. *North Carolina Central Law Journal* 18:67-86.

Dworkin, G. 1972. Paternalism. *The Monist* 56 (January):64-84.

Edwards, M. G. 1990. Teenage Childbearing: Redefining the Problem for Public Policy. Paper presented at the American Political Science Association Meeting, San Francisco, September 1.

Elias, S., and G. J. Annas. 1983. Perspectives on Fetal Surgery. *American Journal of Obstetrics and Gynecology* 145 (4):807-12.

——. 1987. *Reproductive Genetics and the Law.* Chicago: Year Book Medical Publishers.

Elias, S., J. L. Simpson, L. P. Shulman et al. 1989. Transabdominal Chorionic Villus Sampling for First-Trimester Prenatal Diagnosis. *American Journal of Obstetrics and Gynecology* 160 (4):879-86.

Elkins, T. E., H. F. Andersen, M. Barclay et al. 1989. Court-Ordered Cesarean Section: An Analysis of Ethical Concerns in Compelling Cases. *American Journal of Obstetrics and Gynecology* 161 (1):150-54.

Equal Employment Opportunity Commission. 1988. Policy Guidance on Reproductive and Fetal Hazards. 193 Daily Lab. Rep. D-1.

_____. 1990. 18 Daily Lab. Rep. (BNA) D-1.

Eriksen, P. S., Gerhard Gennser, Olof Löfgren, Karin Nilsson et al. 1983. Acute Effects of Maternal Smoking on Fetal Breathing and Movement. *Obstetrics and Gynecology* 61 (3):367-72.

Etzioni, A. 1974. Social Implications of the Use or Non-Use of New Genetic and Medical Techniques. In *Protection of Human Rights in Light of Scientific and Technological Progress in Biology and Medicine.* Geneva: World Health Organization.

Evans, M. I., A. Drugan, F. C. Koppitch et al. 1989. Genetic Diagnosis in the First Trimester: the Norm for the 1990s. *American Journal of Obstetrics and Gynecology* 160 (6):1332-39.

The Evolution of the Right to Privacy after *Roe* v. *Wade.* 1987. *American Journal of Law and Medicine* 13 (2-3):365-525.

Field, M. A. 1988. *Surrogate Motherhood.* Cambridge, Mass.: Harvard University Press.

_____. 1989. Controlling the Woman to Protect the Fetus. *Law, Medicine and Health Care* 17 (2):114-29.

Finamore, E. P. 1983. *Jefferson* v. *Griffin Spaulding County Hospital Authority:* Court-Ordered Surgery to Protect the Life of an Unborn Child. *American Journal of Law and Medicine* 9 (1):83-101.

Fineberg, K. S. 1984. *Obstetrics/Gynecology and the Law.* Ann Arbor: Health Administration Press.

Fletcher, J. C. 1983. Emerging Ethical Issues in Fetal Therapy. In *Research Ethics,* edited by Kare Berg and Knut E. Tranoy. New York: Alan R. Liss.

Fletcher, J. F. 1974. *The Ethics of Genetic Control: Ending Reproductive Roulette.* Garden City, N.Y.: Doubleday.

_____. 1979. *Humanhood.* Buffalo, N.Y.: Prometheus Books.

Food and Drug Administration. 1977. Fetal Alcohol Syndrome. *FDA Drug Bulletin* 7:18.

Freeman, R. K., and S. C. Pescar. 1982. *Safe Delivery: Protecting Your Baby during High Risk Pregnancy.* New York: Facts on File.

Friedman, J. M. 1974. Legal Implications of Amniocentesis. *University of Pennsylvania Law Review* 123:150-68.

Friedman, J. M., B. B. Little, R. L. Brent et al. 1990. Potential Human Teratogenicity of Frequently Prescribed Drugs. *Obstetrics and Gynecology* 75 (4):594-99.

Fuchs, V. R., and L. Perreault. 1986. Expenditures for Reproduction-Related Health Care. *Journal of the American Medical Association* 255:76–81.

Furnish, H. A. 1980. Prenatal Exposure to Fetally Toxic Work Environments: The Dilemma of the 1978 Pregnancy Amendment to Title VII of the Civil Rights Act of 1964. *Iowa Law Review* 66:63-129.

Furstenberg, F. F., J. Brooks-Gunn, and S. P. Morgan. 1987. *Adolescent Mothers in Later Life.* New York: Cambridge University Press.

Gallagher, J. 1987. Prenatal Invasions and Interventions: What's Wrong with Fetal Rights? *Harvard Women's Law Journal* 10:9-58.

Geronimus, A. 1987. On Teenage Childbearing and Neonatal Mortality in the United States. *Population and Development Review* 13 (2):245-79.

Glass, B. 1975. Ethical Problems Raised by Genetics. In *Genetics and the Quality of Life,* edited by C. Birch and P. Albrecht. Australia: Pergamon Press.

———. 1983. Concluding Reflections. In *Defining Human Life,* edited by A. Edward Doudera and Margery W. Shaw. Ann Arbor: Health Administration Press.

Glass, R. H., and R. J. Ericsson. 1982. *Getting Pregnant in the 1980s.* Berkeley: University of California Press.

Golbus, M. S., W. D. Loughman, C. J. Epstein et al. 1979. Prenatal Genetic Diagnosis in 3000 Amniocenteses. *New England Journal of Medicine* 300:157-63.

Golbus, M. S., M. Harrison, R. A. Filly et al. 1982. In Utero Treatment of Urinary Tract Obstruction. *American Journal of Obstetrics and Gynecology* 142:383-86.

Goldberg, S. 1989. Medical Choices during Pregnancy: Whose Decision is it Anyway? *Rutgers Law Review* 41:591-623.

Grobstein, C. 1981. *From Chance to Purpose: An Appraisal of External Human Fertilization.* Reading, Mass.: Addison-Wesley.

———. 1988. *Science and the Unborn: Choosing Human Features.* New York: Basic Books.

Gustaitis, R., E. Gustaitis, and W. D. Young. 1986. *A Time To Be Born. A Time To Die.* Reading, Mass.: Addison-Wesley.

Hackett, K. 1987. The Fragil X Omen: Scientific Advances Compel a Legislative Treatment of Wrongful Life and Wrongful Birth. *The Journal of Law and Technology* 2:249-72.

Hanson, J. W. 1980. Reproductive Wastage and Prenatal Ethanol Exposure: Human and Animal Studies. In *Human Embryonic and Fetal Death,* edited by I. H. Porter and Ernest B. Hook. New York: Academic Press.

———. 1981. Counseling for Fetal Alcohol Syndrome. In *Genetic Screening and Counseling: A Multidisciplinary Perspective,* edited by S. R. Applewhite et al. Springfield, Ill.: Charles C. Thomas.

Hanson, J. W. et al. 1978. The Effects of Moderate Alcohol Consumption during Pregnancy on Fetal Growth and Morphogensis. *Journal of Pediatrics* 92:457-60.

Harrigan, J. 1980. Prenatal and Obstetrical Factors in Mental Retardation. In *Prevention of Mental Retardation and Other Developmental Disabilities,* edited by M. K. McCormack. New York: Marcel Dekker.

Harrison, M. R. 1982. Unborn: Historical Perspective of the Fetus as a Patient. *Pharos* 45:19-24.

Harrison, M. R., M. S. Golbus, and R. A. Filly. 1981. Management of the Fetus with a Correctable Congenital Defect. *Journal of the American Medical Association* 146 (7):774-77.

Harrison, M. R., M. S. Golbus, R. A. Filly et al. 1982. Fetal Surgery for Congenital Hydronephrosis. *New England Journal of Medicine* 306 (10):591-93.

Harrison, M. R., N. S. Adzick, M. Longaker et al. 1990. Successful Repair in Utero of a Fetal Diaphragmatic Hernia after Removal of Herniated Viscera from the Left Thorax. *New England Journal of Medicine* 322 (22): 1582-84.

Hastings Center Report. 1983. Case: AID and the Single Welfare Mother. *Hastings Center Report* 13 (1):22-23.

Hauth, J. C., J. Hauth, R. B. Drawbaugh et al. 1984. Passive Smoking and Thiocyanate Concentrations in Pregnant Women and Newborns. *Obstetrics and Gynecology* 63 (4):519-22.

Heinonen, O. P. et al. 1977. *Birth Defects and Drugs in Pregnancy.* Littleton, Mass.: Publishing Sciences Group.

Henshaw, S. K., and J. Van Vort. 1989. Teenage Abortion, Birth, and Pregnancy Statistics: An Update. *Family Planning Perspectives* 21 (2):85-88.

Hodgson, J. E., ed. 1981. *Abortion and Sterilization: Medical and Social Aspects.* New York: Academic Press.

Hoff, R., V. P. Beradi, B. J. Weiblen et al. 1989. Seroprevalence of Human Immunodeficiency Virus among Childbearing Women: Estimation by Testing Samples of Blood from Newborns. *New England Journal of Medicine* 318:525–30.

Hofferth, S. L. 1987. Social and Economic Consequences of Teenage Childbearing. In *Risking the Future,* Vol. 2, edited by Sandra L. Hofferth and Cheryl D. Hayes. Washington, D.C.: National Academy Press.

Hook, E. B., and I. H. Porter. 1980. Terminological Conventions, Methodological Considerations, Temporal Trends, Specific Genes, Environmental Hazards, & Some Other Factors Pertaining to Embryonic and Fetal Deaths. In *Human Embryonic and Fetal Death,* edited by I. H. Porter and E. B. Hook. New York: Academic Press.

Howard, L. G. 1981. Hazardous Substances in the Workplace: Rights of Women. *University of Pennsylvania Law Review* 129:798-845.

Hoyme, H. E., K. Lyon Jones, S. D. Dixon et al. 1990. Prenatal Cocaine Exposure and Fetal Vascular Disruption. *Pediatrics* 85 (5):743–47.

Hubbard, R. 1985. Prenatal Diagnosis and Eugenic Ideology. *Women's Studies International Forum* 8 (6):567-76.

———. 1990. *The Politics of Women's Biology.* New Brunswick, N.J.: Rutger's University Press.

Huckle, P. 1982. The Womb Factor: Pregnancy Policies and Employment of Women. In *Women, Power and Policy,* edited by Ellen Boneparth. New York: Pergamon Press.

Hume, R. F., K. J. O'Donnell, C. L. Stanger, A. P. Killam, and J. L. Gingras. 1989. In Utero Cocaine Exposure: Observations of Fetal Behavioral State May Predict Neonatal Outcome. *American Journal of Obstetrics and Gynecology* 161 (3):685-90.

Hunt, V. R. 1975. *Occupational Health Problems of Pregnant Women.* Report to DHEW, Office of the Secretary.

———. 1978. Occupational Radiation Exposure of Women Workers, *Preventive Medicine* 7:294-99.

Infante, P. F. et al. 1976. Genetic Risks of Vinyl Chloride. *Lancet* 1:734-35.

———. 1980. Chloroprene: Adverse Effects on Reproduction. In *Proceedings of a Workshop on Methodology for Assessing Reproductive Hazards in the Workplace,* edited by Peter F. Infante and Marvin S. Legator. Washington, D.C.: National Institute for Occupational Safety and Health.

Institute of Medicine. 1985. *Preventing Low Birthweight.* Washington, D.C.: National Academy Press.

———. 1988. *Prenatal Care.* Washington, D.C.: National Academy Press.

Isaacs, S. L., and R. J. Holt. 1987. Redefining Procreation: Facing the Issues. *Population Bulletin* 42 (3):1-37.

Isenberg, S. J., A. Spierer, and S. H. Inkelis. 1987. Ocular Signs of Cocaine Intoxication in Neonates. *American Journal of Ophtamology* 103:211-14.

Jack, B. W., and L. Culpepper. 1990. "Preconception Care: Risk Reduction and Health Promotion in Preparation for Pregnancy." *Journal of the American Medical Association* 264 (9):1147-49.

Jacob, A. J., J. Epstein, D. L. Madden, and J. L. Sever. 1984. Genital Herpes Infection in Pregnant Women Near Term. *Obstetrics and Gynecology* 63 (4): 480-84.

Janerik, D. T. et al. 1974. Oral Contraceptives and Congenital Limb Reduction Defects. *New England Journal of Medicine* 291:697-700.

Johnsen, D. 1986. The Creation of Fetal Rights: Conflicts with Women's Constitutional Rights to Liberty, Privacy, and Equal Protection. *Yale Law Journal* 95:599-625.

———. 1989. From Driving to Drugs: Governmental Regulation of Pregnant Women's Lives after *Webster. University of Pennsylvania Law Review* 138: 179-215.

Johnson, A. M., G. E. Palomaki, and J. E. Haddow. 1990. Maternal Serum-α-Fetoprotein Levels in Pregnancies among Black and White Women with Fetal Open Spina Bifida: A United States Collaborative Study. *American Journal of Obstetrics and Gynecology* 162 (3):328-31.

Kadar, D. 1980. The Law of Tortuous Prenatal Death since *Roe* v. *Wade. Missouri Law Review* 45:639-66.

Kashi, J. S. 1977. The Case of the Unwanted Blessing: Wrongful Life. *University of Miami Law Review* 31:1432.

Kass, L. R. 1975. Determining Death and Viability in Fetuses and Abortuses. In *Research on the Fetus,* edited by the National Commission for the Protection of Human Subjects. Washington, D.C.: U.S. Government Printing Office.

———. 1976. Implications of Prenatal Diagnosis for the Human Right to Life. In *Biomedical Ethics and the Law,* edited by J. M. Humber and R. F. Almeder. New York: Plenum Press.

Katz, J. F. 1989. Hazardous Working Conditions and Fetal Protection Policies: Women Are Going Back to the Future. *Environmental Affairs* 17:201-30.

Kaufman, F. 1990. The Fetus's Mother. *Hastings Center Report* 20 (3):3-4.

Keane, N. P. 1980. Legal Problems of Surrogate Motherhood. *Southern Illinois University Law Journal* 1980:147.

Keane, N. P., and D. L. Breo. 1981. *The Surrogate Mother.* New York: Everest House.

Keith, L. G., S. MacGregor, S. Friedell, M. Rosner, I. J. Chasnoff, and J. J. Sciarra. 1989. Substance Abuse in Pregnant Women. *Obstetrics and Gynecology* 73 (5):715-19.

Kerenyi, T. D., and U. Chitkara. 1981. Selective Birth in Twin Pregnancy with Discordancy for Down's Syndrome. *New England Journal of Medicine* 304:1525.

King, P. A. 1980. The Juridical Status of the Fetus: A Proposal for the Protection of the Unborn. In *The Law and Politics of Abortion,* edited by C. E. Schneider and M. A. Vinovskis. Lexington, Mass.: Lexington Books.

_____. 1989. Should Mom Be Constrained in the Best Interests of the Fetus? *Nova Law Review* 13 (2):393-404.

Kline, J. et al. 1977. Smoking: A Risk Factor for Spontaneous Abortion. *New England Journal of Medicine* 297 (15):793-96.

Kolder, V. E. B., J. Gallagher, and M. T. Parsons. 1987. Court-Ordered Obstetrical Interventions. *New England Journal of Medicine* 316 (19):1192-96.

Lagrew, D. C., T. G. Furlow, W. D. Hager, and R. L. Yarrish. 1984. Disseminated Herpes Simplex Virus Infection in Pregnancy: Successful Treatment with Acyclovir. *Journal of the American Medical Association* 252:2058-59.

Lambert, T. F. 1983. Law in the Future: Tort Law 2003. *Trial* 19 (7):65-70.

Lantos, J. D., S. H. Miles, M. D. Silverstein, and C. B. Stocking. 1989. Survival after Cardiopulmonary Resuscitation in Babies of Very Low Birth Weight: Is CPR Futile Therapy? *New England Journal of Medicine* 318 (2):91-95.

Lappé, M. 1972. Moral Obligations and the Fallacies of "Genetic Control." *Theological Studies* 33 (September): 411-27.

_____. 1973. Human Genetics. *Annals of the New York Academy of Sciences* 216 (May):152-59.

Layde, P.M. et al. 1979. Maternal Serum Alpha-Fetoprotein Screening: A Cost-Benefit Analysis. *American Journal of Public Health* 69 (6):566-72.

Ledbetter, D. H., A. O. Martin, Y. Verlinsky et al. 1990. Cytogenetic Results of Chorionic Villus Sampling: High Success Rate and Diagnostic Accuracy in the United States Collaborative Study. *American Journal of Obstetrics and Gynecology* 162 (3):495-501.

Lenow, J. L. 1983. The Fetus as a Patient: Emerging Rights as a Person? *American Journal of Law and Medicine* 9 (1):1-29.

Life with Mother: The Fourth Circuit Reconciles Title VII and Fetal Vulnerability in *Wright* v. *Olin Corp.* 1983. *Alabama Law Review* 34 (2):327-38.

Lipsett, M. B., and J. C. Fletcher. 1983. Do Vitamins Prevent Neural Tube Defects (and Can We Find Out Ethically)? *Hastings Center Report* 13 (4):5-8.

Little, B. B., L. M. Snell, L. C. Gilstrap, N. F. Gant, and C. R. Rosenfeld. 1989. Alcohol Abuse during Pregnancy: Changes in Frequency in Large Urban Hospital *Obstetrics and Gynecology* 74 (4):547-51.

Little, B. B., L. M. Snell, V. R. Klein, and L. C. Gilstrap. 1989. Cocaine Abuse during Pregnancy: Maternal and Fetal Implications. *Obstetrics and Gynecology* 73 (2):157-60.

Locke, N. J. 1987. Mother v. Her Unborn Child: Where Should Texas Draw the Line? *Houston Law Review* 24:549-76.

Logli, P. A. 1990. Drugs in the Womb: the Newest Battlefield in the War on Drugs. *Criminal Justice Ethics* 9 (1):23-29.

Longo, L. M. 1982. Health Consequences of Maternal Smoking. In *Alternative Di-*

etary Practices and Nutritional Abuses in Pregnancy, edited by the National Research Council. Washington, D.C.: National Academy Press.

Losco, J. 1989. Fetal Abuse: An Exploration of Emerging Philosophic, Legal, and Policy Issues. *Western Political Quarterly* 42 (2):265-86.

Lubs, H. A., and F. H. Ruddle. 1970. Chromosomal Abnormalities in the Human Population. *Science* 169:495-98.

MacGregor, S. N., L. G. Keith, J. A. Bachicha, and I. J. Chasnoff. 1989. Cocaine Abuse during Pregnancy: Correlation between Prenatal Care and Perinatal Outcome. *Obstetrics and Gynecology* 74 (6):882-85.

Macklin, R. 1983. When Human Rights Conflict: Two Persons, One Body. In *Defining Human Life: Medical, Legal and Ethical Implications,* edited by A. E. Doudera and M. W. Shaw. Ann Arbor: Health Administration Press.

McNulty, M. 1988. Pregnancy Police: The Health Policy and Legal Implications of Punishing Pregnant Women for Harm to their Fetuses. *Review of Law and Social Change* 16:277-319.

Macri, J. N., and R. R. Weiss. 1982. Prenatal Serum Alpha-Fetoprotein Screening for Neural Tube Defects. *Obstetrics and Gynecology* 59 (5):633.

Mady, T. M. 1981. Surrogate Mothers: The Legal Issues. *American Journal of Law and Medicine* 7 (3):323-52.

Mahowald, M. B. 1990. Symbols and Rights (letter). *Hastings Center Report* 20 (3):43-44.

Main, D. M., and M. T. Mennuti. 1986. Neural Tube Defects: Issues in Prenatal Diagnosis and Counselling. *Obstetrics and Gynecology* 67 (1):1-16.

Makinson, C. 1985. The Health Consequences of Teenage Pregnancy. *Family Planning Perspectives* 17 (3):132-39.

Manson, R., and J. Marolt. 1988. A New Crime, Fetal Neglect: State Intervention to Protect the Unborn—Protection at What Cost? *California Western Law Review* 24:161-82.

Mascola, L., R. Pelosi, J. H. Blount et al. 1984. Congenital Syphilis: Why Is It Still Occurring? *Journal of the American Medical Association* 252:1719-22.

Mathieu, D. 1985. Respecting Liberty and Preventing Harm: Limits of State Intervention in Prenatal Choice. *Harvard Journal of Law and Policy* 8 (1):19-55.

Mattson, L. P. 1981. The Pregnancy Amendment: Fetal Rights and the Workplace. *Case and Comment* (November-December):33-41.

Meade, T. W. 1976. Effects of Smoking in Pregnancy. In *Prevention of Handicap through Antenatal Care,* edited by A. C. Turnbull and F. P. Woodford. New York: Elsevier.

Melnick, M. 1980. Drugs as Etiological Agents in Mental Retardation and Other Developmental Anomalies of the Central Nervous System. In *Prevention of Mental Retardation and Other Developmental Disabilities,* edited by M. K. McCormick. New York: Marcel Dekker.

Mercado, A., G. Johnson, Jr., D. Calver, and R. J. Sokol. 1989. Cocaine, Pregnancy, and Postpartum Intracerebral Hemorrhage. *Obstetrics and Gynecology* 73 (2):467-68.

Merrick, J. C. 1990. Maternal-Fetal Conflict: Adversaries or Allies? Paper presented at the American Political Science Association Annual Meeting, San Francisco, September 2.

Meyer, M. B. et al. 1976. Perinatal Events Associated with Maternal Smoking during Pregnancy. *American Journal of Epidemiology* 103 (5):464-76.

Meyer, M. B., and J. A. Tonascia. 1977. Maternal Smoking, Pregnancy Complications, and Perinatal Mortality. *American Journal of Obstetrics and Gynecology*
128 (5): 494-502.

Mies, M. 1987. Sexist and Racist Implications of New Reproductive Technologies.
Alternatives 12:323-42.

Miller, R. 1983. Surrogate Parenting: An Infant Industry Presents Society with
Legal, Ethical Questions. *Obstetric and Gynecological News* 3:15-19.

Mills, J. L., B. Graubard, E. E. Harley et al. 1984. Maternal Alcohol Consumption
and Birth Weight: How Much Drinking during Pregnancy is Safe? *Journal of
the American Medical Association* 252:1875-79.

Milunsky, A. 1977. *Know Your Genes.* Boston: Houghton-Mifflin.

Moelis, L. S. 1985. Fetal Protection and Potential Liability: Judicial Application of
the Pregnancy Discrimination Act and the Disparate Impact Theory. *American Journal of Law and Medicine* 11 (3):369-90.

Montagu, M. F. A. 1962. *Prenatal Influences.* Springfield, Ill.: Charles C. Thomas.

Muller, H. J. 1959. The Guidance of Human Evolution. *Perspectives in Biology and
Medicine* 3 (1):1-43.

Murphy, E. A., G. Chase, and A. Rodriguez. 1978. Genetic Intervention: Some So-
cial, Psychological, and Philosophical Aspects. In *Genetic Issues in Public
Health and Medicine,* edited by B. H. Cohen et al. Springfield, Ill.: Charles
C. Thomas.

Murphy, J. P. 1982. The Evolution of the Prenatal Duty Rule: Analysis by Inherent
Determinants. *University of Dayton Law Review* 7 (2):351-86.

Naeye, R. L. 1980. Effects of Maternal Nutrition on the Outcome of Pregnancy. In
Human Embryonic and Fetal Death, edited by I. H. Porter and Ernest B.
Hook. New York: Academic Press.

————. 1981. Common Environmental Influences on The Fetus. In *Perinatal Diseases,* edited by R. L. Naeye, J. M. Kissane, and N. Kaufman. Baltimore:
Williams and Wilkins.

National Academy of Sciences, Food and Nutrition Board. 1970. *Maternal Nutrition and the Course of Pregnancy.* Washington, D.C.: U.S. Government Printing Office.

National Commission for the Protection of Human Subjects. 1975. *Research on the
Fetus.* Washington, D.C.: U.S. Government Printing Office.

National Library of Medicine. 1990. Cocaine, Pregnancy and the Newborn. Washington, D.C.: U.S. Government Printing Office.

National Research Council. 1982. *Alternative Dietary Practices and Nutritional
Abuses in Pregnancy.* Washington, D.C: National Academy Press.

NICHD National Registry for Amniocentesis Study Group. 1976. Midtrimester
Amniocentesis for Prenatal Diagnosis: Safety and Accuracy. *Journal of the
American Medical Association* 236:1471-76.

Neerhof, M. G., S. N. MacGregor, S. S. Retzky, and T. P. Sullivan. 1989. Cocaine
Abuse during Pregnancy: Peripartum Prevalence and Perinatal Outcome.
American Journal of Obstetrics and Gynecology 161 (3):633-38.

Nelson, L. J., and N. Milliken. 1988. Compelled Medical Treatment of Pregnant

Women: Life, Liberty, and Law in Conflict. *Journal of the American Medical Association* 259 (7):1060-66.

New York State Task Force on Life and the Law. 1988. *Surrogate Parenting: Analysis and Recommendations for Public Policy.* Albany: New York State Task Force.

Niebyl, J. R., ed. 1982. *Drug Use in Pregnancy.* Philadelphia: Lea and Febiger.

NIOSH (National Institute for Occupational Safety and Health). 1988. *Proposed National Strategies for the Prevention of Leading Work-Related Diseases and Injuries, Part 2.* Washington, D.C.: Association of Schools of Public Health.

Nishimura, H., and T. Tanimura. 1976. *Clinical Aspects of the Teratogenicity of Drugs.* Amsterdam: Excerpta Medica.

Note. 1988. "Maternal Rights and Fetal Wrongs: The Case Against Criminalization of 'Fetal Abuse.'" *Harvard Law Review* 101:994-1012.

Nothstein, G. Z., and J. P. Ayres. 1981. Sex-Based Considerations of Differentiation in the Workplace: Exploring the Biomedical Interface between OSHA and Title VII. *Villanova Law Review* 26 (2):239-61.

Nurses' Drug Alert. 1982. *American Journal of Nursing* 6 (6):977-82.

Oakley, A. 1984. *The Captured Womb: A History of the Medical Care of Pregnant Women.* Oxford: Oxford University Press.

Office of Medical Applications of Research, National Institutes of Health. 1984. The Use of Diagnostic Ultrasound Imaging during Pregnancy. *Journal of the American Medical Association* 252 (5):669-72.

Office of Technology Assessment. 1988. *Healthy Children.* Washington, D.C.: U.S. Government Printing Office.

———. 1990. *Neurotoxicity: Identifying and Controlling Poisons of the Nervous System.* Washington, D.C.: U.S. Government Printing Office.

O'Neill, O. 1979. Begetting, Bearing and Rearing. In *Having Children: Philosophical and Legal Reflections on Parenthood,* edited by O. O'Neill and W. Ruddick. New York: Oxford University Press.

Overall, C. 1987. *Ethics and Human Reproduction: A Feminist Analysis.* Boston: Allen and Unwin.

Parker, P. 1983. Motivation of Surrogate Mothers: Initial Findings. *American Journal of Psychiatry* 140 (1):115-18.

Parness, J. A. 1983. The Duty to Prevent Handicaps: Laws Promoting the Prevention of Handicaps to Newborns. *Western New England Law Review* 5 (3):431-64.

———. 1986. The Abuse and Neglect of the Human Unborn: Protecting Potential Life. *Family Law Quarterly* 20 (2):197-212.

Parness, J. A., and S. K. Pritchard. 1982. To Be or Not To Be: Protecting the Unborn's Potentiality of Life. *University of Cincinnati Law Review* 51 (2):257-98.

Peacock, J. E., and F. A. Sarubbi. 1983. Disseminated Herpes Simplex Virus Infection during Pregnancy. *Obstetrics and Gynecology* 61 (3):13S-18S.

Perdue, J. M. 1981. An Analysis of the Physician's Professional Liability for Radiation of the Fetus. *Houston Law Review* 18:801-18.

Perkoff, R. 1970. Renal Diseases. *Genetic Disorders of Man* 1: 443.

Perry, T. B. 1985. Fetoscopy. *Progress in Clinical and Biological Research* 163B: 207-12.

Petchesky, R. P. 1980. Reproductive Freedom: Beyond a Woman's Right to Choose. *Signs: Journal of Women in Culture and Society* 5:661-85.

————. 1981. Anti-abortion, Anti-feminism, and the Rise of the New Right. *FS: Feminist Studies* 7 (2):206-47.

Phelan, M. C. et al. 1982. Discordant Expression of Fetal Hydantoin Syndrome in Heteropaternal Dizygotic Twins. *New England Journal of Medicine* 307: 99-101.

Philip, J., and J. Bang. 1985. Prenatal Diagnosis in Multiple Gestations. In *Human Prenatal Diagnosis,* edited by Karen Filkins and Joseph F. Russo. New York: Marcel Dekker.

Phillips, J. W. 1983. Employment Discrimination—Fetal Vulnerability and the 1978 Pregnancy Amendments—*Wright* v. *Olin Corp. Wake Forest Law Review* 19:905-29.

Pilpel, H. F. 1983. Personhood, Abortion and the Right to Privacy. In *Defining Human Life,* edited by A. Edward Doudera and Margery W. Shaw. Ann Arbor: Health Administration Press.

Pinkney, D. S. 1990. Education Urged in War on Maternal Drug Abuse. *American Medical News* (July 6–13):8.

Poe, M. 1981. Health Law: Preservation of Life—A Right To Be Born. *American Journal of Trial Advocacy* 5 (Fall):383-88.

Prager, K. et al. 1983. Maternal Smoking and Drinking Behavior before and during Pregnancy. In *Health and Prevention Profile, United States, 1983.* Washington, D.C.: National Center for Health Statistics.

President's Commission for Study of Ethical Problems in Medicine and Biomedical and Behavioral Research. 1982. *Splicing Life: The Social and Ethical Issues of Genetic Engineering with Human Beings.* Washington, D.C.: U.S. Government Printing Office.

Prosser, W. L. 1971. *Handbook of the Law of Torts,* 4th ed. St. Paul, MN: West Publishing Co.

Public Health Service Expert Health Panel on the Content of Prenatal Care. 1989. *Caring for Our Future: The Content of Prenatal Care.* Washington, D.C.: Department of Health and Human Services.

Ramsey, P. 1975. *The Ethics of Fetal Research.* New Haven: Yale University Press.

Rauscher, K. 1987. Fetal Surgery: A Developing Legal Dilemma. *Saint Louis University Law Journal* 31:775-95.

Rawls, J. 1971. *A Theory of Justice.* Cambridge, Mass.: Harvard University Press.

Rawls, R. L. 1980. Reproductive Hazards in the Workplace. *Chemical and Engineering News* (February):28-30.

Reilly, P. 1977. *Genetics, Law and Social Policy.* Cambridge, Mass.: Harvard University Press.

————. 1978. Government Support of Genetic Services. *Social Biology* 25 (1): 23-32.

Ricci, J. M., R. M. Fojaco, and M. O'Sullivan. 1989. Congenital Syphilis: The University of Miami/Jackson Memorial Medical Center Experience, 1986-1988. *Obstetrics and Gynecology* 74 (5):687-91.

Rice, J. E. 1983. Fetal Rights: Defining "Person" under 42 U.S.C. 1983. *University of Illinois Law Review* 1:347-66.

Risemberg, H. M. 1989. Fetal Neglect and Abuse. *New York State Journal of Medicine* (March):148-51.

Robertson, J. A. 1982. The Right to Procreate and In Utero Therapy. *The Journal of Legal Medicine* 3 (3):333-66.

_____. 1983a. Procreative Liberty and the Control of Conception, Pregnancy, and Childbirth. *Virginia Law Review* 69 (3):405-64.

_____. 1983b. Medicolegal Implications of a Human Life Amendment. In *Defining Human Life,* edited by A. Edward Doudera and Margery W. Shaw. Ann Arbor: Health Administration Press.

_____. 1987. Gestational Burdens and Fetal Status: Justifying *Roe* v. *Wade. American Journal of Law and Medicine* 13 (213):189-212.

Roe, D. A. 1982. Adverse Effects of Over-the-Counter Drugs in Pregnancy. In *Alternative Dietary Practices and Nutritional Abuses in Pregnancy,* edited by National Research Council. Washington D.C.: National Academy Press.

Rogers, T. D. 1982. Wrongful Life and Wrongful Birth: Medical Malpractice in Genetic Counseling and Prenatal Testing. *South Carolina Law Review* 33:713-57.

Rom, W. N. 1980. Effects of Lead on Reproduction. In *Proceedings of a Workshop on Methodology for Assessing Reproductive Hazards on the Workplace,* edited by Peter F. Infante and Marvin S. Legator. Washington, D.C.: National Institute for Occupational Safety and Health.

Rosendahl, H., and S. Kivinen. 1989. Antenatal Detection of Congenital Malformations by Routine Ultrasonography. *Obstetrics and Gynecology* 73 (6): 947-51.

Rosenfeld A. 1982. The Patient in the Womb. *Science* 82:18-23.

Rosett, H. L., L. Weiner, A. Lee et al. 1983. Patterns of Alcohol Consumption and Fetal Development. *Obstetrics and Gynecology* 61 (5):539-46.

Rothman, B. K. 1986. *The Tentative Pregnancy: Prenatal Diagnosis and the Future of Motherhood.* New York: Viking Press.

_____. 1987. Surrogacy: A Question of Values. *Conscience* 8 (3):1-15.

_____. 1989. *Recreating Motherhood: Ideology and Technology in a Patriarchal Society.* New York: W. W. Norton.

Rowland, R. 1985. Quoted in *New Birth Techologies.* Wellington, New Zealand: Department of Justice, Law-Reform Commission.

Rubin, E. R. 1982. *Abortion, Politics, and the Courts: Roe* v. *Wade and Its Aftermath.* Westport, Conn.: Greenwood Press.

Rubin, S. P. 1980. *It's Not Too Late for a Baby: For Women and Men Over 35.* Englewood Cliffs, N.J.: Prentice-Hall.

Ruddick, W., and W. Wilcox. 1982. Operating on the Fetus. *Hastings Center Report* 12 (5):10-14.

Rush, D. 1980. Cigarette Smoking, Nutrition, Social Status, and Perinatal Loss: A Look at Their Interactive Relationships. In *Human Embryonic and Fetal Death,* edited by I. H. Porter and Ernest B. Hook. New York: Academic Press.

Rush, S. E. 1987. Prenatal Caretaking: Limits of State Intervention with and without *Roe. University of Florida Law Review* 39:55-109.

Ryan, M. A. 1990. The Argument for Unlimited Procreative Liberty: A Feminist Critique. *Hastings Center Report* 20 (4):6-12.

Sales, B. D., D. M. Powell, and R. Van Duizend. 1982. *Disabled Persons and the Law.* New York: Plenum Press.

Scofield, T. J. 1982. Recovery for Tortuous Death of the Unborn. *South Carolina Law Review* 33:797-817.

Scott, G. G. et al. 1985. Mothers of Infants with the Acquired Immunodeficiency Syndrome: Evidence for Both Symptomatic and Asymptomatic Carriers. *Journal of the American Medical Association* 253 (3):363-66.

Scriver, C. R. 1985. Population Screening: Report of a Workshop. *Progress in Clinical and Biological Research* 163B:89-152.

Seksay, E. H. 1983. Tort Law—Begetting a Cause of Action for Those Injured by a Drug Prior to Birth. *Suffolk University Law Review* 17:257-68.

Sever, J. L. 1980. Infectious Causes of Human Reproductive Loss. In I. H. Porter and Ernest B. Hook, eds., *Human Embryonic and Fetal Death.* New York: Academic Press.

Sexton, M., and J. R. Hebel. 1984. A Clinical Trial of Change on Maternal Smoking and Its Effect on Birth Weight. *Journal of the American Medical Association* 251 (7):911-15.

Shankaran, S., S. N. Cohen, M. Linver, and S. Zonia. 1988. Medical Care Costs of High-Risk Infants after Neonatal Intensive Care: A Controlled Study. *Pediatrics* 81 (3):372-78.

Shaw, M. W. 1978. Genetically Defective Children: Emerging Legal Considerations. *American Journal of Law and Medicine* 3:333-40.

———. 1980. Preconception and Prenatal Torts. In *Genetics and the Law II,* edited by Aubrey Milunsky and George Annas. New York: Plenum Press.

Shelley, B. 1988. Maternal Substance Abuse: The Next Step in the Protection of Fetal Rights? *Dickinson Law Review* 92:691-714.

Shepard, R. J. 1982. *The Risks of Passive Smoking.* New York: Oxford University Press.

Shepard, T. H. 1989. *Catalog of Teratogenic Agents,* 6th ed. Baltimore: Johns Hopkins University Press.

Simon, C. A. 1978. Parental Liability for Prenatal Injury. *Columbia Journal of Law and Social Relations* 14:47-90.

Simpson, J. L. 1986. Methods for Detecting Neural Tube Defects. *Contemporary OB/Gyn* 1986:202-22.

Smith, C. A. 1947. Effects of Maternal Undernutrition upon the Newborn Infant in Holland (1944-1945). *Journal of Pediatrics* 30:229-41.

Smith, J. M. 1977. Congenital Minimata Disease: Methyl Mercury Poisoning and Birth Defects in Japan. In *Proceedings: Conference on Women and the Workplace,* edited by E. Bingham. Washington, D.C.: Society for Occupational and Environmental Health.

Smithells, R. W. et al. 1983. Further Experience of Vitamin Supplementation on Prevention of Neural Tube Defects. *The Lancet* 1:1027-31.

Snyder, D. B. 1989. Mother and Fetus—The Case of "Do or Die": *In Re A.C. Journal of Contemporary Health Law and Policy* 5:319-37.

Southgate, D. A. T., and E. Hey. 1976. Chemical and Biochemical Development of the Human Fetus. In *The Biology of Human Fetal Growth,* edited by D. F. Roberts and A. M. Thomson. New York: Halsted Press.

Spallone, P. 1989. *Beyond Conception: The New Politics of Reproduction.* Granby, Mass.: Bergin and Garvey Publishers.

Spielberg, S. P. 1982. Pharmacogenetics and the Fetus. *New England Journal of Medicine* 307 (2):115-16.

Stearns, M. L. 1986. Maternal Duties during Pregnancy: Toward a Conceptual Framework. *New England Law Review* 21 (3):595-634.

Steinbrook, R. 1986. In California, Voluntary Mass Prenatal Screening, *Hastings Center Report* 16 (5):5-7.

Stone, K. M. et al. 1989. National Surveillance for Neonatal Herpes Simplex Virus Infections. *Sexually Transmitted Diseases* 16:152-56.

Strong, C. 1983. The Tiniest Newborns. *Hastings Center Report* 13 (1):14-19.

Sun, M. 1988. Anti-Acne Drug Poses Dilemma for FDA. *Science* 240:714-15.

Susser, M., and Z. Stein. 1980. Prenatal Diet and Reproductive Loss. In *Human Embryonic and Fetal Death,* edited by I. H. Porter and Ernest B. Hook. New York: Academic Press.

Syphilis—United States, 1983. 1984. *Journal of the American Medical Association* 252 (8):992-93.

Tedeschi, G. 1966. On Tort Liability for "Wrongful Life." *Israel Law Review* 1:529-56.

Thompson, E. L. 1989. The Criminalization of Maternal Conduct during Pregnancy: A Decisionmaking Model for Lawmakers. *Indiana Law Journal* 64:357-74.

Thorp, J. M., V. L. Katz, L. J. Fowler, J. T. Kurtzman, and W. A. Bowes, Jr. 1989. Fetal Death from Chlamydial Infection across Intact Amniotic Membranes. *American Journal of Obstetrics and Gynecology* 161:1245-46.

Trotzig, M. A. 1980. The Defective Child and the Actions for Wrongful Life and Wrongful Birth. *Family Law Quarterly* 14:16-28.

Twiss, S. B. 1974. Ethical Issues in Genetic Screening: Models of Genetic Responsibility. In *Ethical, Social and Legal Dimensions of Screening for Human Genetic Disease,* edited by D. Bergsma. New York: Stratton.

Universal Declaration of Human Rights. 1948. New York: The United Nations.

Upchurch, D. M., and J. McCarthy. 1990. The Timing of a First Birth and High School Completion. *American Sociological Review* 55:224-34.

U.S. Surgeon General. 1979. Chapter 8 in *Smoking and Health.* Washington, D.C.: U.S. Government Printing Office.

Valentine, J. M., and A. L. Plough. 1982. Protecting the Reproductive Health of Workers: Problems in Science and Public Policy. *Journal of Health Politics, Policy and Law* 8 (1):144-63.

Van Hoften, E. L. 1981. Surrogate Motherhood in California: Legislative Proposals. *San Diego Law Review* 18:341-85.

Vaupel, J. W. 1980. Prospects for Saving Lives: A Policy Analysis. House Subcommittee on Science, Research and Technology, *Hearings on Compara-*

tive Risk Assessment. Washington, D.C.: U.S. Government Printing Office.

Verni, T., and J. Kelly. 1981. *The Secret Life of the Unborn Child.* New York: Summit Books.

Verp, M. S., and J. L. Simpson. 1985. Amniocentesis for Cytogenatic Studies. In *Human Prenatal Diagnosis,* edited by K. Filkins and J. F. Russo. New York: Marcel Dekker.

Vinovskis, M. A. 1988. *An "Epidemic" of Adolescent Pregnancy? Some Historical and Policy Considerations.* New York: Oxford University Press.

Warner, R. H., and H. L. Rosett. 1975. The Effects of Drinking on Offspring: An Historical Survey of the American and British Literature. *Journal of Studies on Alcohol* 36:1395-1420.

Warsof, S. L., D. J. Cooper, D. Little, and S. Campbell. 1986. Routine Ultrasound Screening for Antenatal Detection of Intrauterine Growth Retardation. *Obstetrics and Gynecology* 67 (1):33-38.

Wen, S. W., R. L. Goldenberg, G. R. Cutter et al. 1990. Smoking, Maternal Age, Fetal Growth, and Gestational Age at Delivery. *American Journal of Obstetrics and Gynecology* 162 (1):53-58.

Wentz, A. 1982. Adverse Effects of Danazol in Pregnancy. *Annals of Internal Medicine* 96:672-73.

Westfall, D. 1983. Beyond Abortion: The Potential Reach of a Human Life Amendment. In *Defining Human Life,* edited by A. Edward Doudera and Margery W. Shaw. Ann Arbor: Health Administration Press.

Westoff, C. F. 1988. Contraceptive Paths toward Reduction of Unintended Pregnancy and Abortion. *Family Planning Perspectives* 20 (1):4-12.

White, H. M. 1988. Unborn Child: Can You Be Protected? *University of Richmond Law Review* 22:285-302.

Williams, W. W. 1981. Firing the Woman to Protect the Fetus: The Reconciliation of Fetal Protection with Employment Opportunity Goals under Title VII. *Georgetown Law Journal* 69:641-704.

Williamson, R. A., C. P. Weiner, W. T. C. Yuh, and M. M. Abu-Yousef. 1989. Magnetic Resonance Imaging of Anomalous Fetuses. *Obstetrics and Gynecology* 73 (6):952-57.

Wilson, J. G. 1977. Embryotoxicity of Drugs in Man. In *Handbook of Teratology,* Vol. 1, edited by J. G. Wilson and F. C. Fraser. *General Principles and Etiology.* New York: Plenum Press.

Winborne, W. H., ed. 1983. *Handling Pregnancy and Birth Cases.* New York: McGraw-Hill.

Winick, M. 1976. *Malnutrition and Brain Development.* New York: Oxford University Press.

Winslade, W. J. 1981. Surrogate Mothers: Private Right or Public Wrong? *Journal of Medical Ethics* 7:153-54.

Witwer, M. 1989. One-Third of Infants Born to HIV-Positive Mothers Face Illness or Death during Their First Year of Life. *Family Planning Perspectives* 21 (6):281-82.

Yaffe, S. J. 1986. Introduction. In *Drugs in Pregnancy and Lactation,* edited by

G. G. Briggs, R. K. Freeman, and S. J. Yaffe. Baltimore: Williams and Wilkins.

Zylke, J. W. 1989. Maternal, Child Health Needs Noted by Two Major National Study Groups. *Journal of the American Medical Association* 261 (12): 1687-88.

Index

About the Author

ROBERT H. BLANK is Professor of Political Science and Associate Director of the Program for Biosocial Research at Northern Illinois University. He is the author of many books, including, most recently, *Biomedical Technology and Public Policy* (Greenwood Press, 1989) and *Regulating Reproduction* (1990).